KEITH GIFFEN & JOHN ROGERS
WRITERS

CULLY HAMNER
CYNTHIA MARTIN
DUNCAN ROULEAU
KEVIN WEST
PENCILLERS

CULLY HAMNER
PHIL MOY
DUNCAN ROULEAU
JACK PURCELL
INKERS

**DAVID SELF
GUY MAJOR**
COLORISTS

PHIL BALSMAN
PAT BROSSEAU
LETTERERS

BLUE BEETLE SHELLSHOCKED

DAN DIDIO Senior VP-Executive Editor

JOAN HILTY Editor-original series

RACHEL GLUCKSTERN Assistant Editor-original series

ANTON KAWASAKI Editor-collected edition

ROBBIN BROSTERMAN Senior Art Director

PAUL LEVITZ President & Publisher

GEORG BREWER VP-Design & DC Direct Creative

RICHARD BRUNING Senior VP-Creative Director

PATRICK CALDON Executive VP-Finance & Operations

CHRIS CARAMALIS VP-Finance

JOHN CUNNINGHAM VP-Marketing

TERRI CUNNINGHAM VP-Managing Editor

STEPHANIE FIERMAN Senior VP-Sales & Marketing

ALISON GILL VP-Manufacturing

HANK KANALZ VP-General Manager, WildStorm

JIM LEE Editorial Director-WildStorm

PAULA LOWITT Senior VP-Business & Legal Affairs

MARYELLEN MCLAUGHLIN VP-Advertising & Custom Publishing

JOHN NEE VP-Business Development

GREGORY NOVECK Senior VP-Creative Affairs

CHERYL RUBIN Senior VP-Brand Management

JEFF TROJAN VP-Business Development, DC Direct

BOB WAYNE VP-Sales

BLUE BEETLE: SHELLSHOCKED

DC Comics, 1700 Broadway, New York, NY 10019.
A Warner Bros. Entertainment Company
Printed in Canada. First Printing.
ISBN: 1-4012-0965-3
ISBN-13: 978-1-4012-0965-0
Cover by Cully Hamner
Publication design by Amelia Grohman
Logo design by Brainchild Studios/NYC

BLUE BEETLE #1
Cover and interior art by Cully Hamner

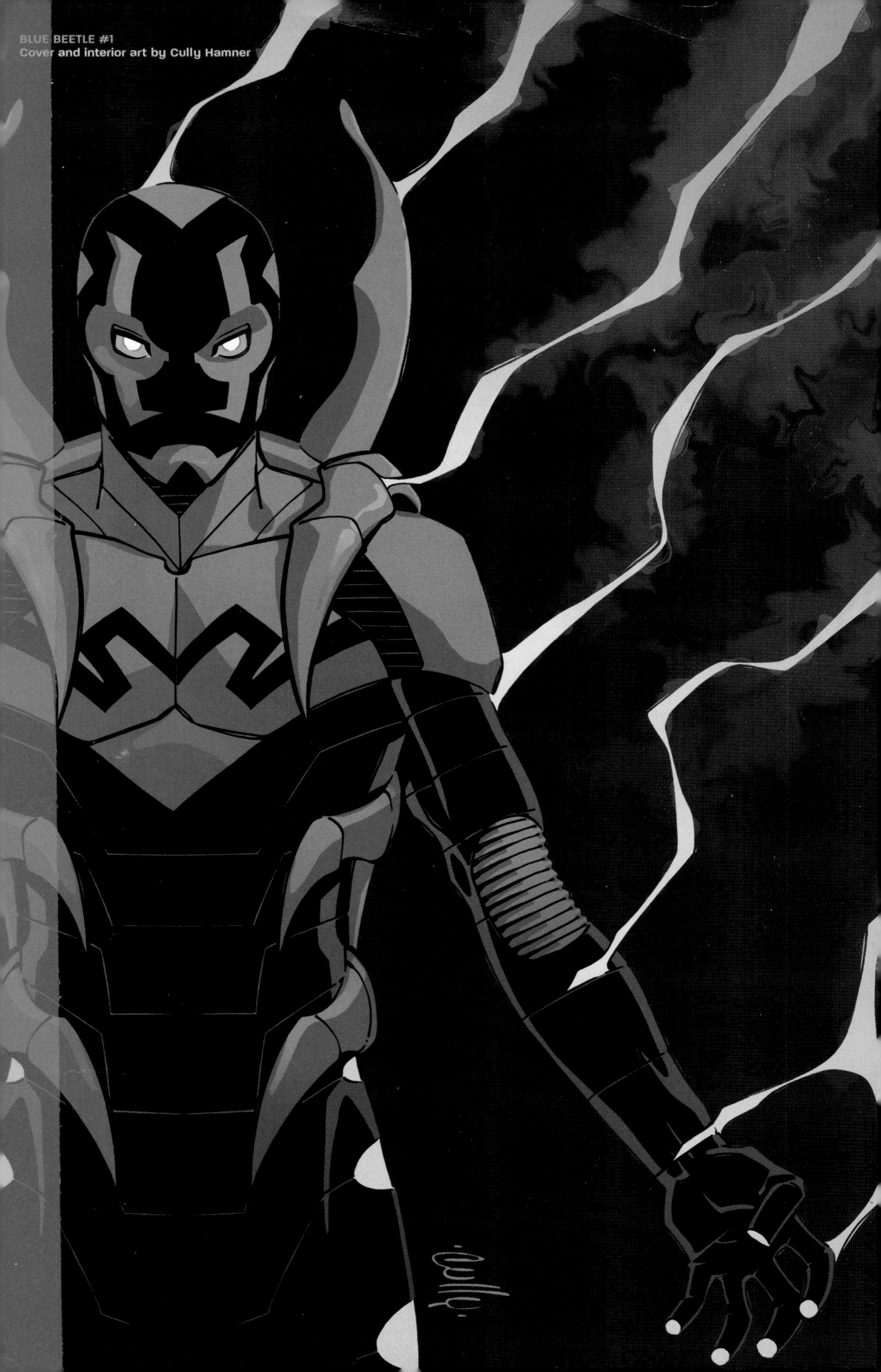

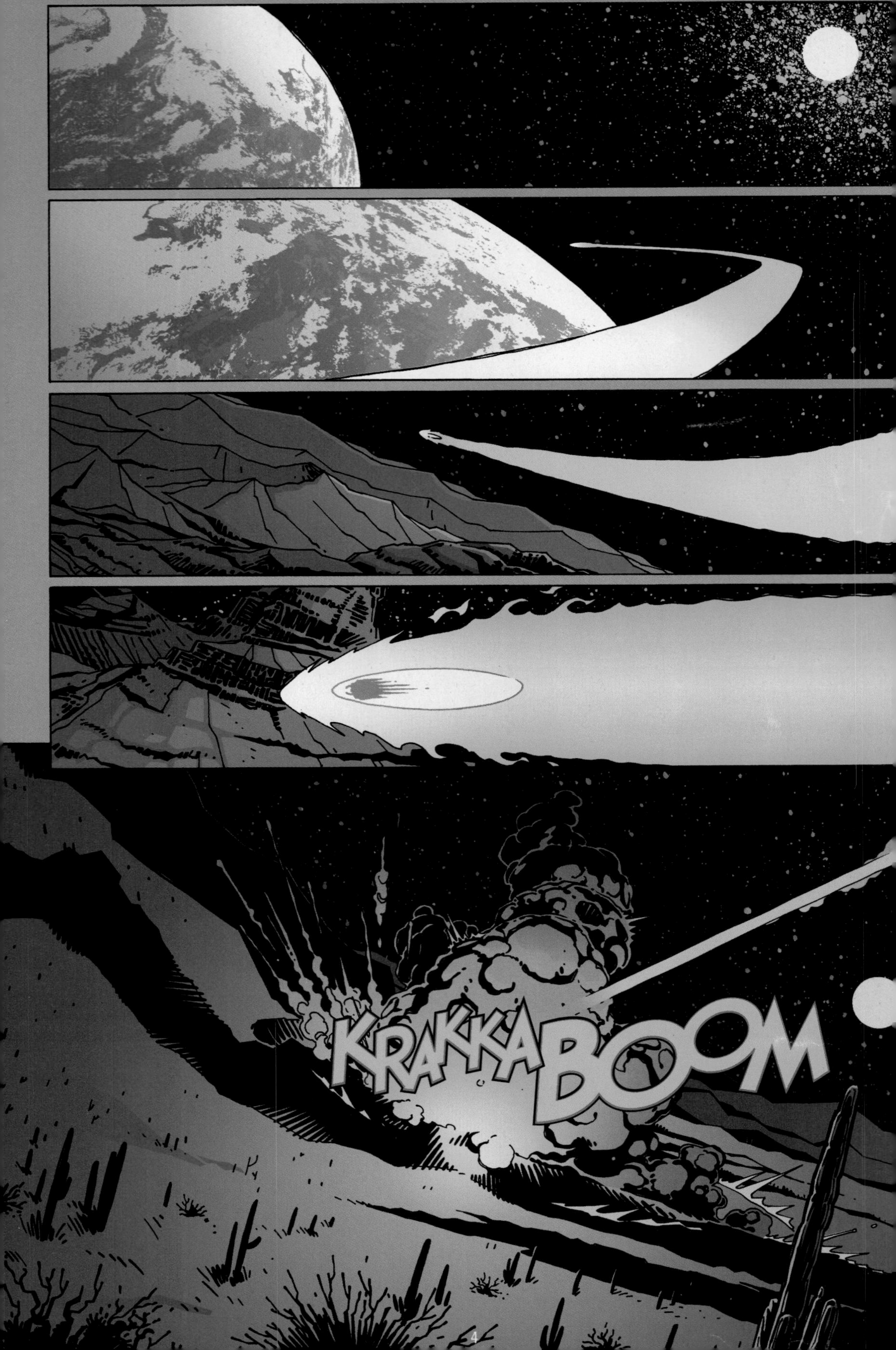
KRAKKABOOM

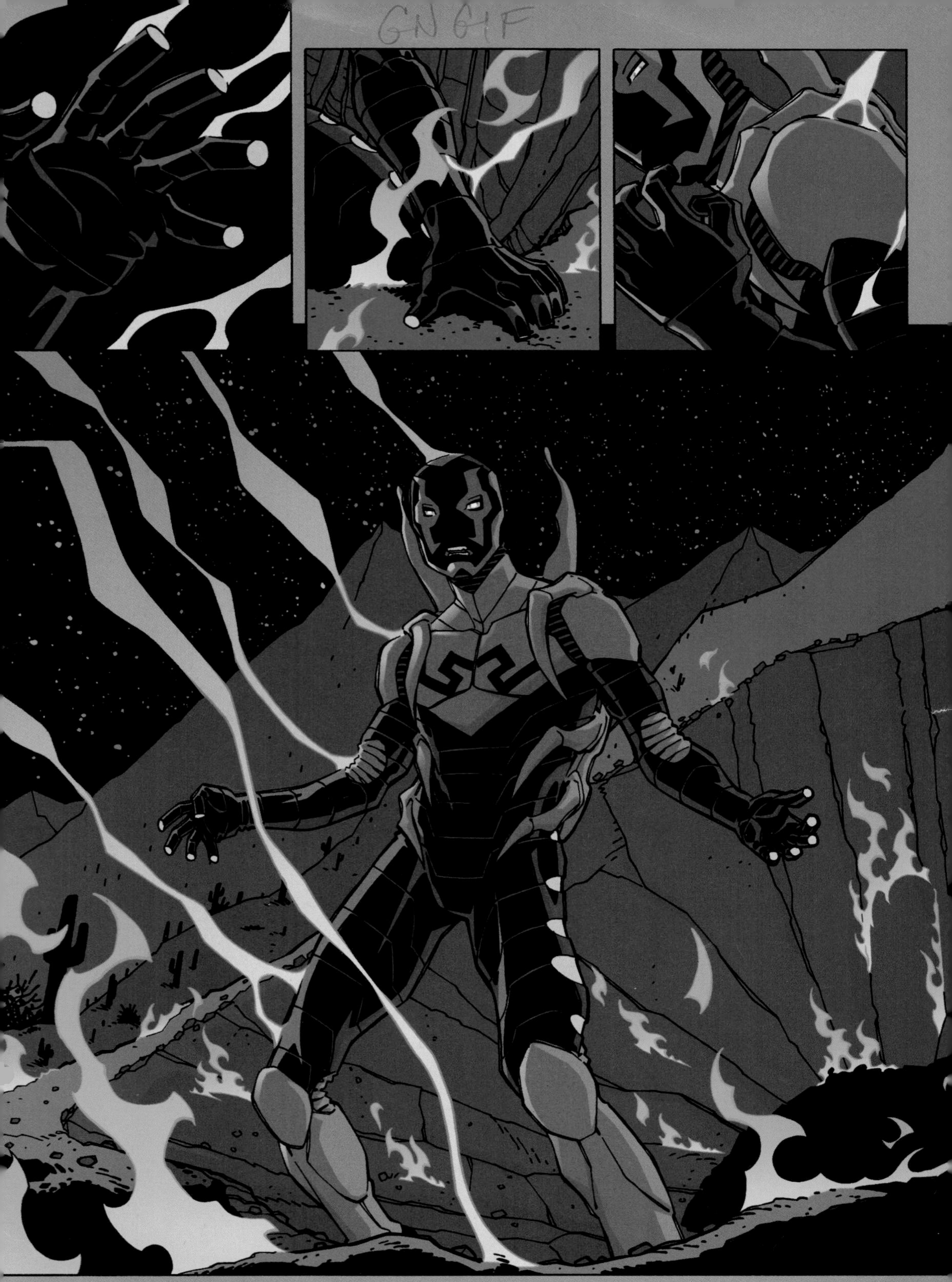

BLUE MONDAY

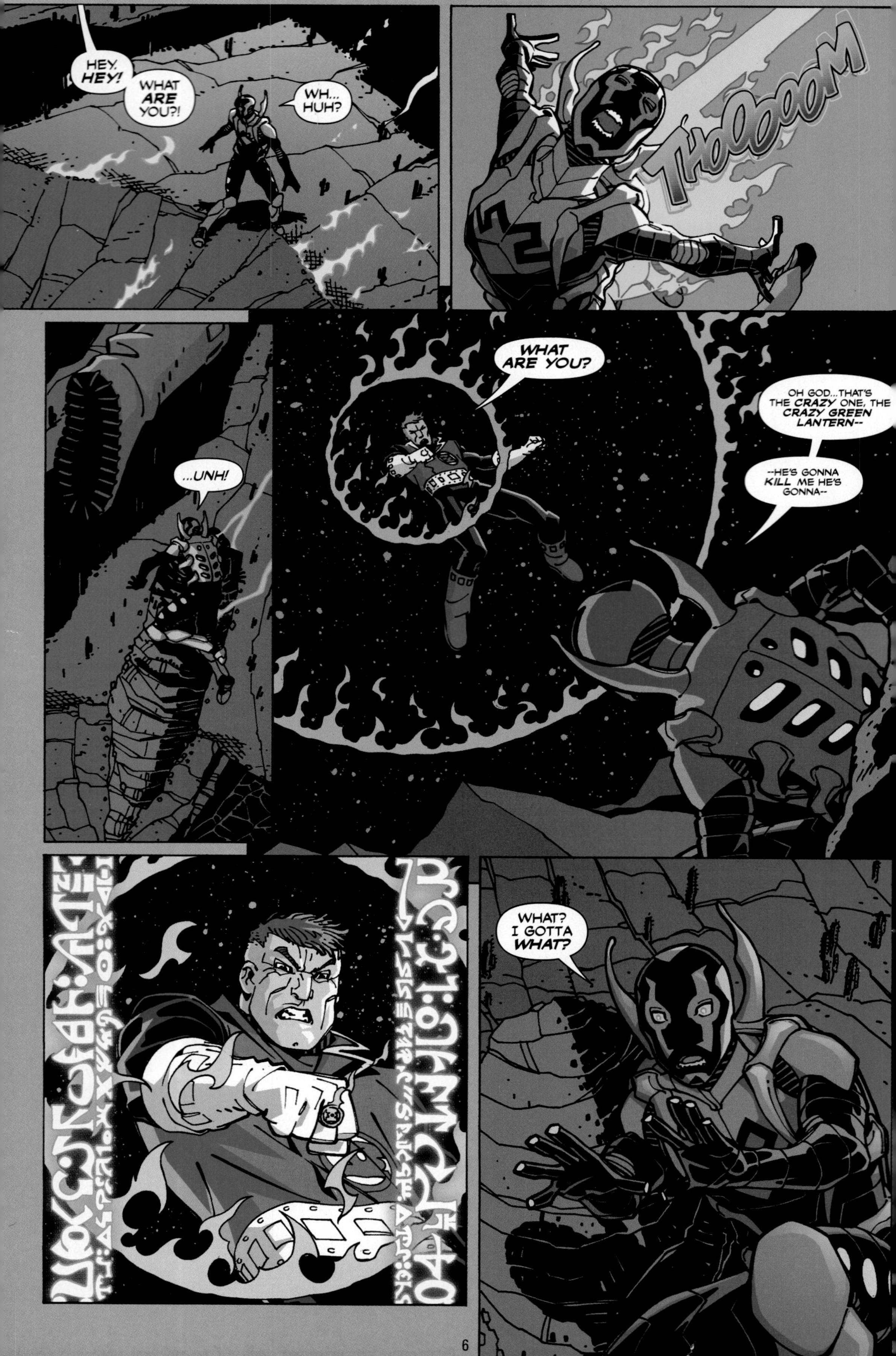
HEY. HEY!
WHAT ARE YOU?!
WH... HUH?
THOOOOOM
...UNH!
WHAT ARE YOU?
OH GOD...THAT'S THE CRAZY ONE, THE CRAZY GREEN LANTERN--
--HE'S GONNA KILL ME HE'S GONNA--
WHAT? I GOTTA WHAT?

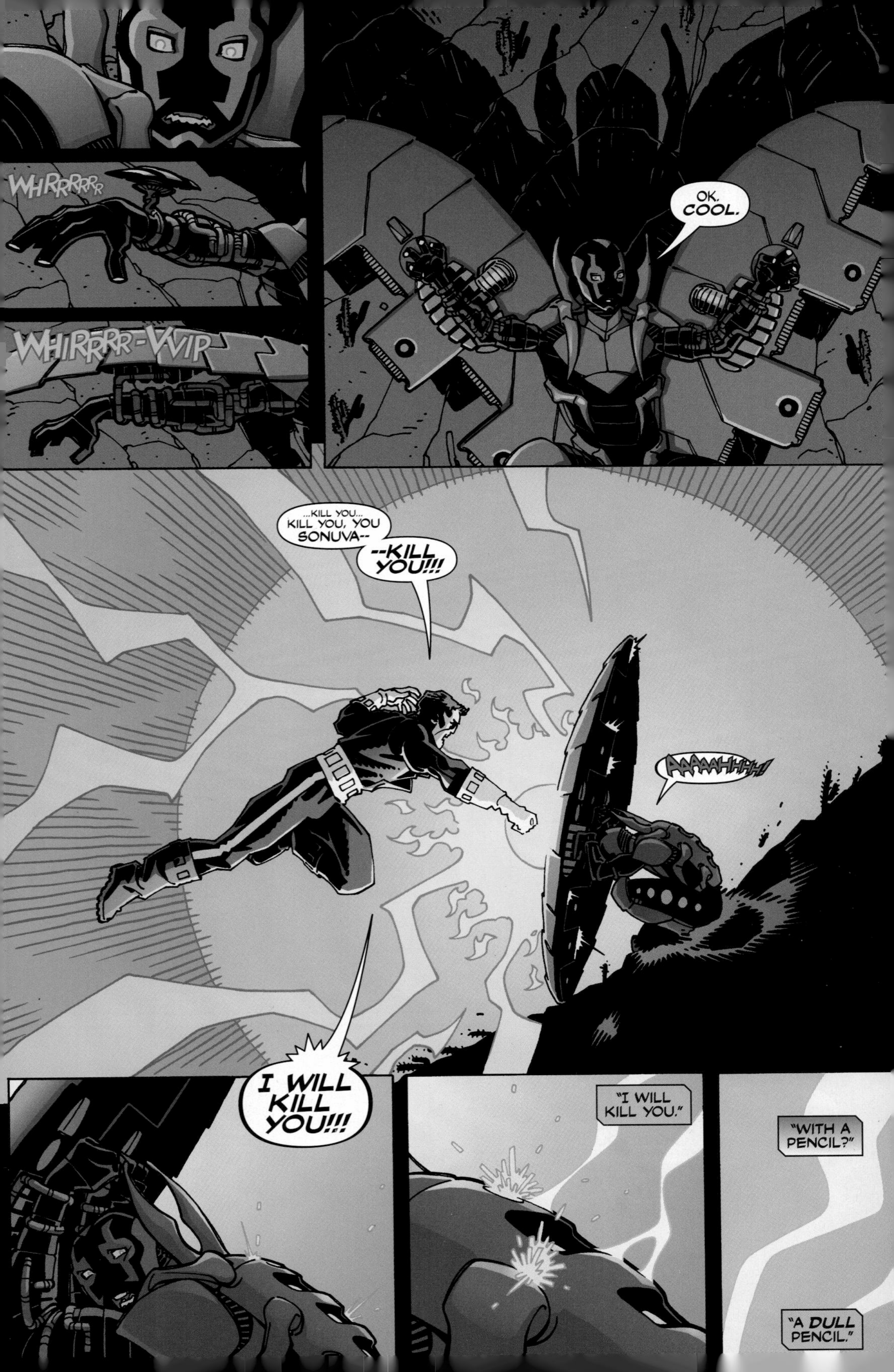
WHRRRRRR
WHIRRRR-VVIP
OK. COOL.
...KILL YOU... KILL YOU, YOU SONUVA--
--KILL YOU!!!
AAAAAHHHH!
I WILL KILL YOU!!!
"I WILL KILL YOU."
"WITH A PENCIL?"
"A DULL PENCIL."

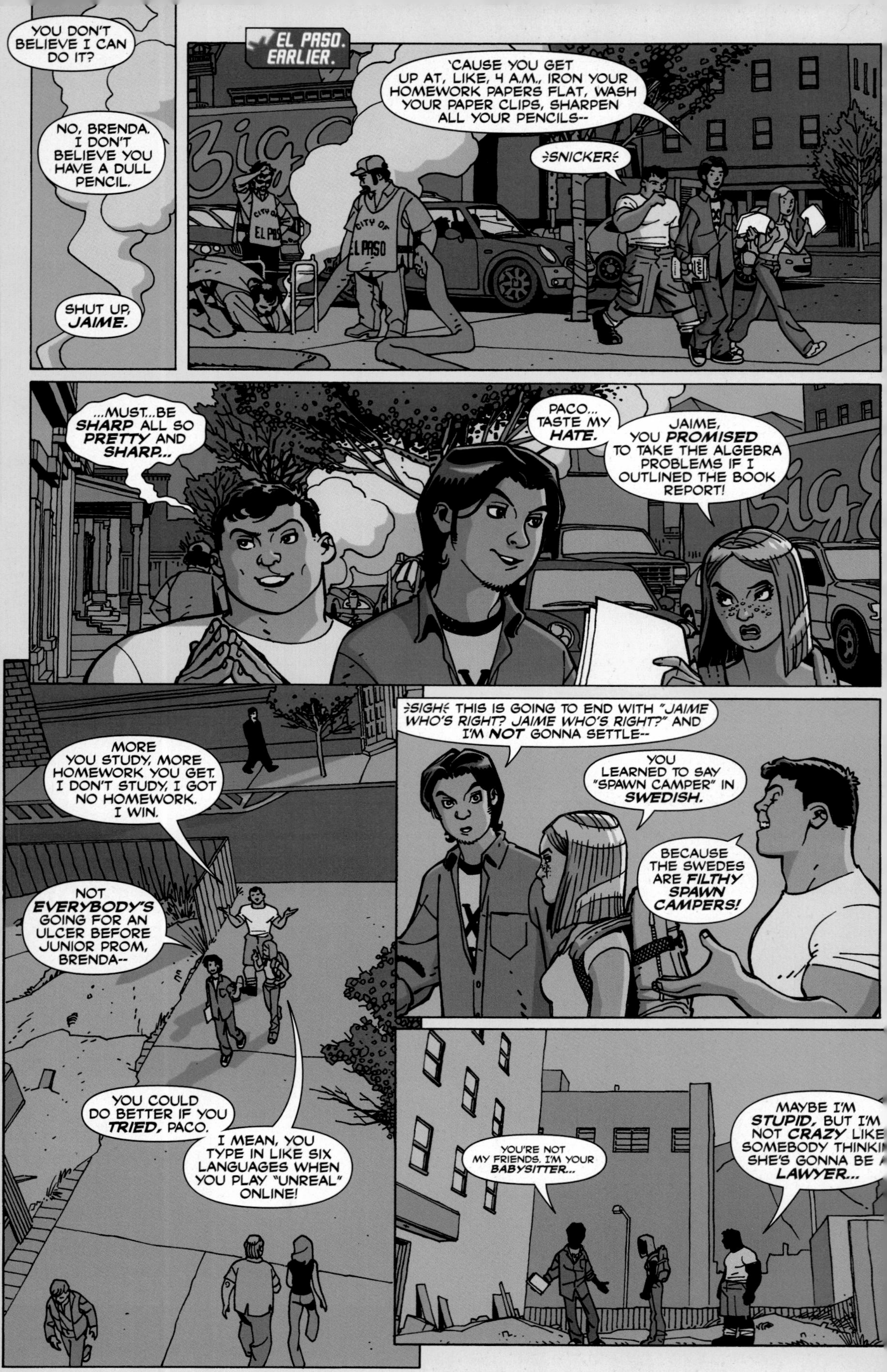
YOU DON'T BELIEVE I CAN DO IT?
NO, BRENDA. I DON'T BELIEVE YOU HAVE A DULL PENCIL.
SHUT UP, JAIME.
EL PASO. EARLIER.
'CAUSE YOU GET UP AT, LIKE, 4 A.M., IRON YOUR HOMEWORK PAPERS FLAT, WASH YOUR PAPER CLIPS, SHARPEN ALL YOUR PENCILS--
SNICKER
CITY OF EL PASO
CITY OF EL PASO
...MUST...BE SHARP ALL SO PRETTY AND SHARP...
PACO... TASTE MY HATE.
JAIME, YOU PROMISED TO TAKE THE ALGEBRA PROBLEMS IF I OUTLINED THE BOOK REPORT!
MORE YOU STUDY, MORE HOMEWORK YOU GET. I DON'T STUDY, I GOT NO HOMEWORK. I WIN.
NOT EVERYBODY'S GOING FOR AN ULCER BEFORE JUNIOR PROM, BRENDA--
YOU COULD DO BETTER IF YOU TRIED, PACO.
I MEAN, YOU TYPE IN LIKE SIX LANGUAGES WHEN YOU PLAY "UNREAL" ONLINE!
SIGH THIS IS GOING TO END WITH "JAIME WHO'S RIGHT? JAIME WHO'S RIGHT?" AND I'M NOT GONNA SETTLE--
YOU LEARNED TO SAY "SPAWN CAMPER" IN SWEDISH.
BECAUSE THE SWEDES ARE FILTHY SPAWN CAMPERS!
YOU'RE NOT MY FRIENDS. I'M YOUR BABYSITTER...
MAYBE I'M STUPID, BUT I'M NOT CRAZY LIKE SOMEBODY THINKIN' SHE'S GONNA BE A LAWYER...

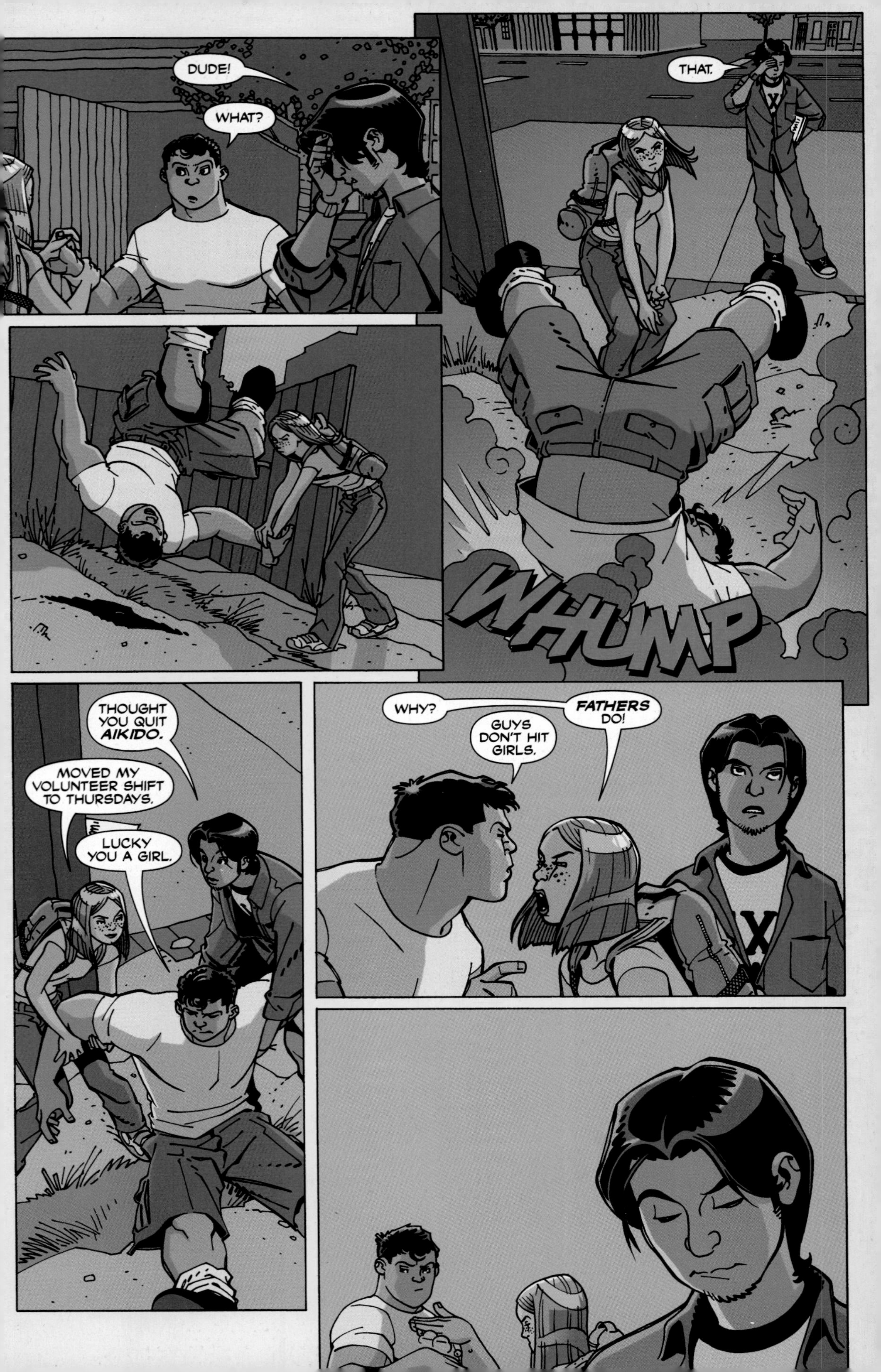
DUDE!
WHAT?
THAT.
WHUMP
THOUGHT YOU QUIT AIKIDO.
MOVED MY VOLUNTEER SHIFT TO THURSDAYS.
LUCKY YOU A GIRL.
WHY?
GUYS DON'T HIT GIRLS.
FATHERS DO!

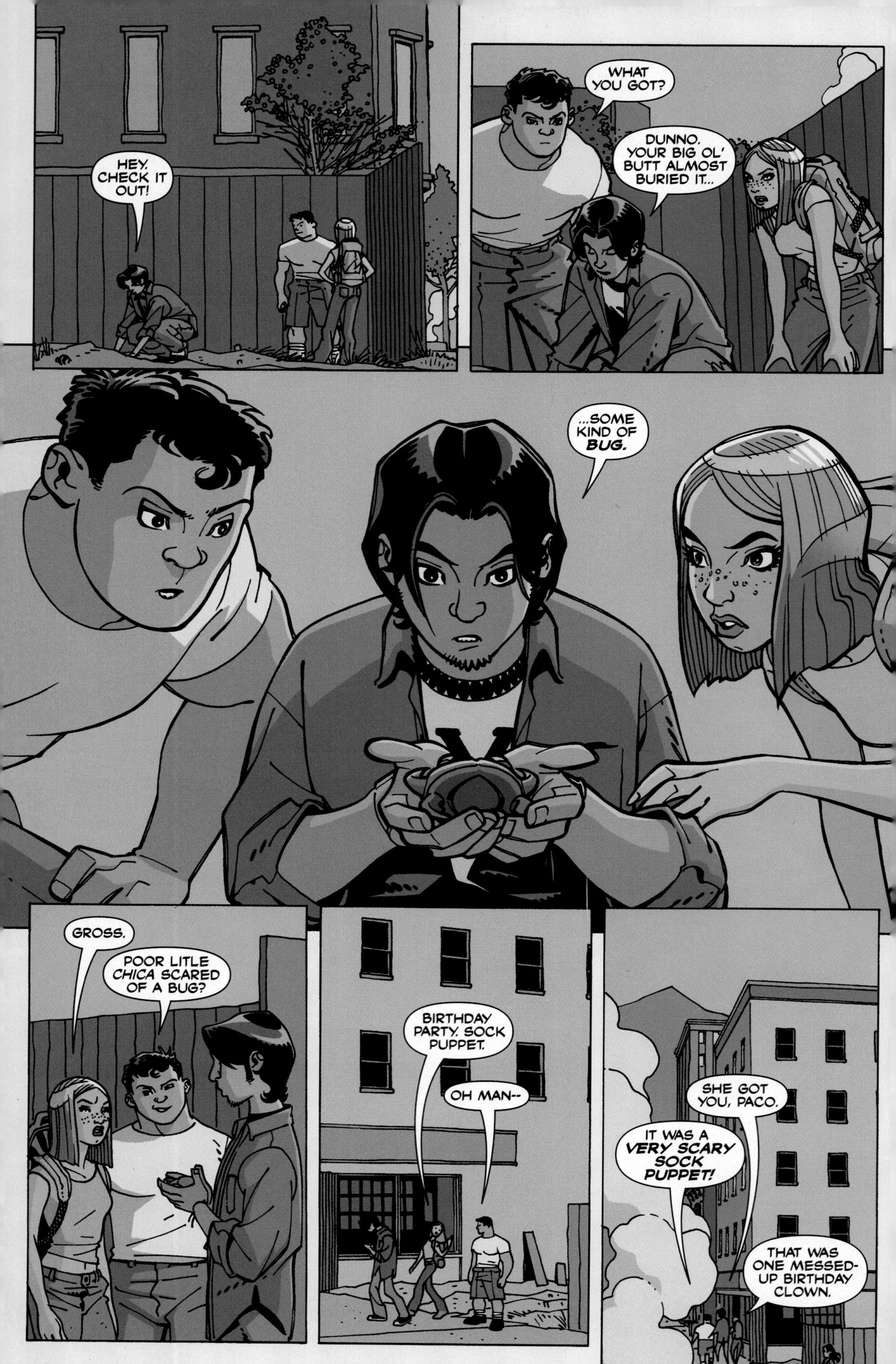
HEY, CHECK IT OUT!
WHAT YOU GOT?
DUNNO, YOUR BIG OL' BUTT ALMOST BURIED IT...
...SOME KIND OF BUG.
GROSS.
POOR LITLE CHICA SCARED OF A BUG?
BIRTHDAY PARTY. SOCK PUPPET.
OH MAN--
SHE GOT YOU, PACO.
IT WAS A VERY SCARY SOCK PUPPET!
THAT WAS ONE MESSED-UP BIRTHDAY CLOWN.

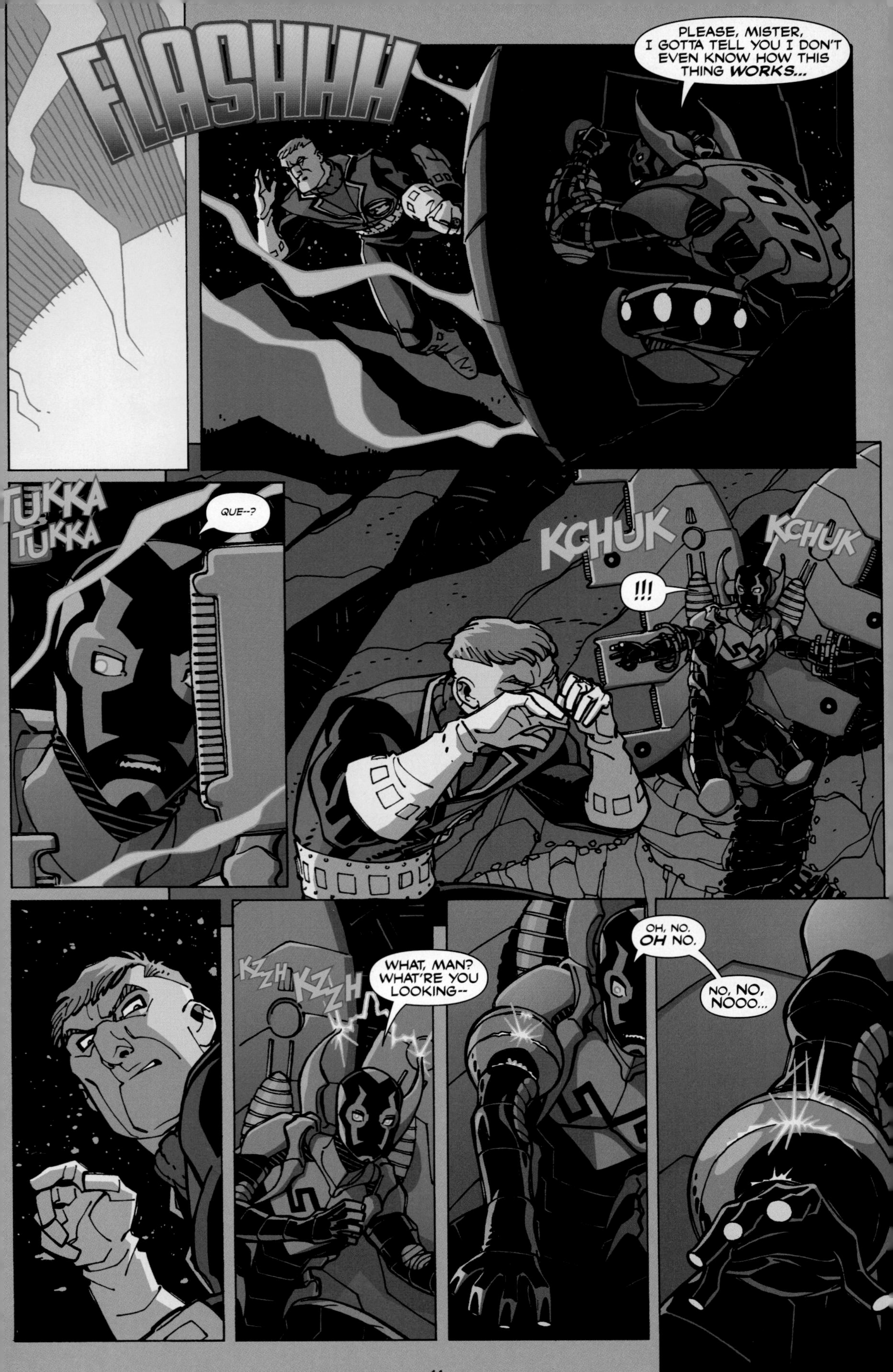
FLASHHH
PLEASE, MISTER, I GOTTA TELL YOU I DON'T EVEN KNOW HOW THIS THING WORKS...
TUKKA TUKKA
QUE--?
KCHUK
KCHUK
!!!
KZZH KZZH
WHAT, MAN? WHAT'RE YOU LOOKING--
OH, NO. OH NO.
NO, NO, NOOO...

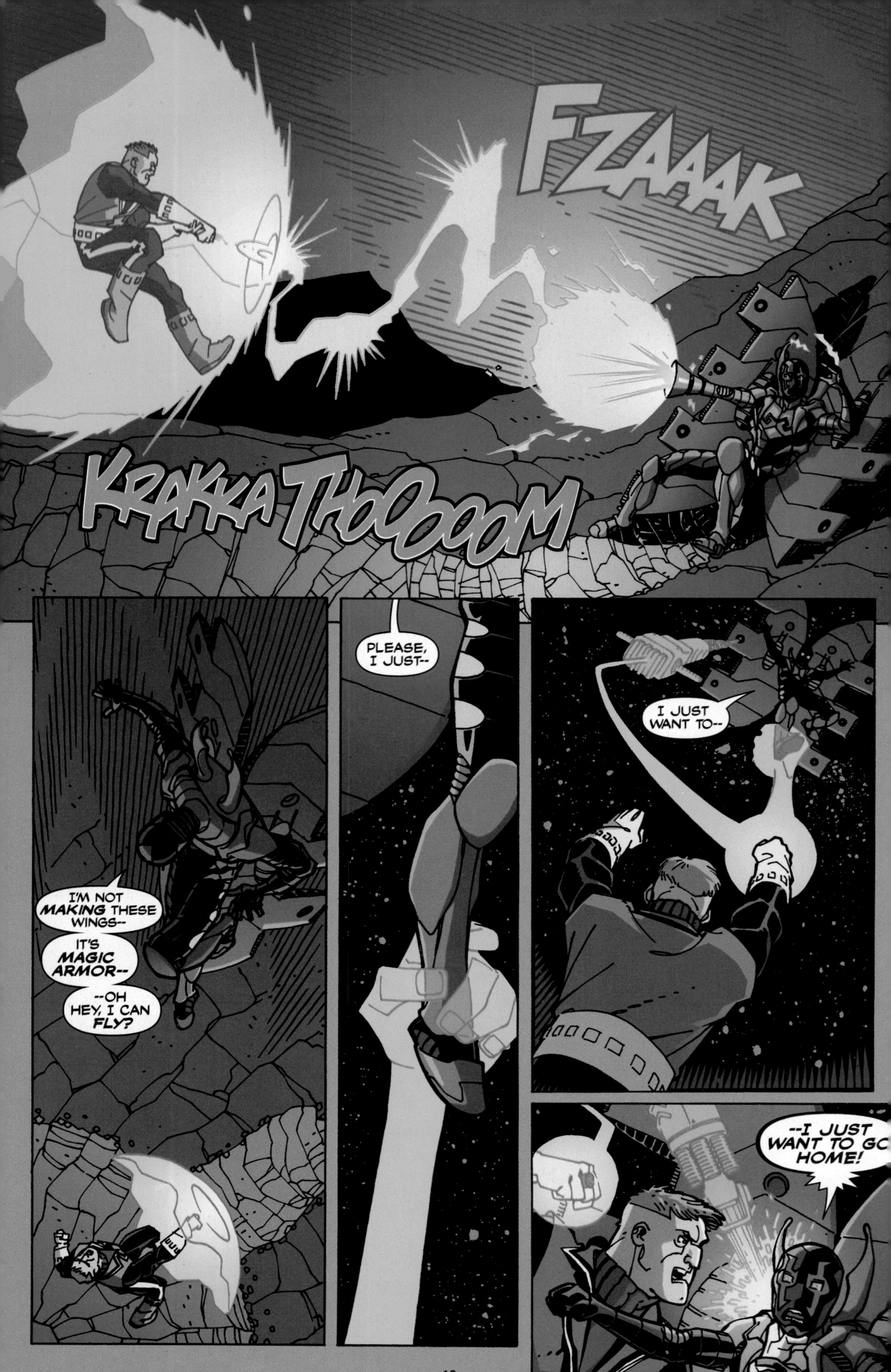
FZAAAK
KRAKKA THOOOOOOM
I'M NOT MAKING THESE WINGS--
IT'S MAGIC ARMOR--
--OH HEY, I CAN FLY?
PLEASE, I JUST--
I JUST WANT TO--
--I JUST WANT TO GO HOME!

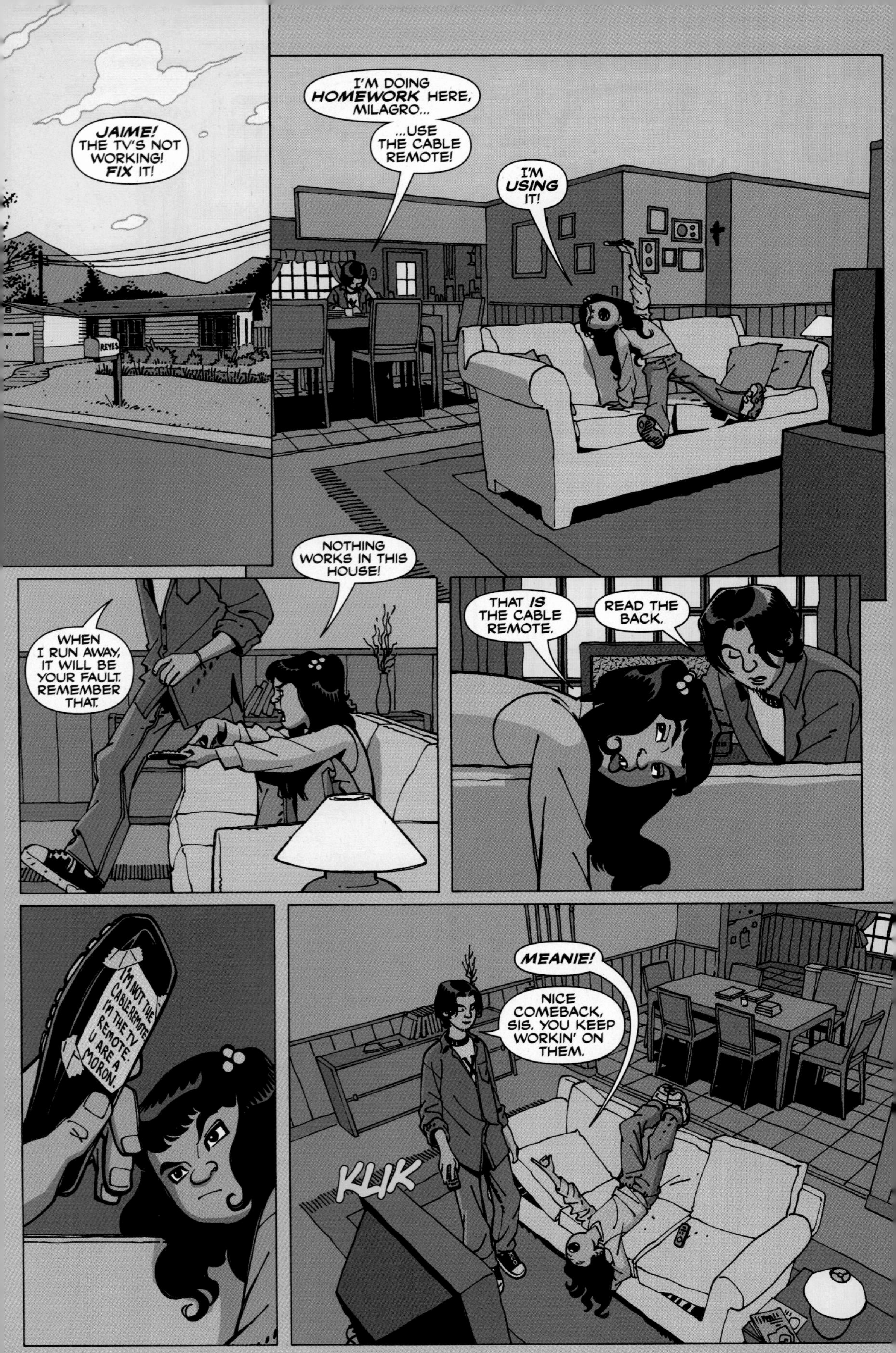
JAIME! THE TV'S NOT WORKING! FIX IT!
I'M DOING HOMEWORK HERE, MILAGRO...
...USE THE CABLE REMOTE!
I'M USING IT!
REYES
NOTHING WORKS IN THIS HOUSE!
WHEN I RUN AWAY, IT WILL BE YOUR FAULT. REMEMBER THAT.
THAT IS THE CABLE REMOTE.
READ THE BACK.
I'M NOT THE CABLE REMOTE. I'M THE TV REMOTE. U ARE A MORON.
MEANIE!
NICE COMEBACK, SIS. YOU KEEP WORKIN' ON THEM.
KLIK

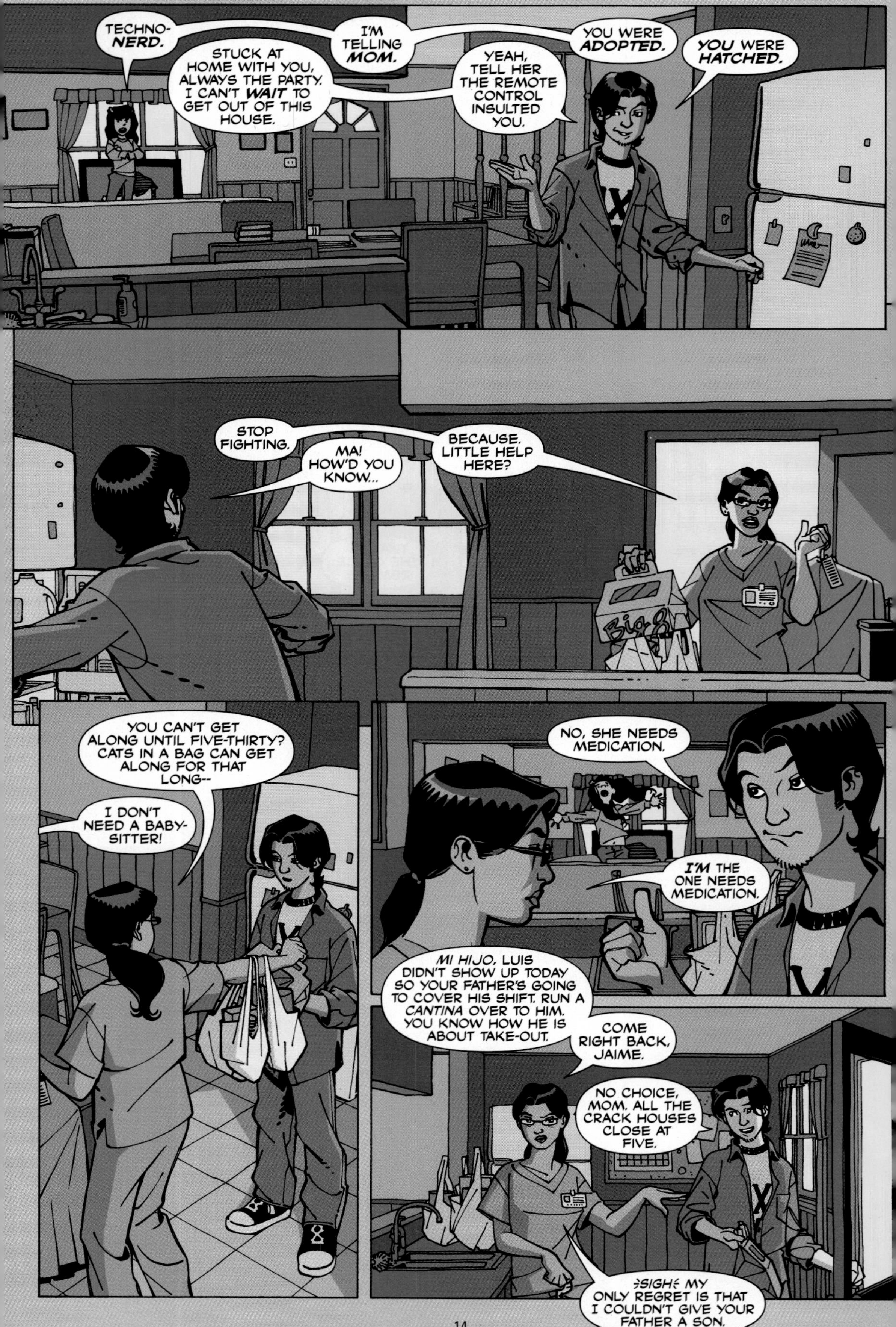

TECHNO-NERD.
I'M TELLING MOM.
YOU WERE ADOPTED.
YOU WERE HATCHED.
STUCK AT HOME WITH YOU, ALWAYS THE PARTY. I CAN'T WAIT TO GET OUT OF THIS HOUSE.
YEAH, TELL HER THE REMOTE CONTROL INSULTED YOU.
STOP FIGHTING.
MA! HOW'D YOU KNOW...
BECAUSE. LITTLE HELP HERE?
YOU CAN'T GET ALONG UNTIL FIVE-THIRTY? CATS IN A BAG CAN GET ALONG FOR THAT LONG--
I DON'T NEED A BABY-SITTER!
NO, SHE NEEDS MEDICATION.
I'M THE ONE NEEDS MEDICATION.
MI HIJO, LUIS DIDN'T SHOW UP TODAY SO YOUR FATHER'S GOING TO COVER HIS SHIFT. RUN A CANTINA OVER TO HIM. YOU KNOW HOW HE IS ABOUT TAKE-OUT.
COME RIGHT BACK, JAIME.
NO CHOICE, MOM. ALL THE CRACK HOUSES CLOSE AT FIVE.
≈SIGH≈ MY ONLY REGRET IS THAT I COULDN'T GIVE YOUR FATHER A SON.

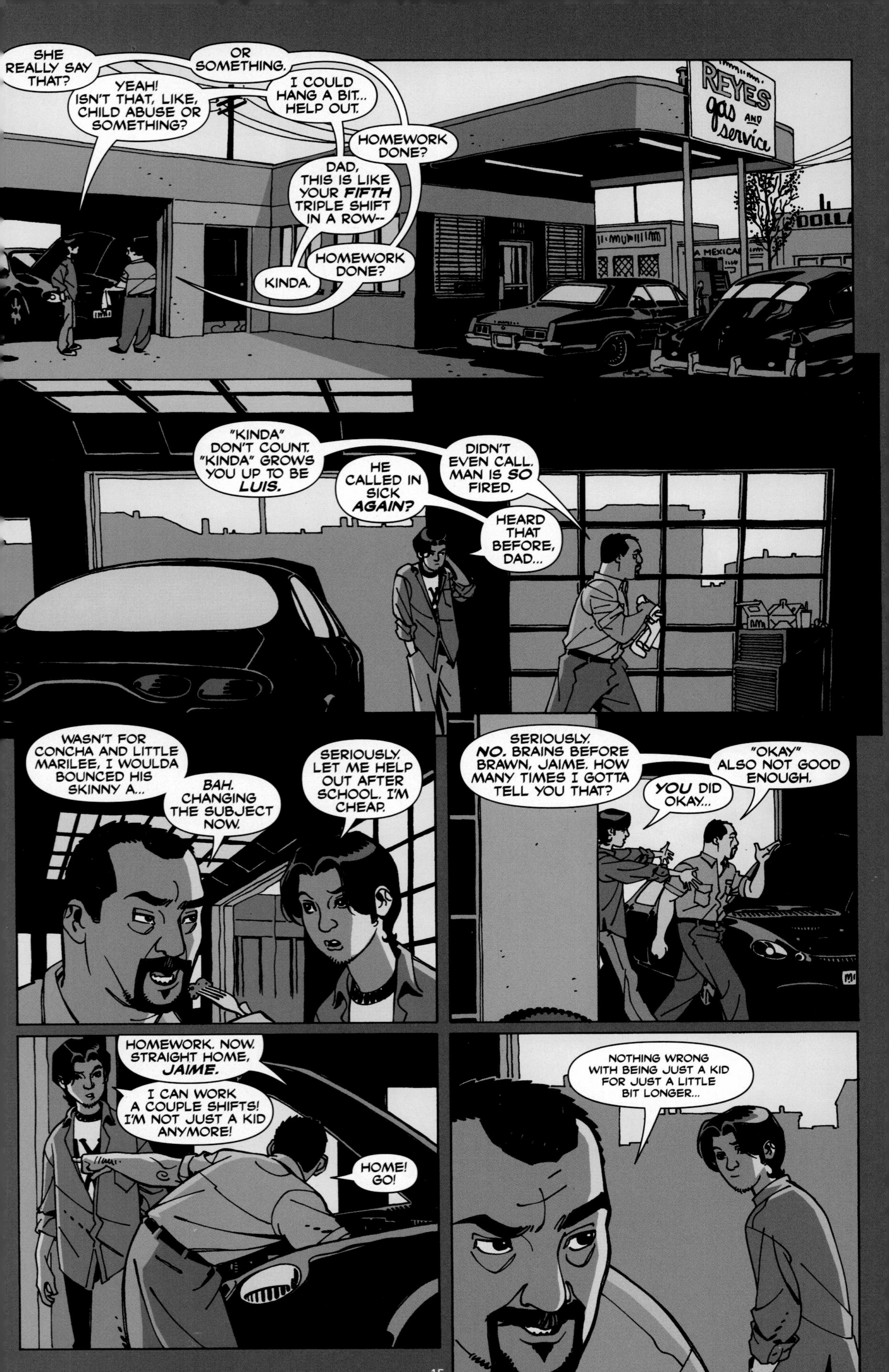
SHE REALLY SAY THAT?
YEAH! ISN'T THAT, LIKE, CHILD ABUSE OR SOMETHING?
OR SOMETHING.
I COULD HANG A BIT... HELP OUT.
HOMEWORK DONE?
DAD, THIS IS LIKE YOUR FIFTH TRIPLE SHIFT IN A ROW--
HOMEWORK DONE?
KINDA.
REYES gas AND service
"KINDA" DON'T COUNT. "KINDA" GROWS YOU UP TO BE LUIS.
HE CALLED IN SICK AGAIN?
DIDN'T EVEN CALL. MAN IS SO FIRED.
HEARD THAT BEFORE, DAD...
WASN'T FOR CONCHA AND LITTLE MARILEE, I WOULDA BOUNCED HIS SKINNY A...
BAH. CHANGING THE SUBJECT NOW.
SERIOUSLY. LET ME HELP OUT AFTER SCHOOL. I'M CHEAP.
SERIOUSLY. NO. BRAINS BEFORE BRAWN, JAIME. HOW MANY TIMES I GOTTA TELL YOU THAT?
YOU DID OKAY...
"OKAY" ALSO NOT GOOD ENOUGH.
HOMEWORK. NOW. STRAIGHT HOME, JAIME.
I CAN WORK A COUPLE SHIFTS! I'M NOT JUST A KID ANYMORE!
HOME! GO!
NOTHING WRONG WITH BEING JUST A KID FOR JUST A LITTLE BIT LONGER...

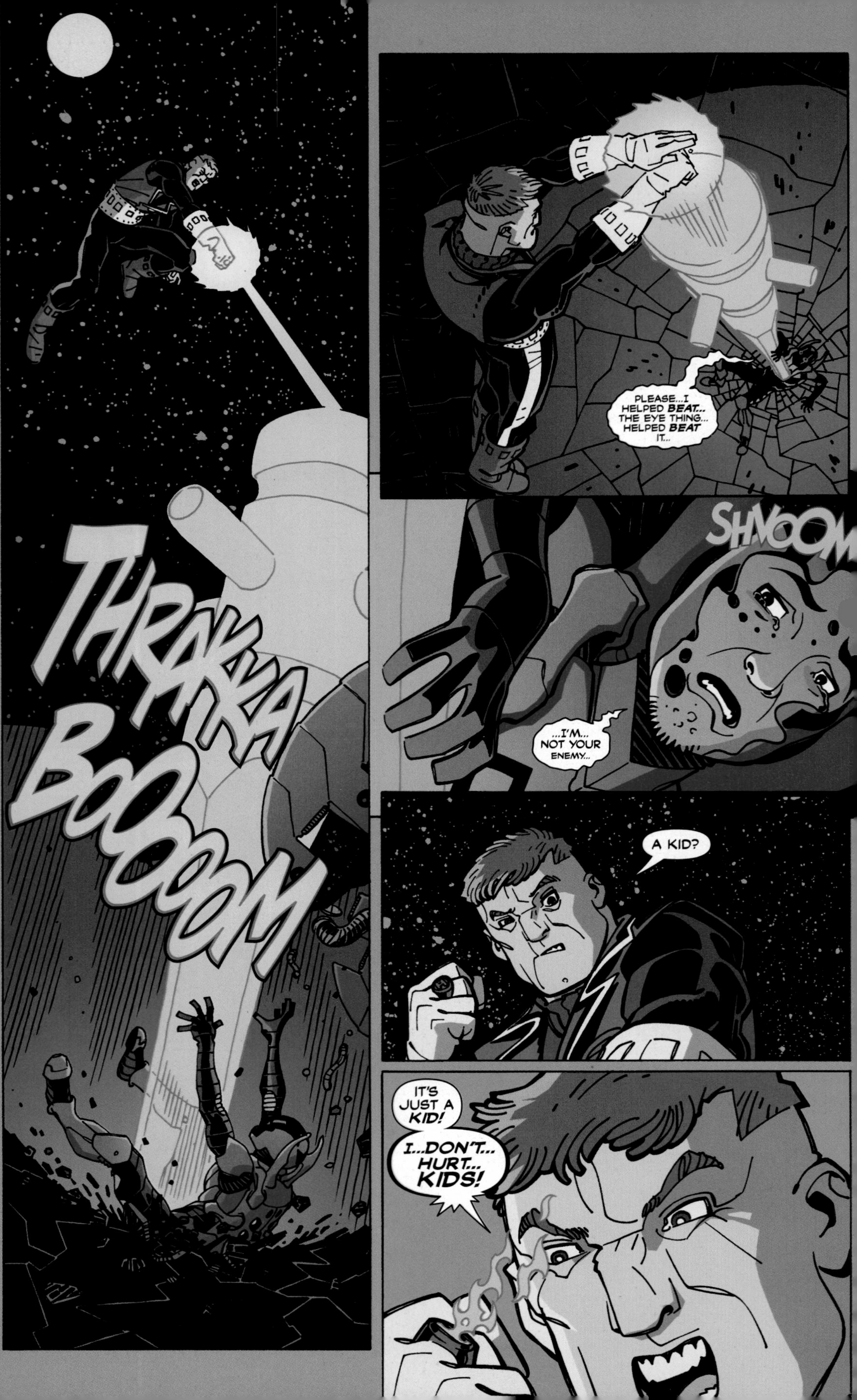
THRAKKA BOOOOOM
PLEASE...I HELPED BEAT... THE EYE THING... HELPED BEAT IT...
SHVOOM
...I'M... NOT YOUR ENEMY...
A KID?
IT'S JUST A KID!
I...DON'T... HURT... KIDS!

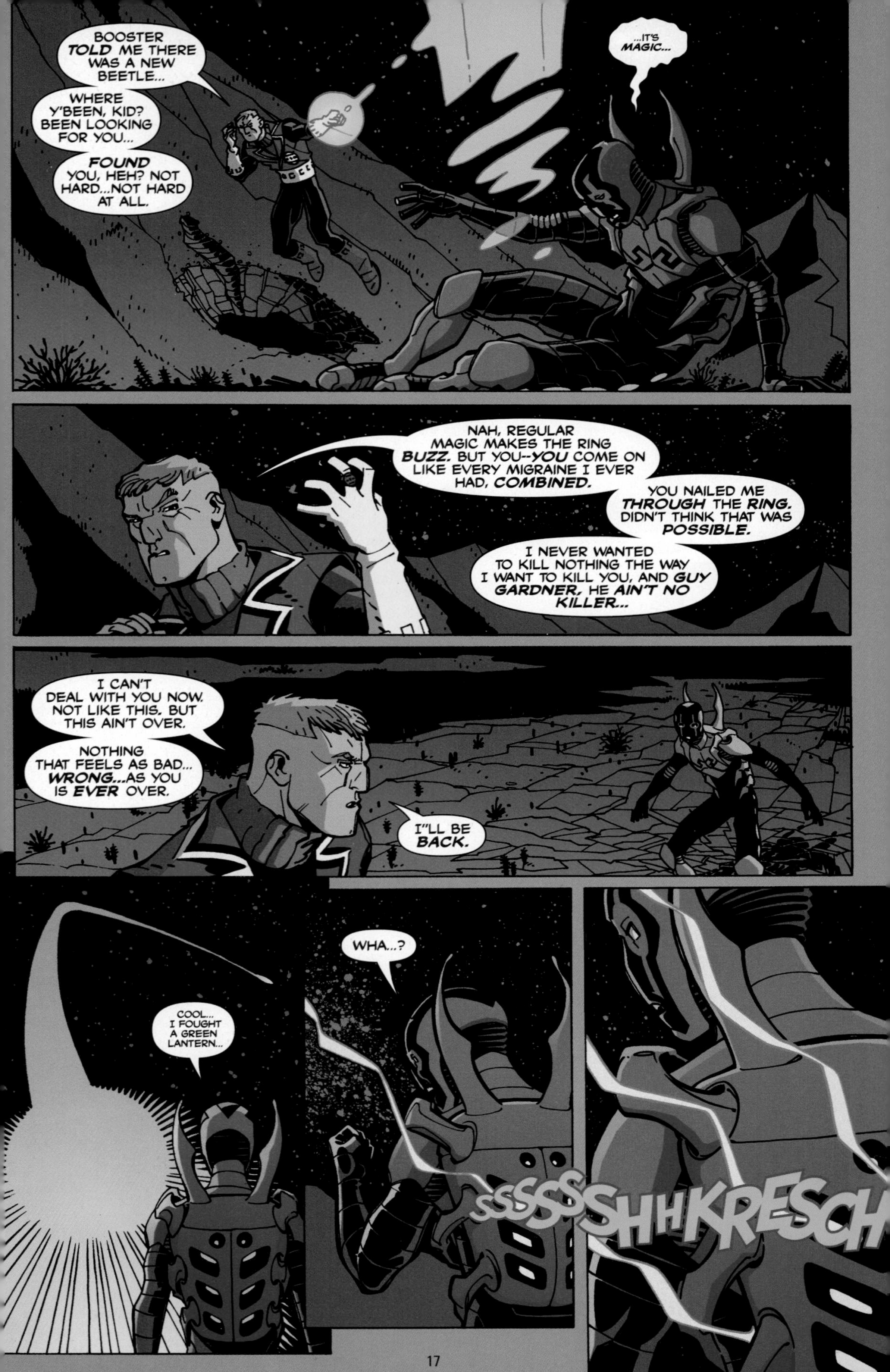
BOOSTER TOLD ME THERE WAS A NEW BEETLE...
WHERE Y'BEEN, KID? BEEN LOOKING FOR YOU...
FOUND YOU, HEH? NOT HARD...NOT HARD AT ALL.
...IT'S MAGIC...
NAH, REGULAR MAGIC MAKES THE RING BUZZ. BUT YOU--YOU COME ON LIKE EVERY MIGRAINE I EVER HAD, COMBINED.
YOU NAILED ME THROUGH THE RING. DIDN'T THINK THAT WAS POSSIBLE.
I NEVER WANTED TO KILL NOTHING THE WAY I WANT TO KILL YOU, AND GUY GARDNER, HE AIN'T NO KILLER...
I CAN'T DEAL WITH YOU NOW. NOT LIKE THIS. BUT THIS AIN'T OVER.
NOTHING THAT FEELS AS BAD... WRONG...AS YOU IS EVER OVER.
I"LL BE BACK.
COOL... I FOUGHT A GREEN LANTERN...
WHA...?
SSSSSSHHKRESCH

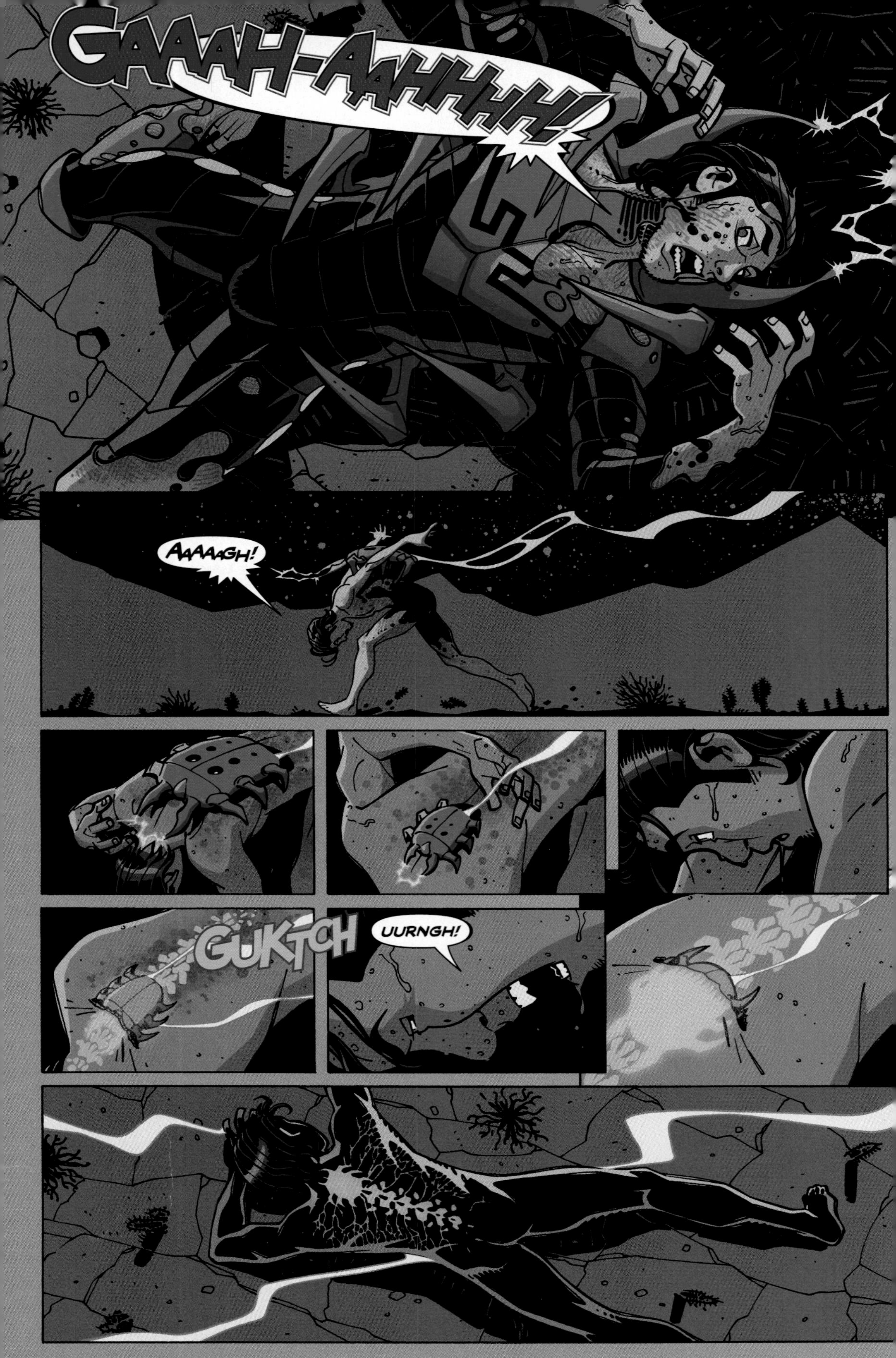
GAAAH-AAHHHH!
AAAAAGH!
GUKTCH
UURNGH!

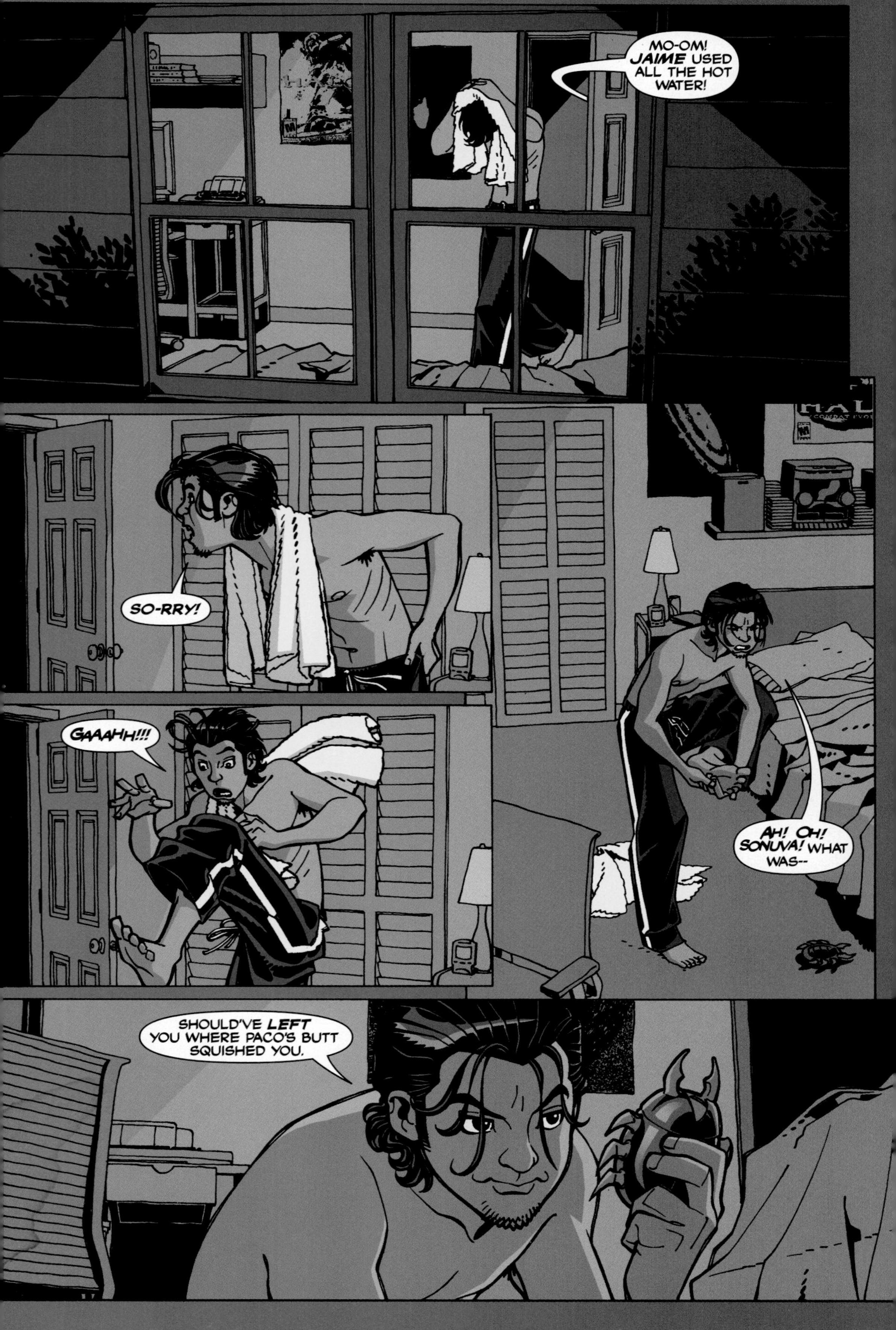
MO-OM! JAIME USED ALL THE HOT WATER!
SO-RRY!
GAAAHH!!!
AH! OH! SONUVA! WHAT WAS--
SHOULD'VE LEFT YOU WHERE PACO'S BUTT SQUISHED YOU.

...URGING CALM AS THE COSMIC STORM CONTINUES...

CRISIS '06

...EVERYONE 'SPECTS ME TO CLEAN UP AFTER 'M...

ASTRONOMERS ARE STILL TRYING TO EXPLAIN THE...

SKSSS

SKFFT

KCKKIK... KIKKICK... KCKKIK

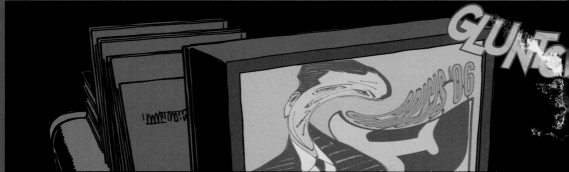

CLUNT

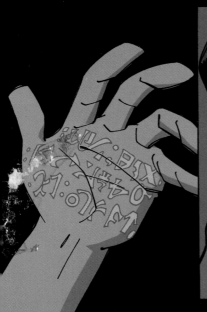

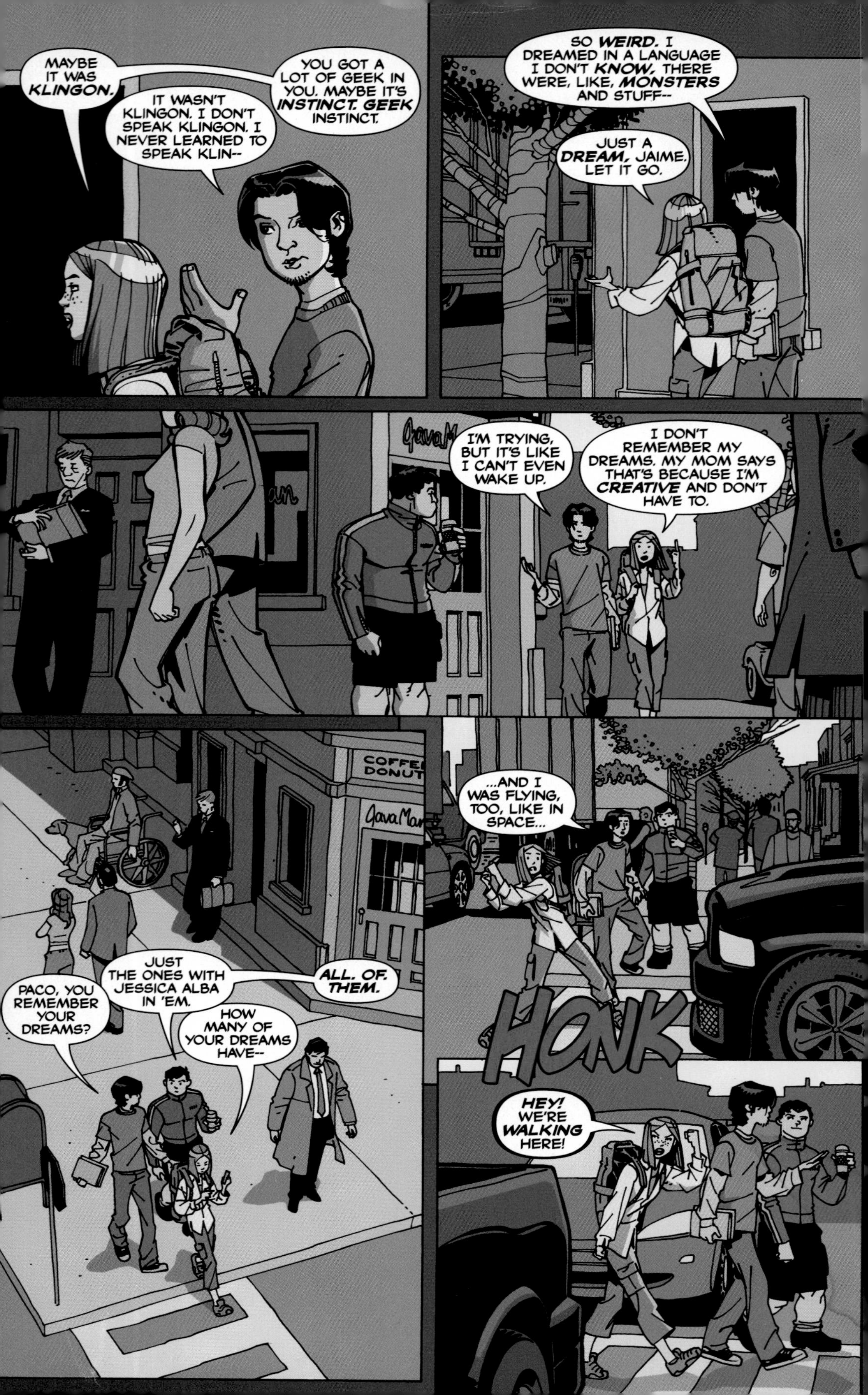
MAYBE IT WAS KLINGON.
IT WASN'T KLINGON. I DON'T SPEAK KLINGON. I NEVER LEARNED TO SPEAK KLIN--
YOU GOT A LOT OF GEEK IN YOU. MAYBE IT'S INSTINCT. GEEK INSTINCT.
SO WEIRD. I DREAMED IN A LANGUAGE I DON'T KNOW. THERE WERE, LIKE, MONSTERS AND STUFF--
JUST A DREAM, JAIME. LET IT GO.
I'M TRYING, BUT IT'S LIKE I CAN'T EVEN WAKE UP.
I DON'T REMEMBER MY DREAMS. MY MOM SAYS THAT'S BECAUSE I'M CREATIVE AND DON'T HAVE TO.
PACO, YOU REMEMBER YOUR DREAMS?
JUST THE ONES WITH JESSICA ALBA IN 'EM.
HOW MANY OF YOUR DREAMS HAVE--
ALL. OF. THEM.
...AND I WAS FLYING, TOO, LIKE IN SPACE...
HONK
HEY! WE'RE WALKING HERE!

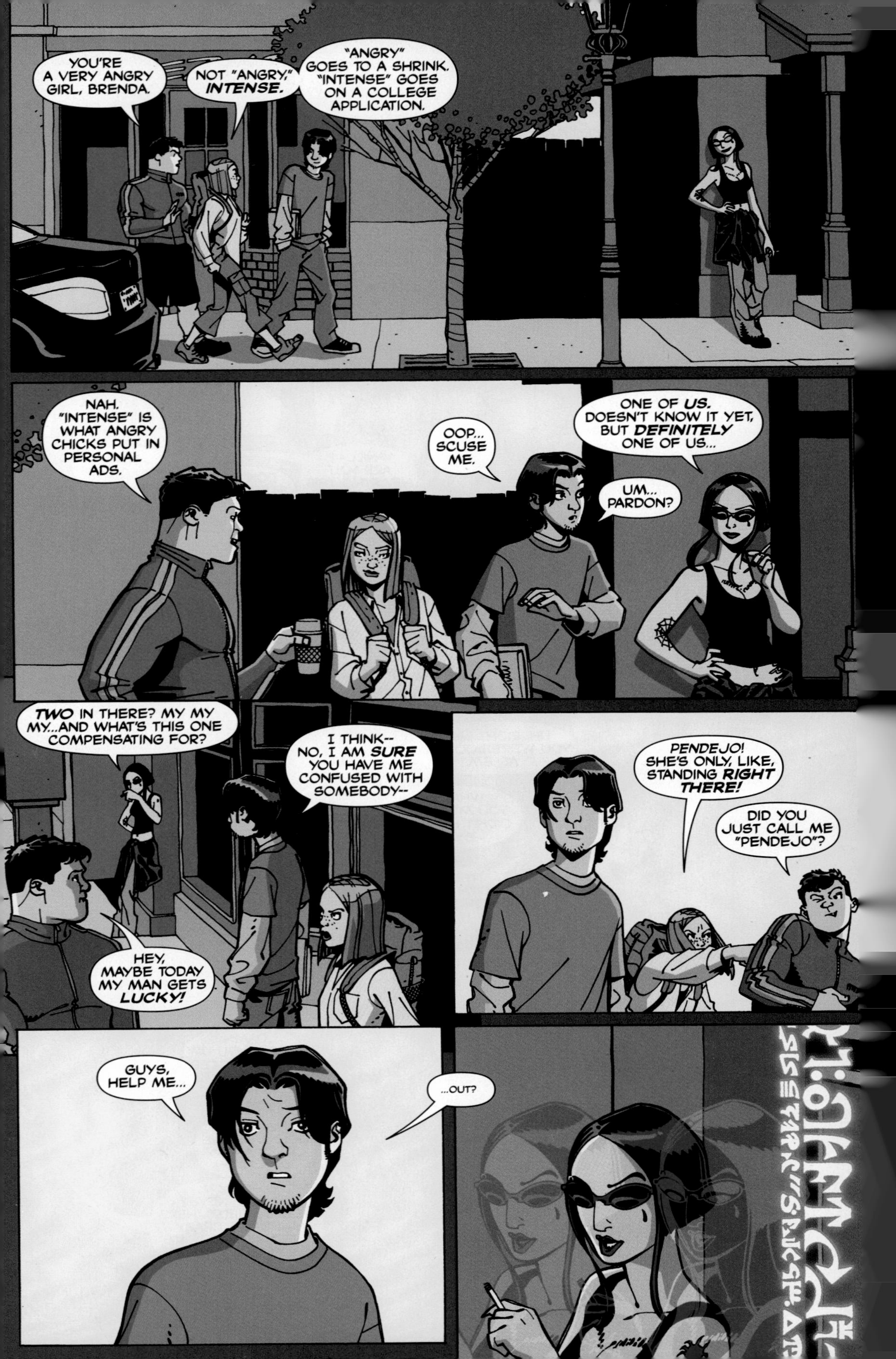

YOU'RE A VERY ANGRY GIRL, BRENDA.
NOT "ANGRY," *INTENSE.*
"ANGRY" GOES TO A SHRINK. "INTENSE" GOES ON A COLLEGE APPLICATION.
NAH. "INTENSE" IS WHAT ANGRY CHICKS PUT IN PERSONAL ADS.
OOP... SCUSE ME.
ONE OF *US.* DOESN'T KNOW IT YET, BUT *DEFINITELY* ONE OF US...
UM... PARDON?
TWO IN THERE? MY MY MY...AND WHAT'S THIS ONE COMPENSATING FOR?
I THINK-- NO, I AM *SURE* YOU HAVE ME CONFUSED WITH SOMEBODY--
HEY, MAYBE TODAY MY MAN GETS *LUCKY!*
PENDEJO! SHE'S ONLY, LIKE, STANDING *RIGHT THERE!*
DID YOU JUST CALL ME "PENDEJO"?
GUYS, HELP ME...
...OUT?

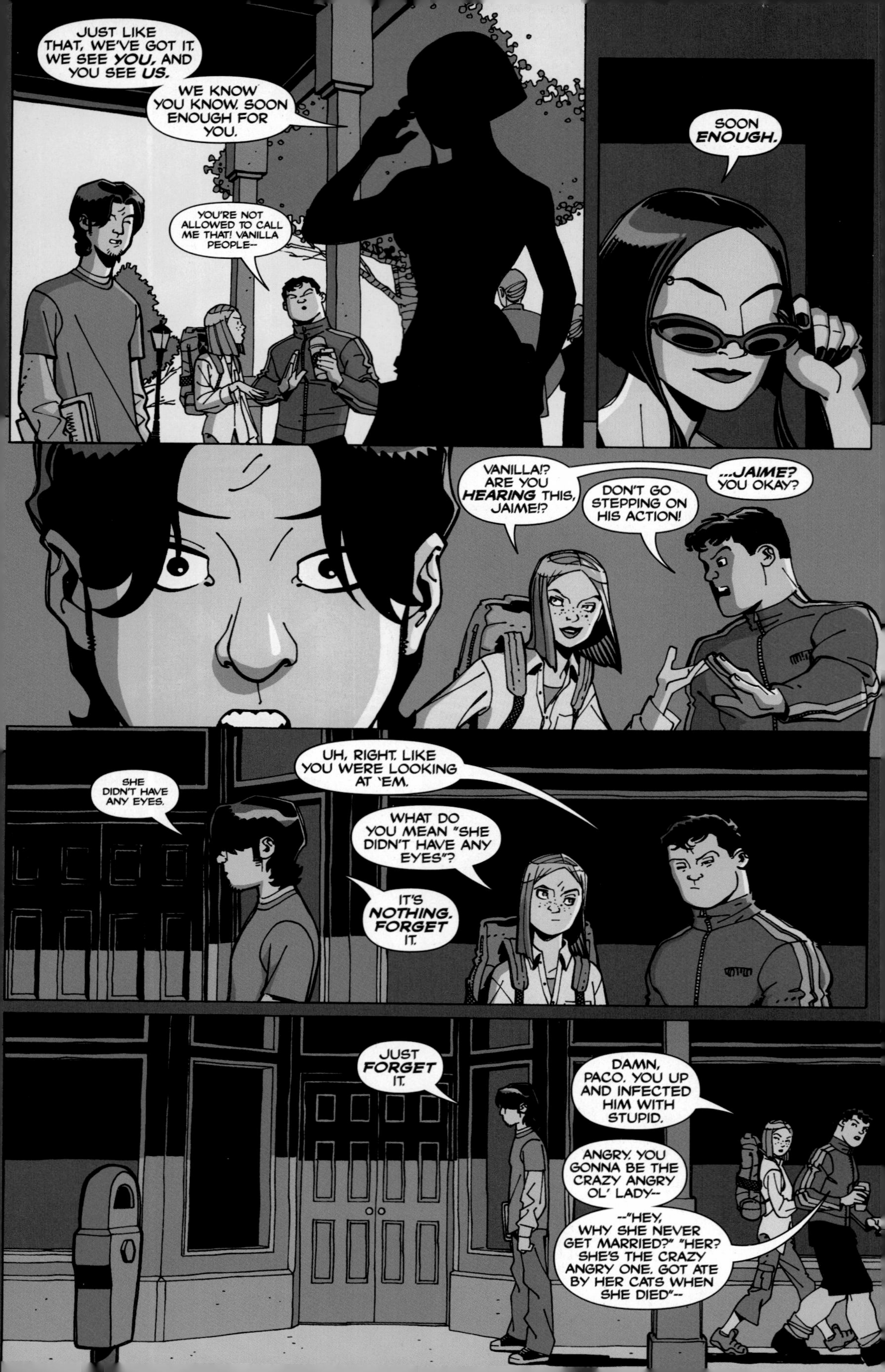

JUST LIKE THAT, WE'VE GOT IT. WE SEE *YOU,* AND YOU SEE *US.*
WE KNOW YOU KNOW. SOON ENOUGH FOR YOU.
YOU'RE NOT ALLOWED TO CALL ME THAT! VANILLA PEOPLE--
SOON *ENOUGH.*
VANILLA!? ARE YOU *HEARING* THIS, JAIME!?
DON'T GO STEPPING ON HIS ACTION!
...JAIME? YOU OKAY?
SHE DIDN'T HAVE ANY EYES.
UH, RIGHT. LIKE YOU WERE LOOKING AT 'EM.
WHAT DO YOU MEAN "SHE DIDN'T HAVE ANY EYES"?
IT'S *NOTHING. FORGET* IT.
JUST *FORGET* IT.
DAMN, PACO. YOU UP AND INFECTED HIM WITH STUPID.
ANGRY. YOU GONNA BE THE CRAZY ANGRY OL' LADY--
--"HEY, WHY SHE NEVER GET MARRIED?" "HER? SHE'S THE CRAZY ANGRY ONE. GOT ATE BY HER CATS WHEN SHE DIED"--

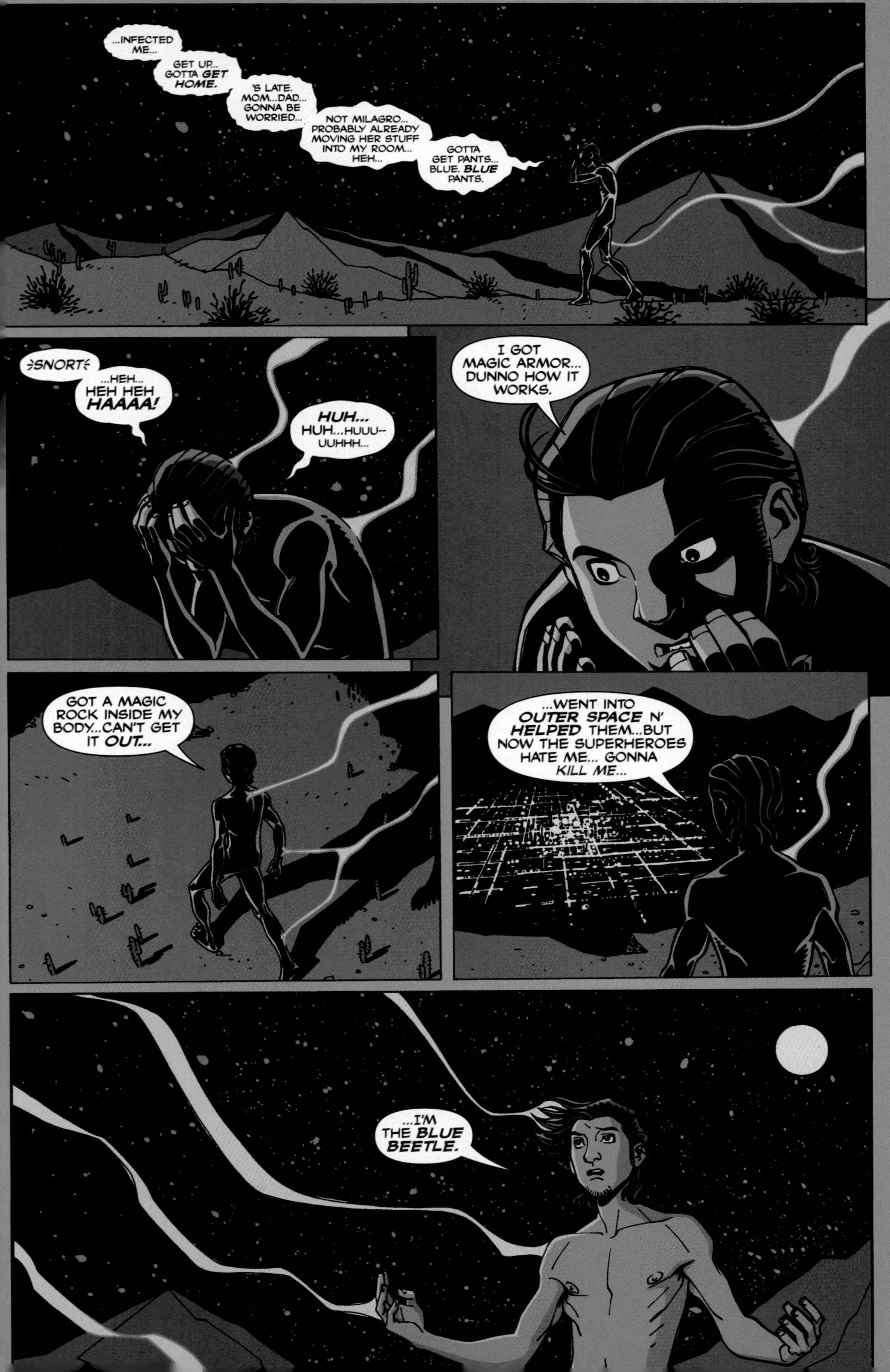

...INFECTED ME...
GET UP... GOTTA GET HOME.
'S LATE. MOM...DAD... GONNA BE WORRIED...
NOT MILAGRO... PROBABLY ALREADY MOVING HER STUFF INTO MY ROOM... HEH...
GOTTA GET PANTS... BLUE. BLUE PANTS.
SNORT
...HEH... HEH HEH HAAAA!
HUH... HUH...HUUU--UUHHH...
I GOT MAGIC ARMOR... DUNNO HOW IT WORKS.
GOT A MAGIC ROCK INSIDE MY BODY...CAN'T GET IT OUT...
...WENT INTO OUTER SPACE N' HELPED THEM...BUT NOW THE SUPERHEROES HATE ME... GONNA KILL ME...
...I'M THE BLUE BEETLE.

BLUE BEETLE #2
Cover and interior art by Cully Hamner

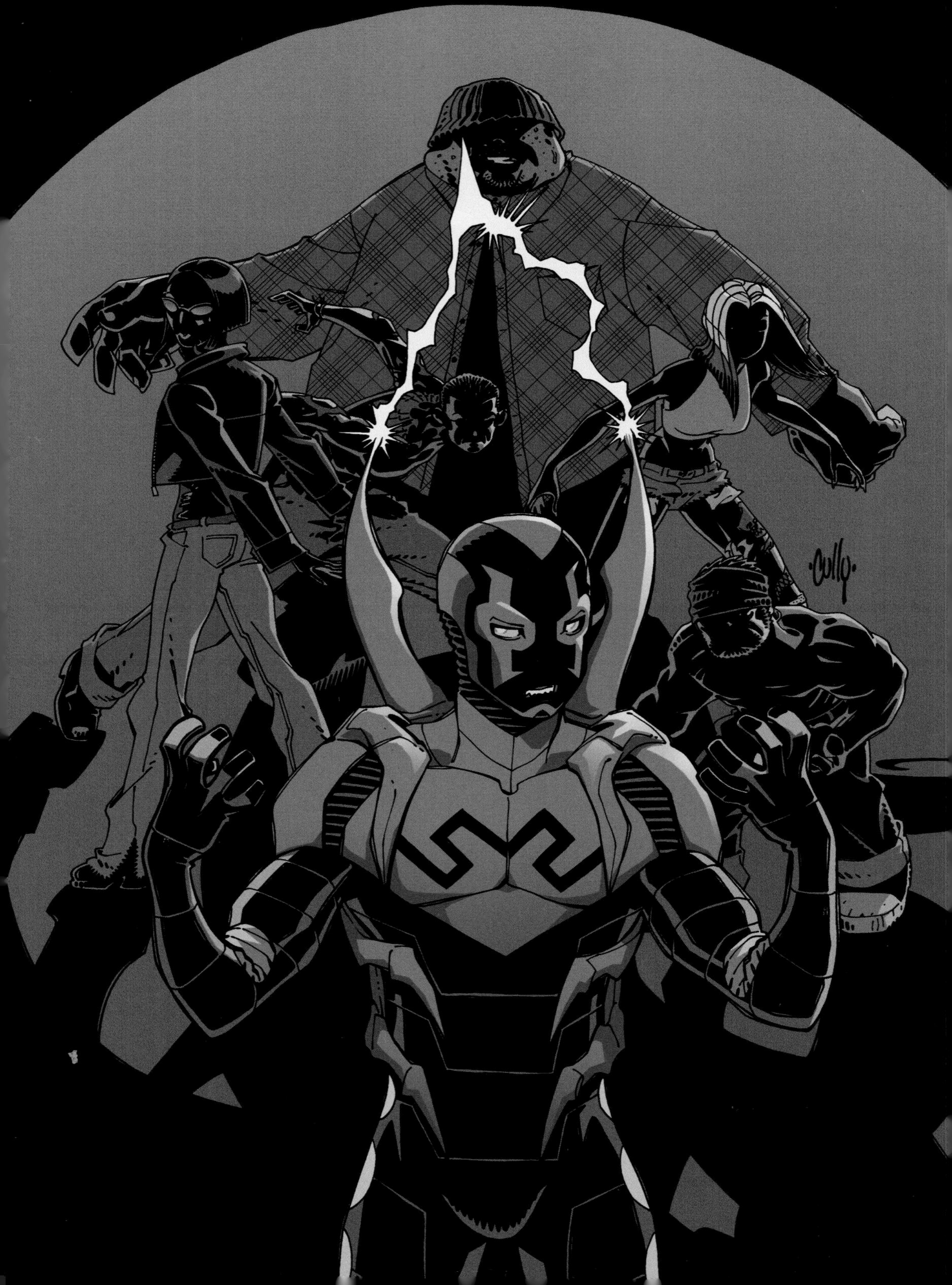
Cully

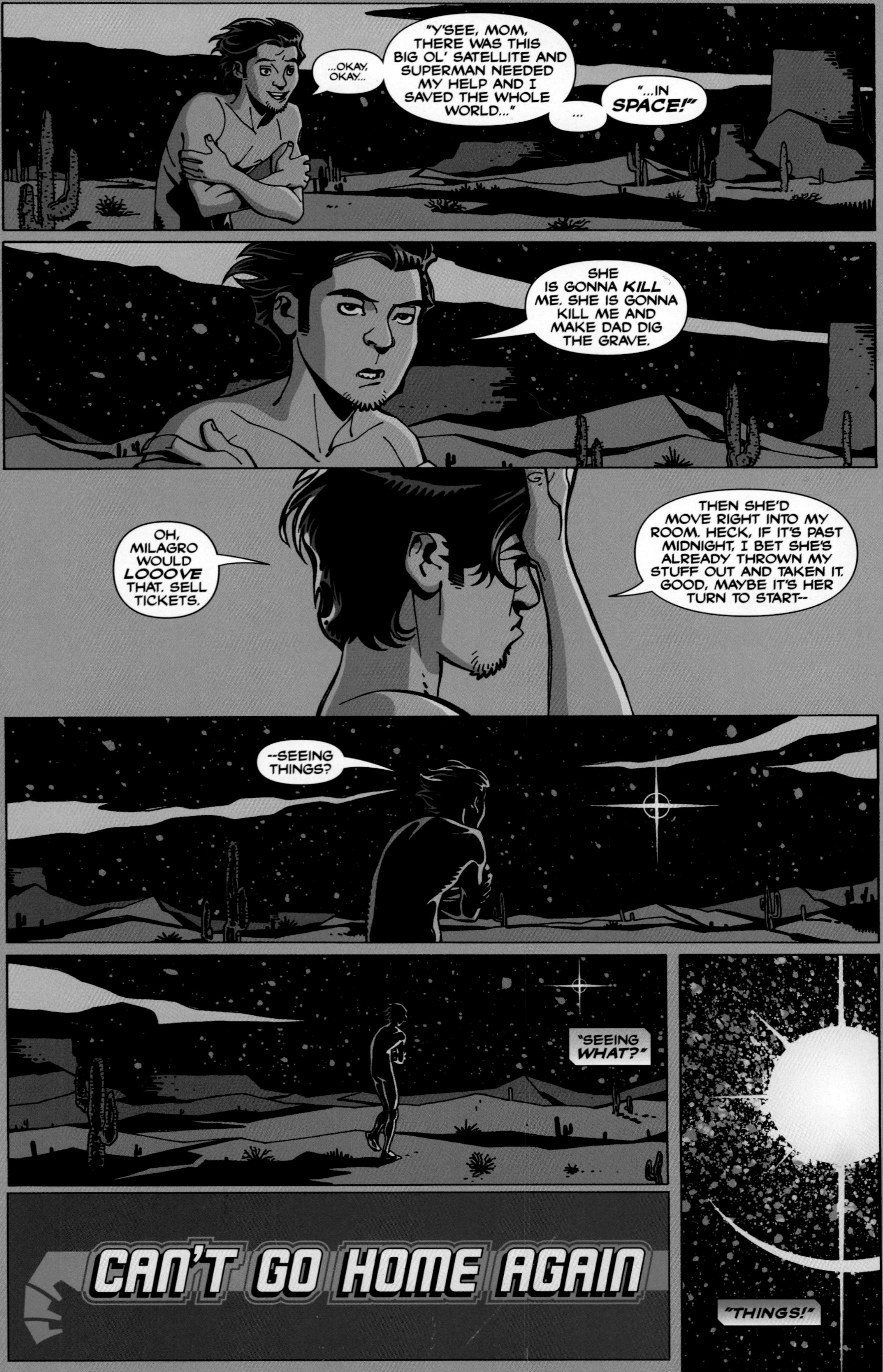
...OKAY, OKAY...
"Y'SEE, MOM, THERE WAS THIS BIG OL' SATELLITE AND SUPERMAN NEEDED MY HELP AND I SAVED THE WHOLE WORLD..."
...
"...IN SPACE!"
SHE IS GONNA KILL ME. SHE IS GONNA KILL ME AND MAKE DAD DIG THE GRAVE.
OH, MILAGRO WOULD LOOOVE THAT. SELL TICKETS.
THEN SHE'D MOVE RIGHT INTO MY ROOM. HECK, IF IT'S PAST MIDNIGHT, I BET SHE'S ALREADY THROWN MY STUFF OUT AND TAKEN IT. GOOD, MAYBE IT'S HER TURN TO START--
--SEEING THINGS?
"SEEING WHAT?"
CAN'T GO HOME AGAIN
"THINGS!"

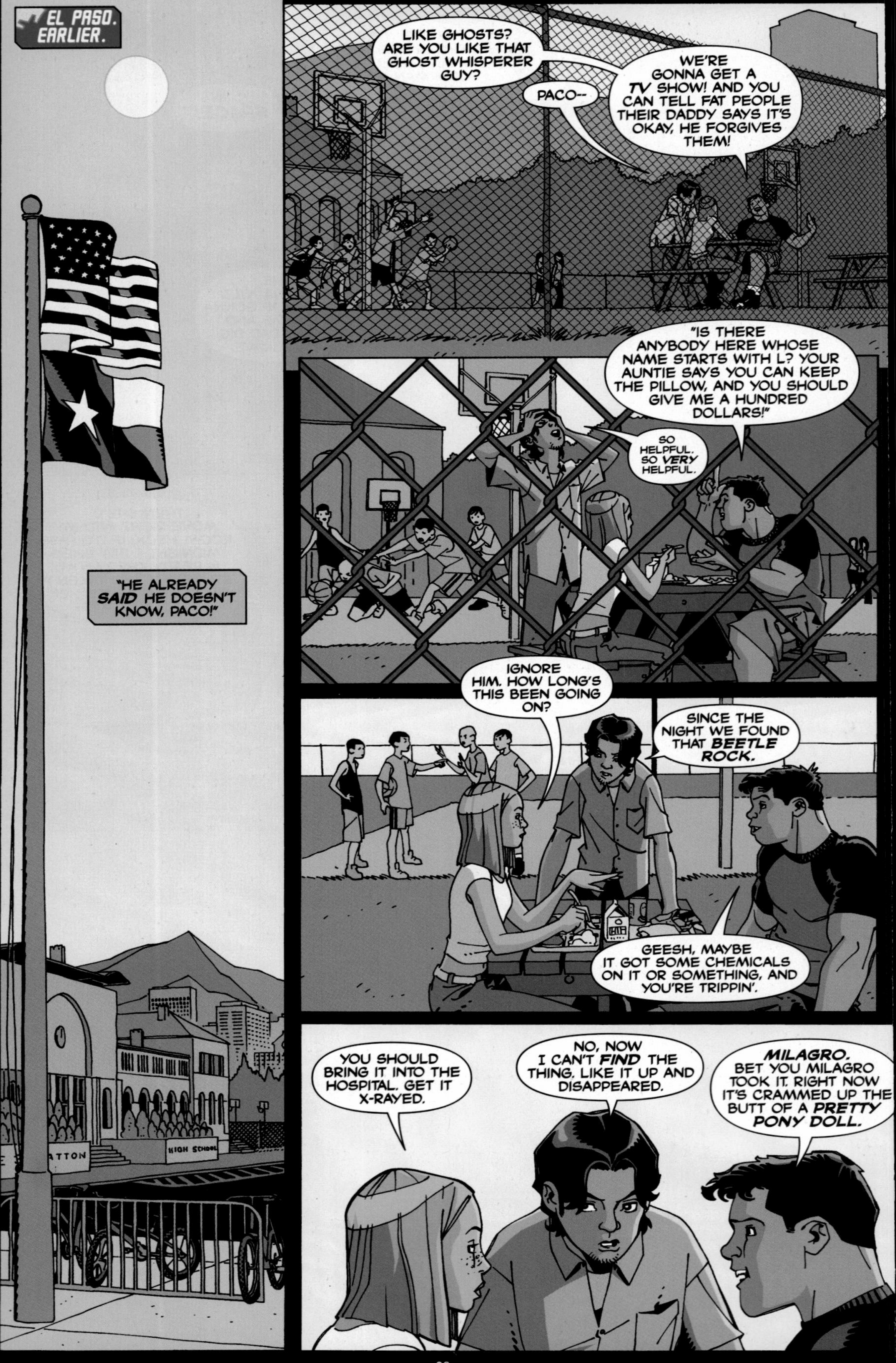
EL PASO. EARLIER.
LIKE GHOSTS? ARE YOU LIKE THAT GHOST WHISPERER GUY?
WE'RE GONNA GET A TV SHOW! AND YOU CAN TELL FAT PEOPLE THEIR DADDY SAYS IT'S OKAY, HE FORGIVES THEM!
PACO--
"HE ALREADY SAID HE DOESN'T KNOW, PACO!"
"IS THERE ANYBODY HERE WHOSE NAME STARTS WITH L? YOUR AUNTIE SAYS YOU CAN KEEP THE PILLOW, AND YOU SHOULD GIVE ME A HUNDRED DOLLARS!"
SO HELPFUL. SO VERY HELPFUL.
IGNORE HIM. HOW LONG'S THIS BEEN GOING ON?
SINCE THE NIGHT WE FOUND THAT BEETLE ROCK.
GEESH, MAYBE IT GOT SOME CHEMICALS ON IT OR SOMETHING, AND YOU'RE TRIPPIN'.
YOU SHOULD BRING IT INTO THE HOSPITAL. GET IT X-RAYED.
NO, NOW I CAN'T FIND THE THING. LIKE IT UP AND DISAPPEARED.
MILAGRO. BET YOU MILAGRO TOOK IT. RIGHT NOW IT'S CRAMMED UP THE BUTT OF A PRETTY PONY DOLL.
HIGH SCHOOL

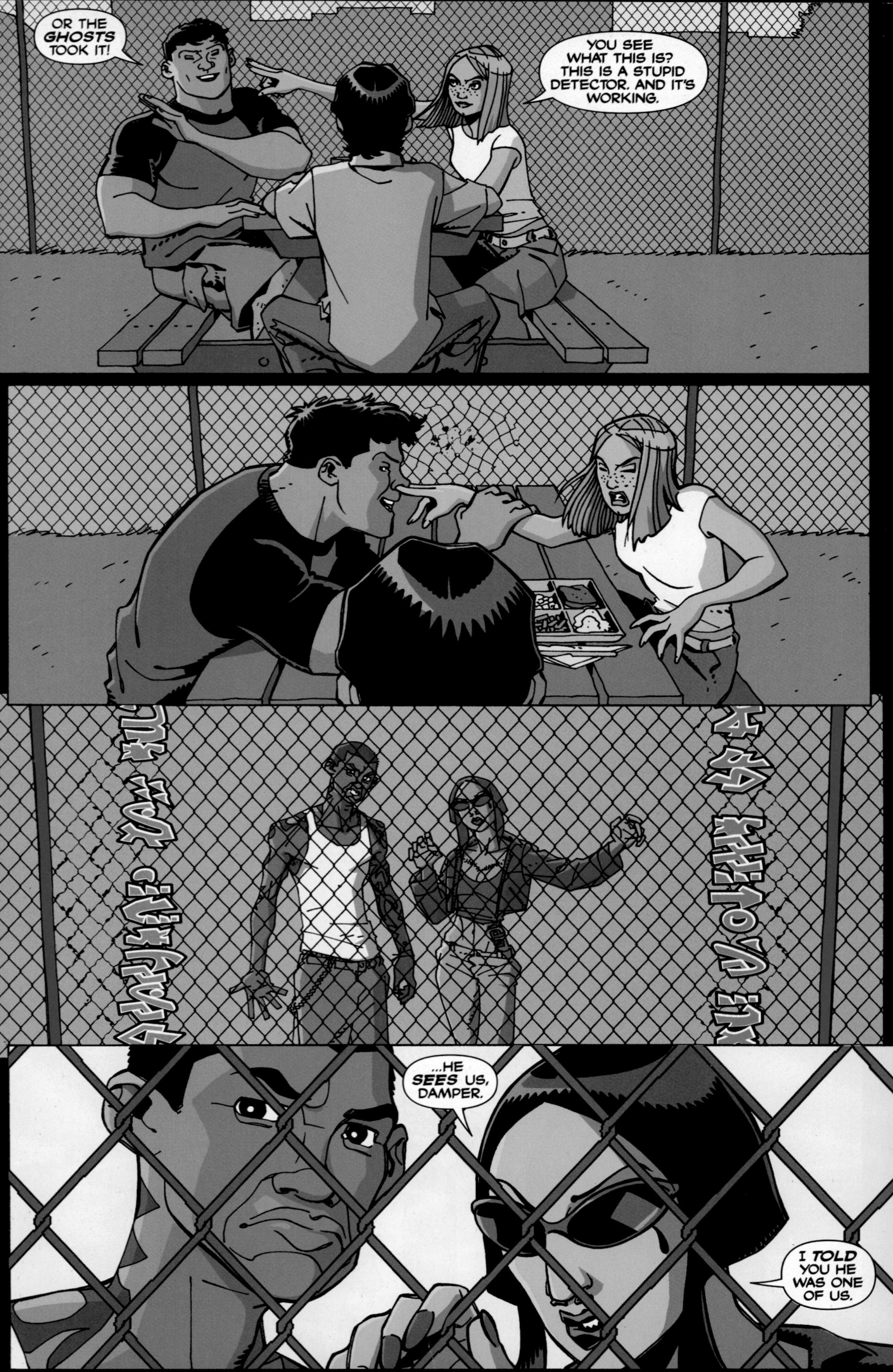
OR THE GHOSTS TOOK IT!
YOU SEE WHAT THIS IS? THIS IS A STUPID DETECTOR. AND IT'S WORKING.
...HE SEES US, DAMPER.
I TOLD YOU HE WAS ONE OF US.

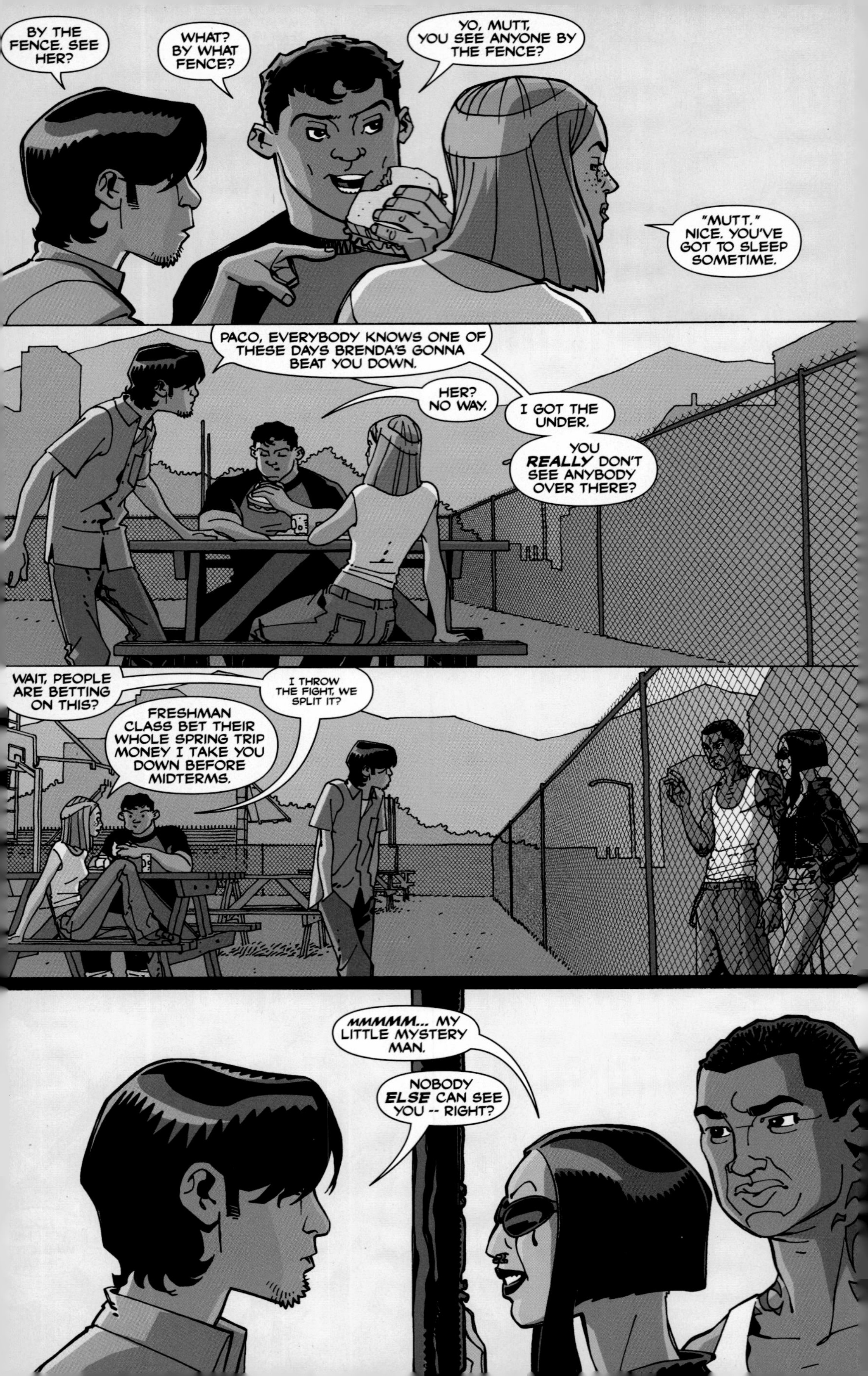
BY THE FENCE. SEE HER?
WHAT? BY WHAT FENCE?
YO, MUTT, YOU SEE ANYONE BY THE FENCE?
"MUTT." NICE. YOU'VE GOT TO SLEEP SOMETIME.
PACO, EVERYBODY KNOWS ONE OF THESE DAYS BRENDA'S GONNA BEAT YOU DOWN.
HER? NO WAY.
I GOT THE UNDER.
YOU REALLY DON'T SEE ANYBODY OVER THERE?
WAIT, PEOPLE ARE BETTING ON THIS?
I THROW THE FIGHT, WE SPLIT IT?
FRESHMAN CLASS BET THEIR WHOLE SPRING TRIP MONEY I TAKE YOU DOWN BEFORE MIDTERMS.
MMMMM... MY LITTLE MYSTERY MAN.
NOBODY ELSE CAN SEE YOU -- RIGHT?

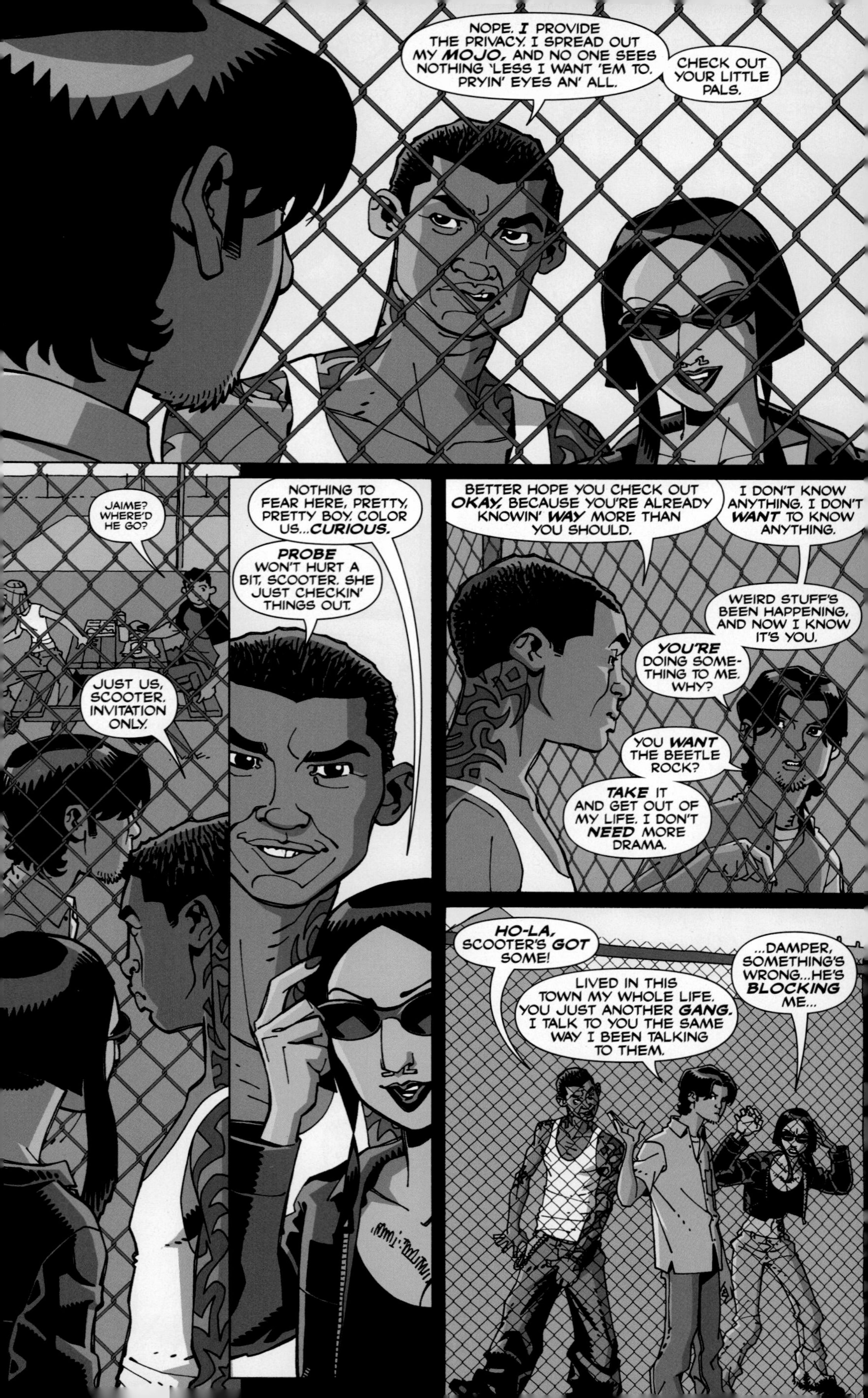
NOPE. I PROVIDE THE PRIVACY. I SPREAD OUT MY MOJO, AND NO ONE SEES NOTHING 'LESS I WANT 'EM TO. PRYIN' EYES AN' ALL.
CHECK OUT YOUR LITTLE PALS.
JAIME? WHERE'D HE GO?
JUST US, SCOOTER. INVITATION ONLY.
NOTHING TO FEAR HERE, PRETTY, PRETTY BOY. COLOR US...CURIOUS.
PROBE WON'T HURT A BIT, SCOOTER. SHE JUST CHECKIN' THINGS OUT.
BETTER HOPE YOU CHECK OUT OKAY, BECAUSE YOU'RE ALREADY KNOWIN' WAY MORE THAN YOU SHOULD.
I DON'T KNOW ANYTHING. I DON'T WANT TO KNOW ANYTHING.
WEIRD STUFF'S BEEN HAPPENING, AND NOW I KNOW IT'S YOU.
YOU'RE DOING SOMETHING TO ME. WHY?
YOU WANT THE BEETLE ROCK?
TAKE IT AND GET OUT OF MY LIFE. I DON'T NEED MORE DRAMA.
HO-LA, SCOOTER'S GOT SOME!
LIVED IN THIS TOWN MY WHOLE LIFE. YOU JUST ANOTHER GANG. I TALK TO YOU THE SAME WAY I BEEN TALKING TO THEM.
...DAMPER, SOMETHING'S WRONG...HE'S BLOCKING ME...

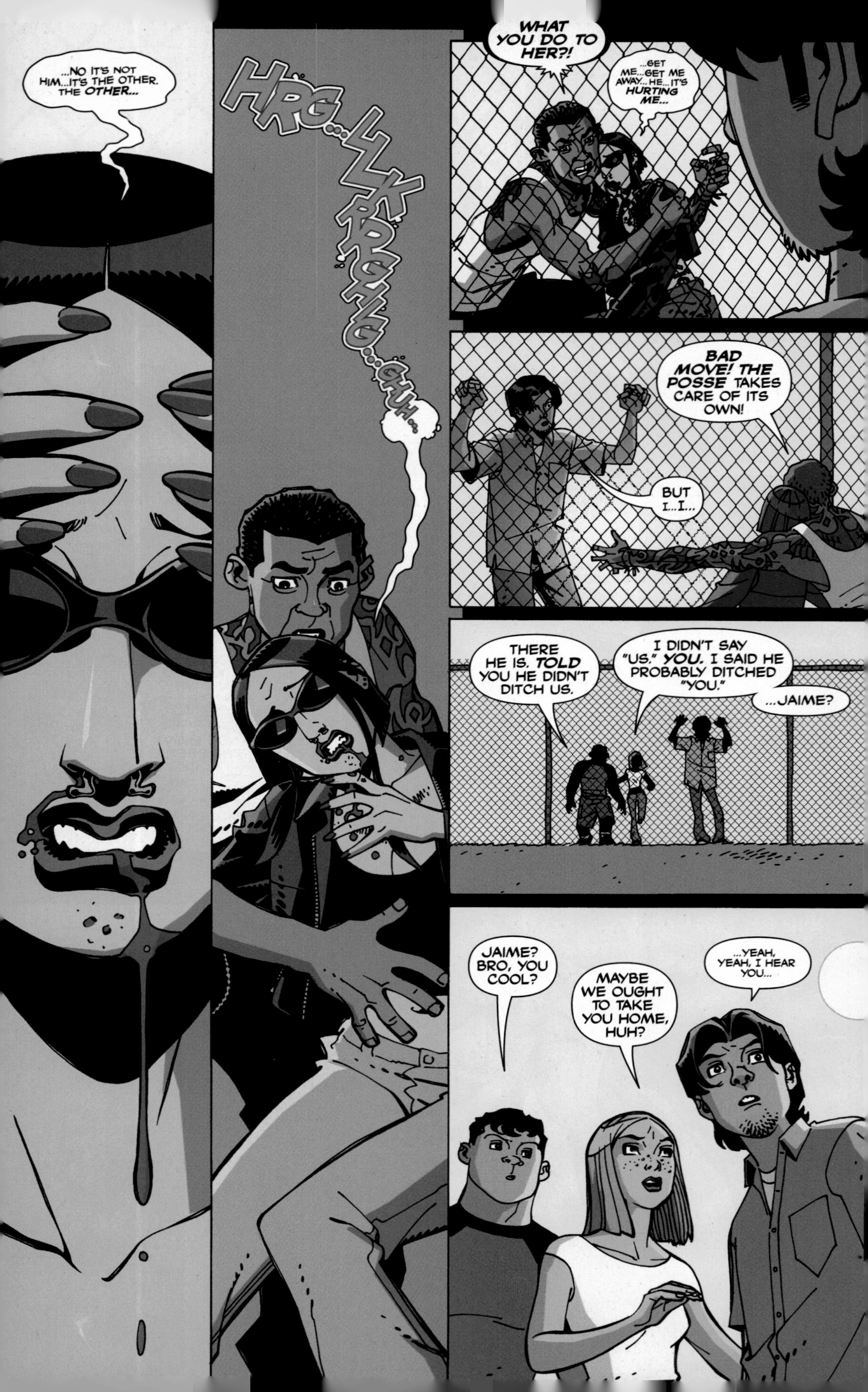
...NO IT'S NOT HIM...IT'S THE OTHER. THE OTHER...
HRG...LLKRGHG...CHUH...
WHAT YOU DO TO HER?!
...GET ME...GET ME AWAY...HE...IT'S HURTING ME...
BAD MOVE! THE POSSE TAKES CARE OF ITS OWN!
BUT I...I...
THERE HE IS. TOLD YOU HE DIDN'T DITCH US.
I DIDN'T SAY "US," YOU. I SAID HE PROBABLY DITCHED "YOU."
...JAIME?
JAIME? BRO, YOU COOL?
MAYBE WE OUGHT TO TAKE YOU HOME, HUH?
...YEAH, YEAH, I HEAR YOU...

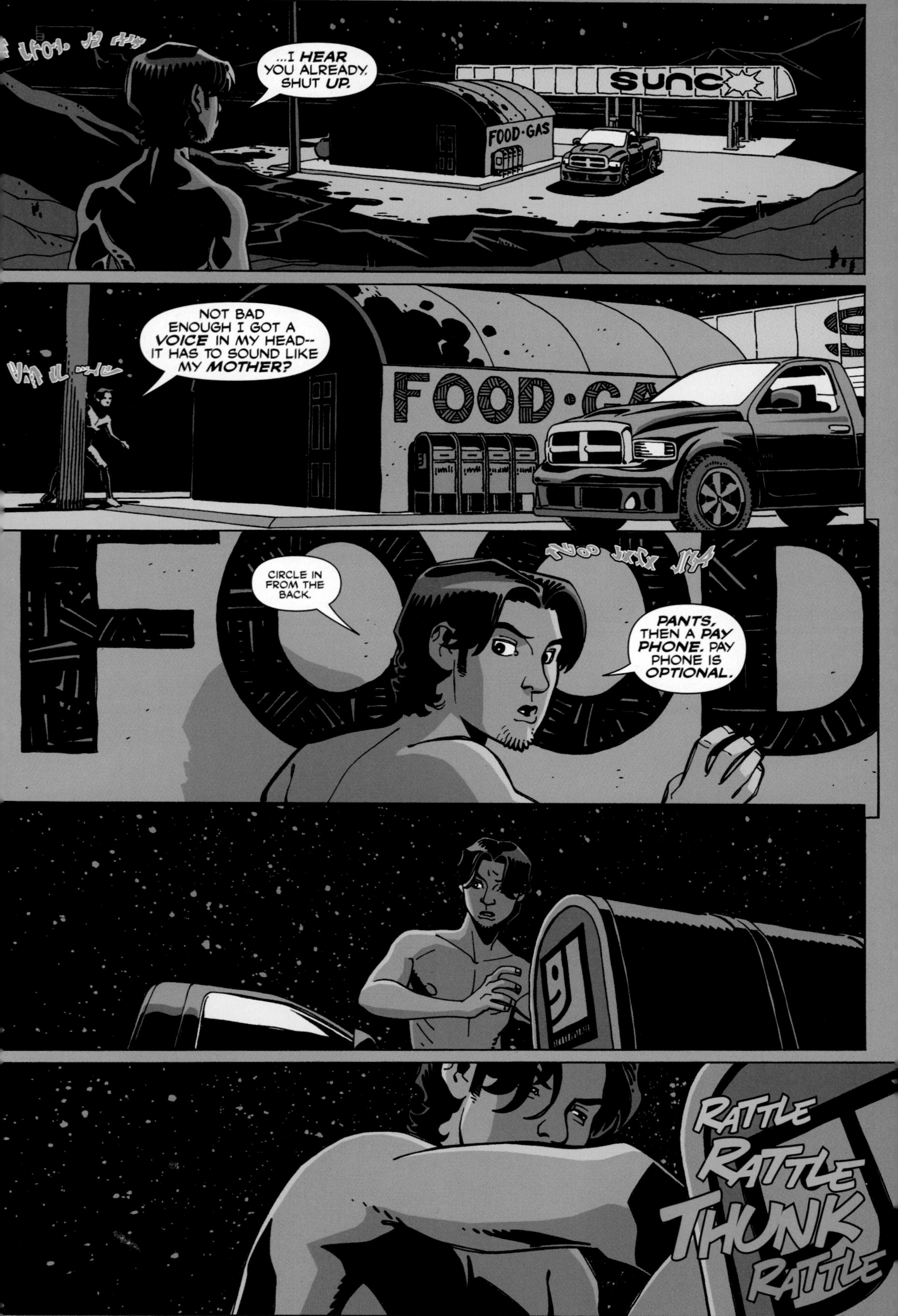

...I HEAR YOU ALREADY. SHUT UP.
SUNCO
FOOD · GAS
NOT BAD ENOUGH I GOT A VOICE IN MY HEAD-- IT HAS TO SOUND LIKE MY MOTHER?
CIRCLE IN FROM THE BACK.
PANTS, THEN A PAY PHONE. PAY PHONE IS OPTIONAL.
RATTLE
RATTLE
THUNK
RATTLE

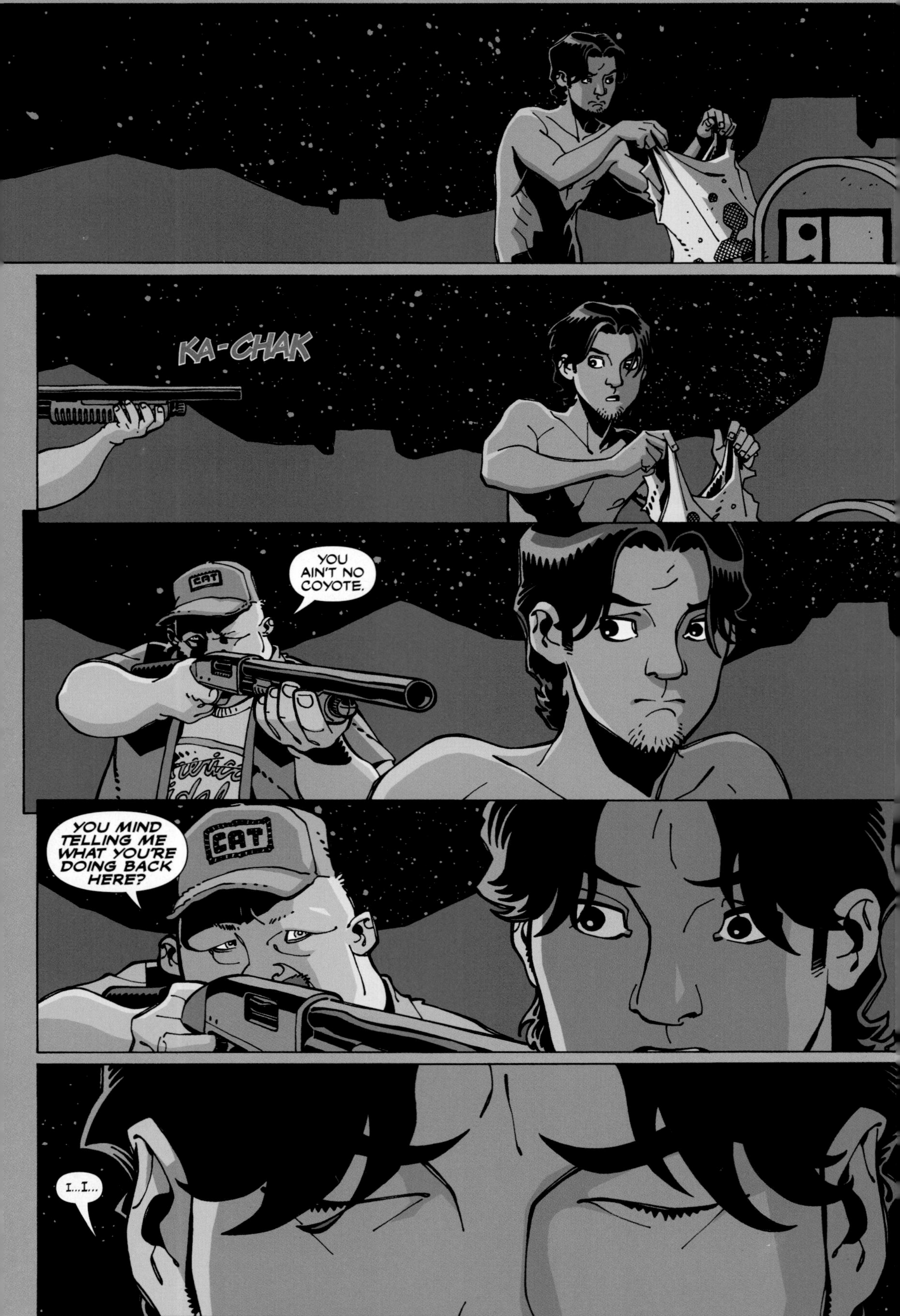
KA-CHAK
YOU AIN'T NO COYOTE.
CAT
YOU MIND TELLING ME WHAT YOU'RE DOING BACK HERE?
CAT
I...I...

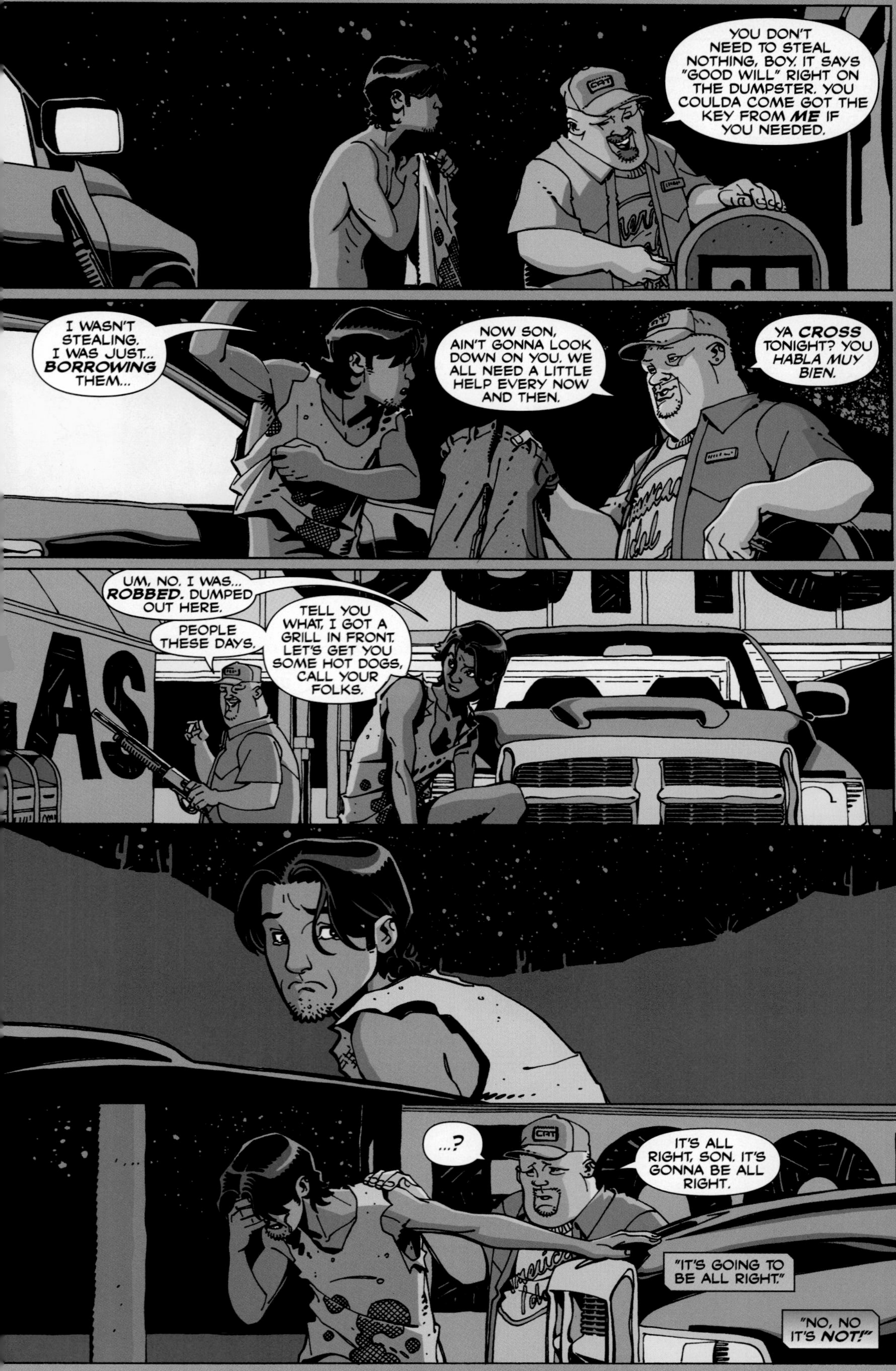
YOU DON'T NEED TO STEAL NOTHING, BOY. IT SAYS "GOOD WILL" RIGHT ON THE DUMPSTER. YOU COULDA COME GOT THE KEY FROM *ME* IF YOU NEEDED.
I WASN'T STEALING. I WAS JUST... ***BORROWING*** THEM...
NOW SON, AIN'T GONNA LOOK DOWN ON YOU. WE ALL NEED A LITTLE HELP EVERY NOW AND THEN.
YA ***CROSS*** TONIGHT? YOU *HABLA MUY BIEN.*
UM, NO. I WAS... ***ROBBED.*** DUMPED OUT HERE.
PEOPLE THESE DAYS.
TELL YOU WHAT, I GOT A GRILL IN FRONT. LET'S GET YOU SOME HOT DOGS, CALL YOUR FOLKS.
...?
IT'S ALL RIGHT, SON. IT'S GONNA BE ALL RIGHT.
"IT'S GOING TO BE ALL RIGHT."
"NO, NO IT'S ***NOT!***"

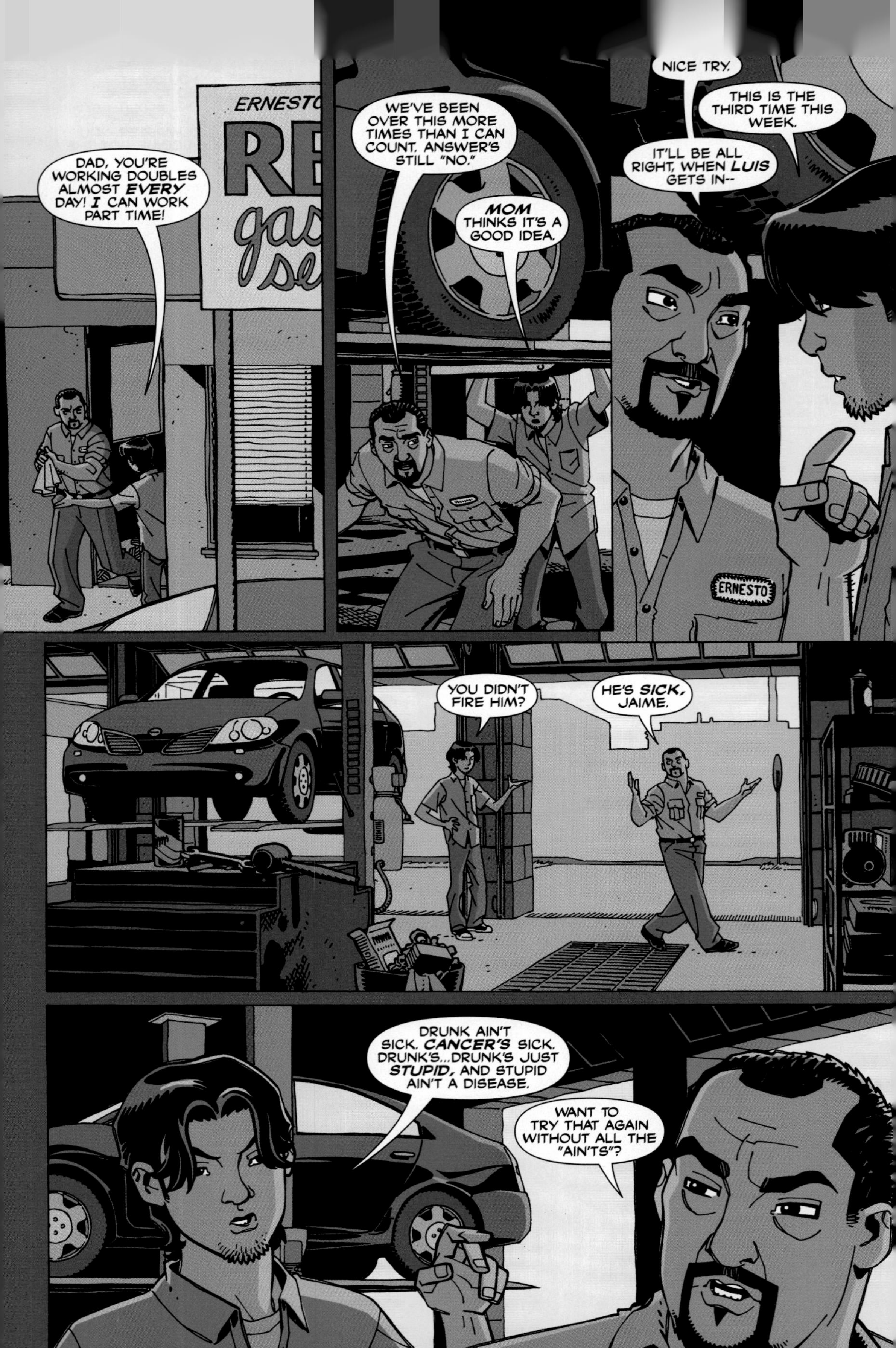
ERNESTO
DAD, YOU'RE WORKING DOUBLES ALMOST EVERY DAY! I CAN WORK PART TIME!
WE'VE BEEN OVER THIS MORE TIMES THAN I CAN COUNT. ANSWER'S STILL "NO."
MOM THINKS IT'S A GOOD IDEA.
NICE TRY.
IT'LL BE ALL RIGHT, WHEN LUIS GETS IN--
THIS IS THE THIRD TIME THIS WEEK.
ERNESTO
YOU DIDN'T FIRE HIM?
HE'S SICK, JAIME.
DRUNK AIN'T SICK. CANCER'S SICK. DRUNK'S...DRUNK'S JUST STUPID, AND STUPID AIN'T A DISEASE.
WANT TO TRY THAT AGAIN WITHOUT ALL THE "AIN'TS"?

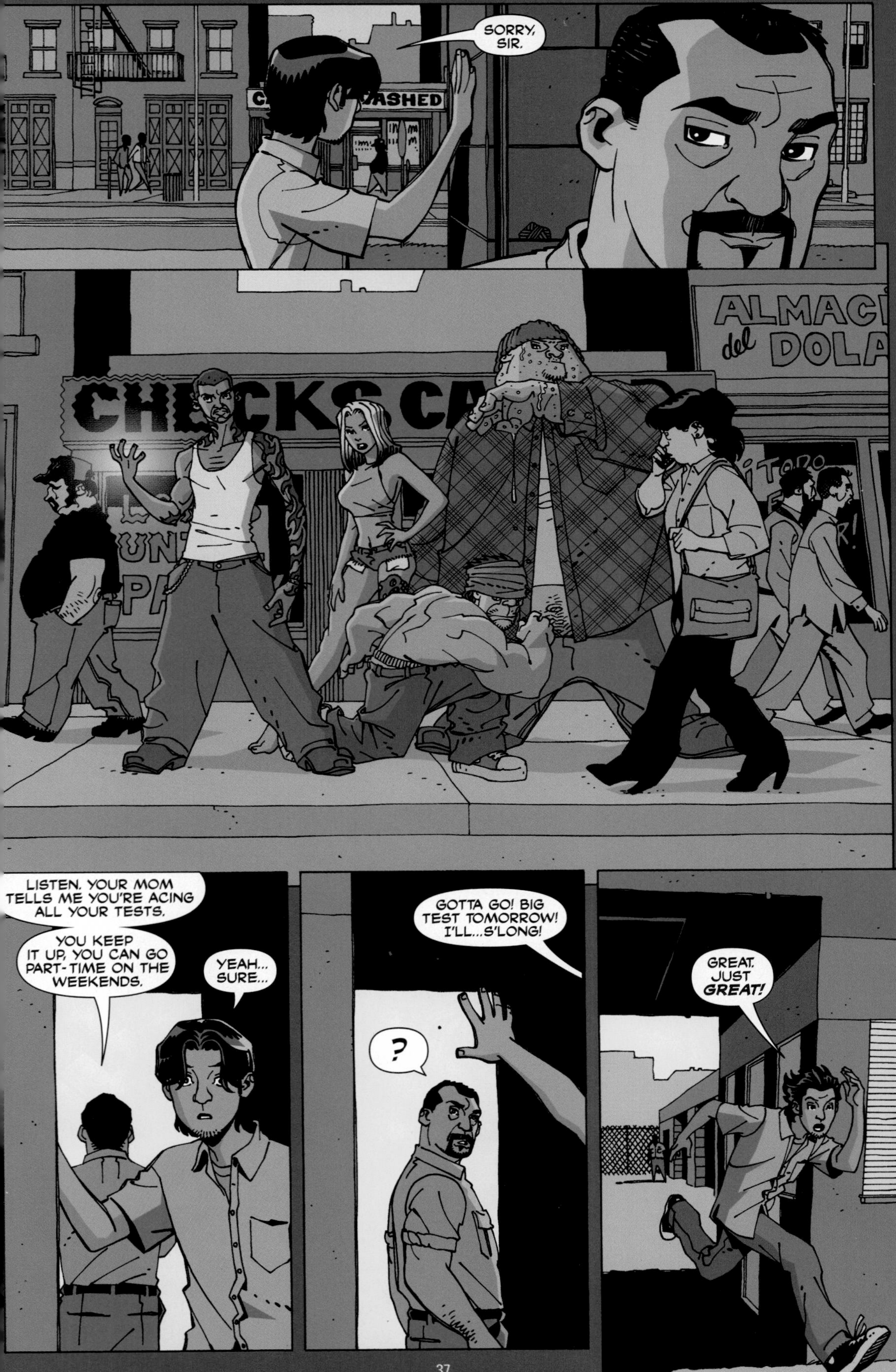
SORRY, SIR.
C ASHED
ALMAC
del DOLA
CH CKS CA
LISTEN. YOUR MOM TELLS ME YOU'RE ACING ALL YOUR TESTS.
YOU KEEP IT UP, YOU CAN GO PART-TIME ON THE WEEKENDS.
YEAH... SURE...
GOTTA GO! BIG TEST TOMORROW! I'LL...S'LONG!
?
GREAT. JUST GREAT!

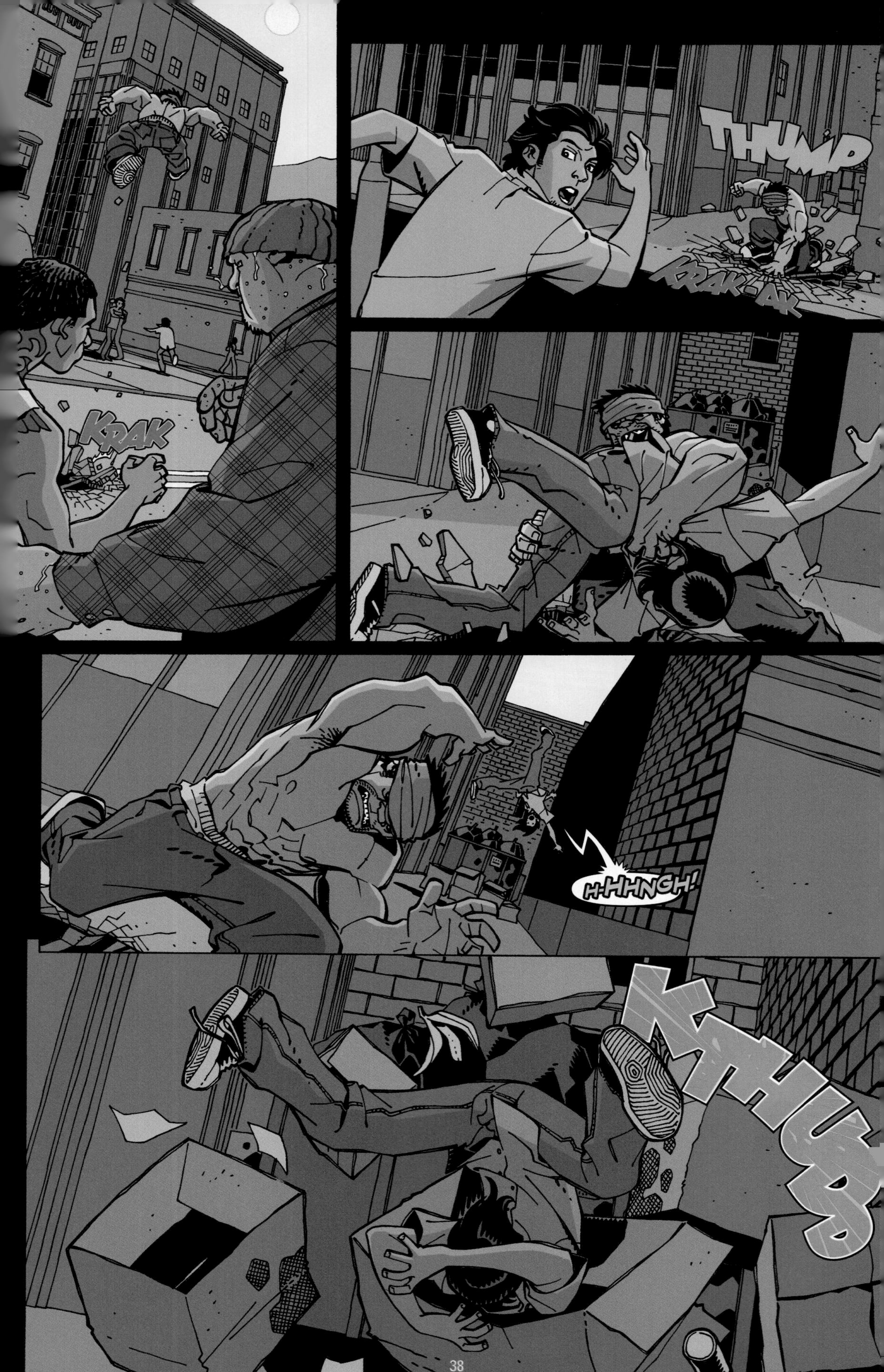
KRAK
THUMP
KRAK-AK
H-HHNGH!
KTHUD

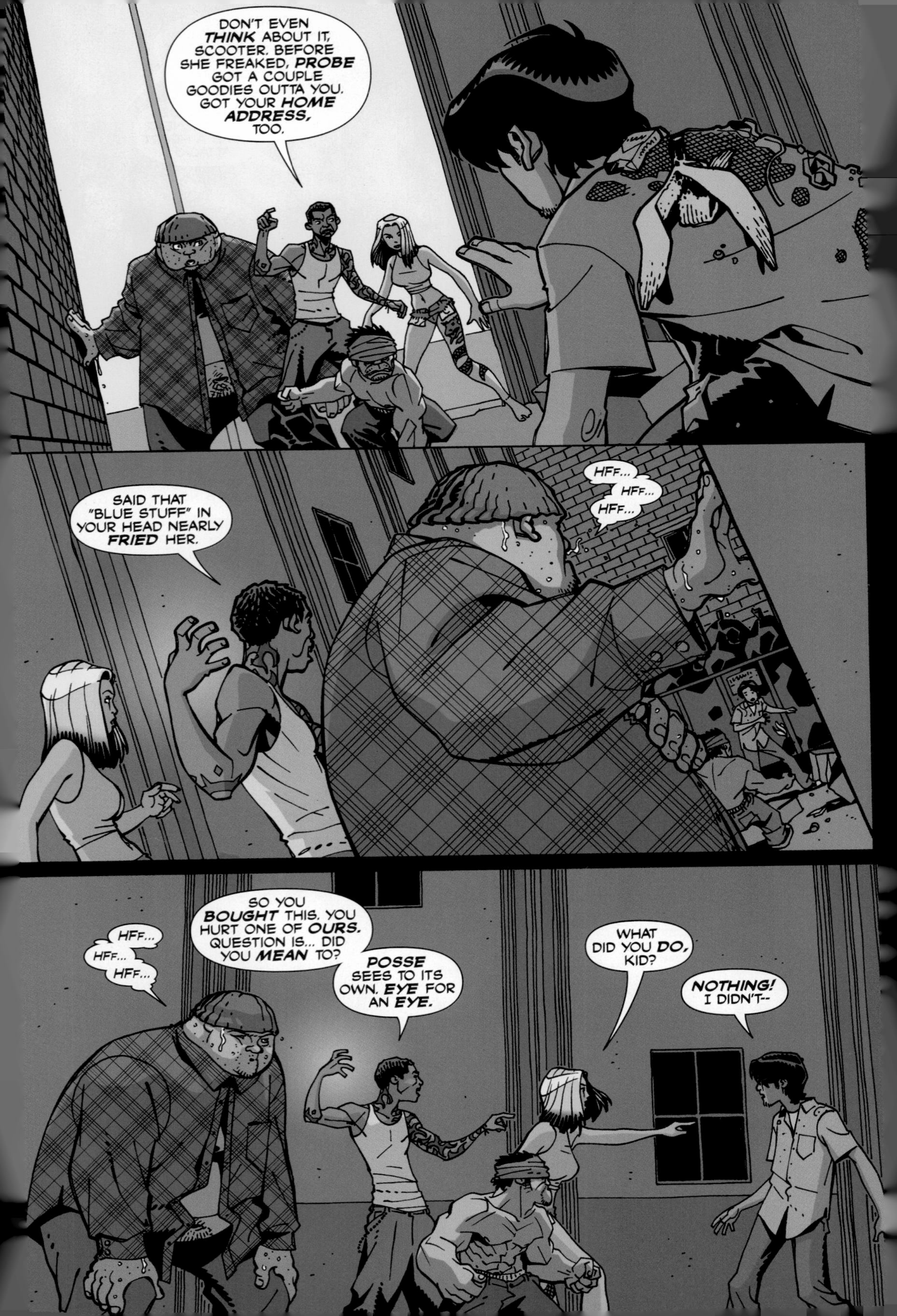

DON'T EVEN THINK ABOUT IT, SCOOTER. BEFORE SHE FREAKED, PROBE GOT A COUPLE GOODIES OUTTA YOU. GOT YOUR HOME ADDRESS, TOO.
SAID THAT "BLUE STUFF" IN YOUR HEAD NEARLY FRIED HER.
HFF... HFF... HFF...
HFF... HFF... HFF...
SO YOU BOUGHT THIS. YOU HURT ONE OF OURS. QUESTION IS... DID YOU MEAN TO?
POSSE SEES TO ITS OWN. EYE FOR AN EYE.
WHAT DID YOU DO, KID?
NOTHING! I DIDN'T--

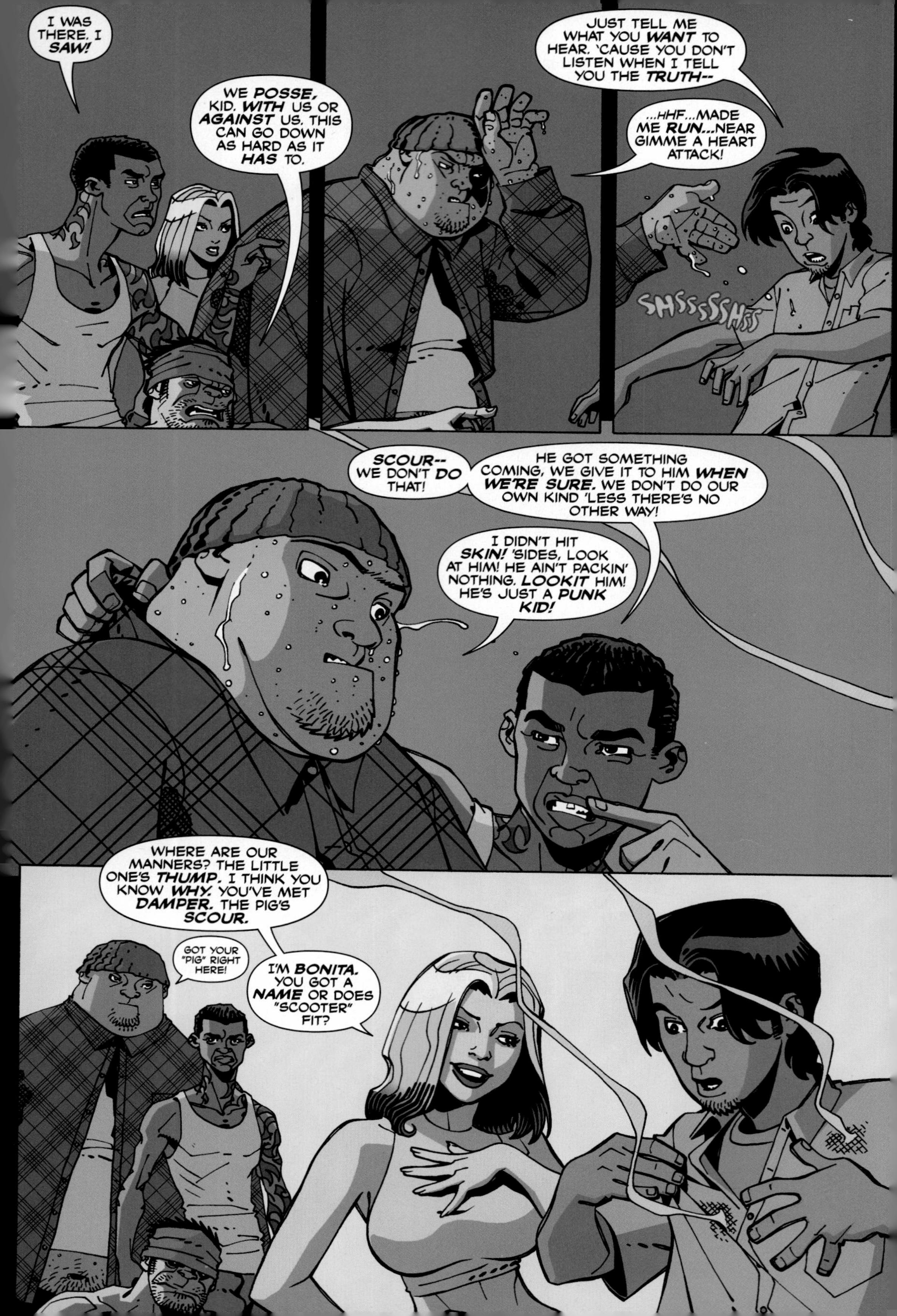
I WAS THERE. I SAW!
WE POSSE, KID. WITH US OR AGAINST US. THIS CAN GO DOWN AS HARD AS IT HAS TO.
JUST TELL ME WHAT YOU WANT TO HEAR. 'CAUSE YOU DON'T LISTEN WHEN I TELL YOU THE TRUTH--
...HHF...MADE ME RUN...NEAR GIMME A HEART ATTACK!
SHSSSSSHSS
SCOUR-- WE DON'T DO THAT!
HE GOT SOMETHING COMING, WE GIVE IT TO HIM WHEN WE'RE SURE. WE DON'T DO OUR OWN KIND 'LESS THERE'S NO OTHER WAY!
I DIDN'T HIT SKIN! 'SIDES, LOOK AT HIM! HE AIN'T PACKIN' NOTHING. LOOKIT HIM! HE'S JUST A PUNK KID!
WHERE ARE OUR MANNERS? THE LITTLE ONE'S THUMP. I THINK YOU KNOW WHY. YOU'VE MET DAMPER. THE PIG'S SCOUR.
GOT YOUR "PIG" RIGHT HERE!
I'M BONITA. YOU GOT A NAME OR DOES "SCOOTER" FIT?

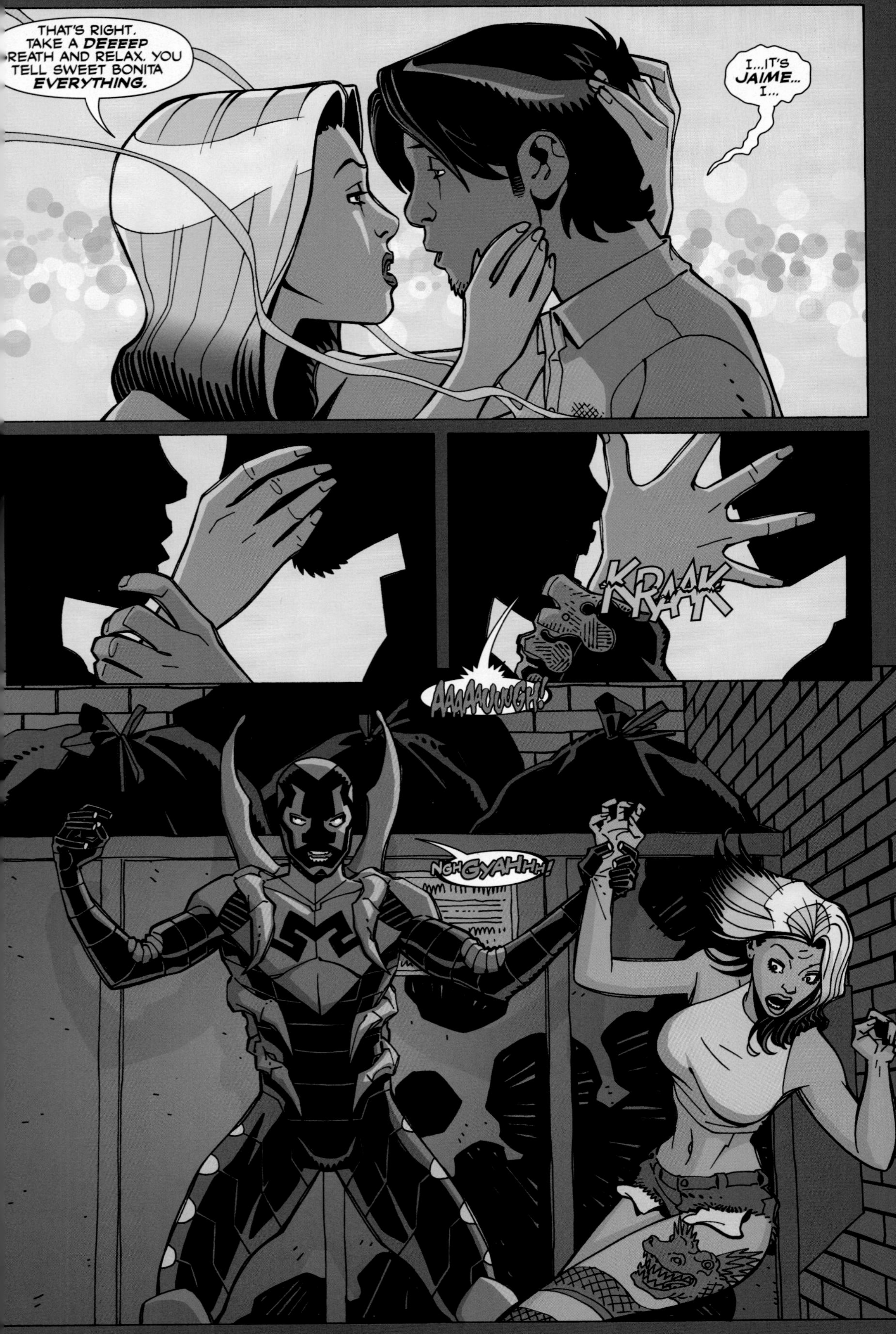
THAT'S RIGHT. TAKE A DEEEEP REATH AND RELAX. YOU TELL SWEET BONITA EVERYTHING.
I...IT'S JAIME... I...
KRAAK
AAAAAUUUGH!
NGHGYAHHH!

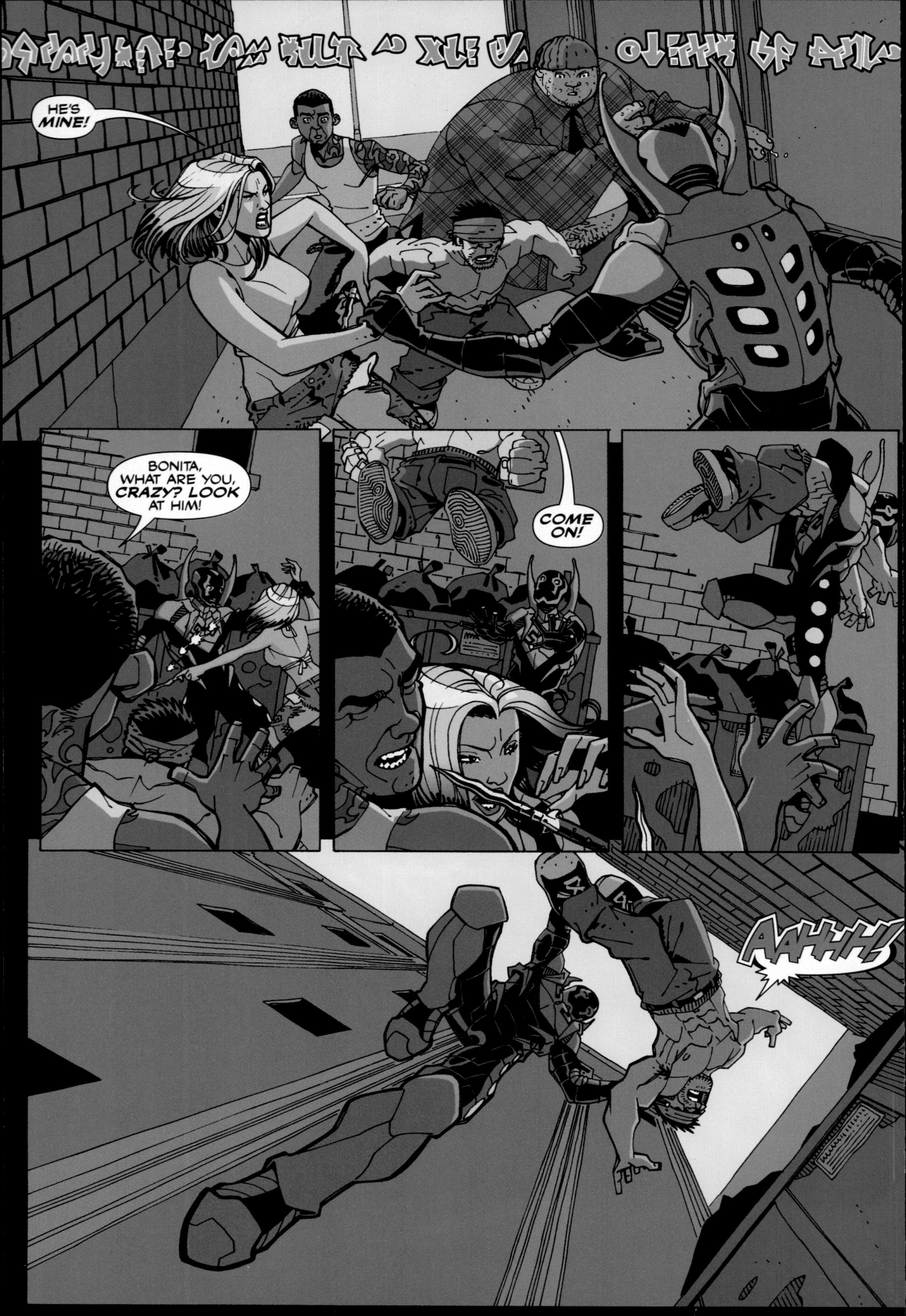
HE'S MINE!
BONITA, WHAT ARE YOU, CRAZY? LOOK AT HIM!
COME ON!
AAHHH!

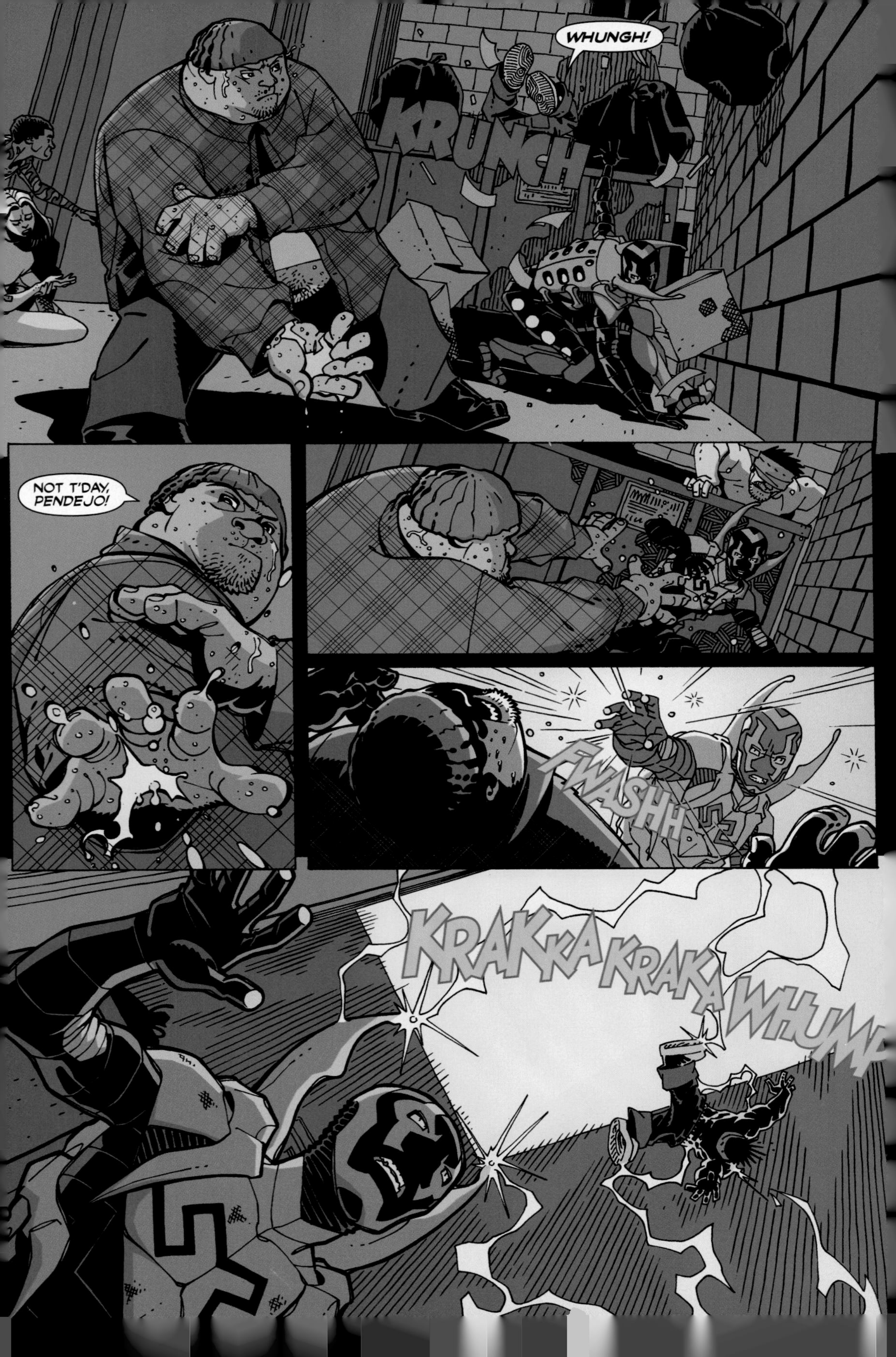
WHUNGH!
KRUNCH
NOT T'DAY, PENDEJO!
FWASHH
KRAKKA KRAKA WHUMP

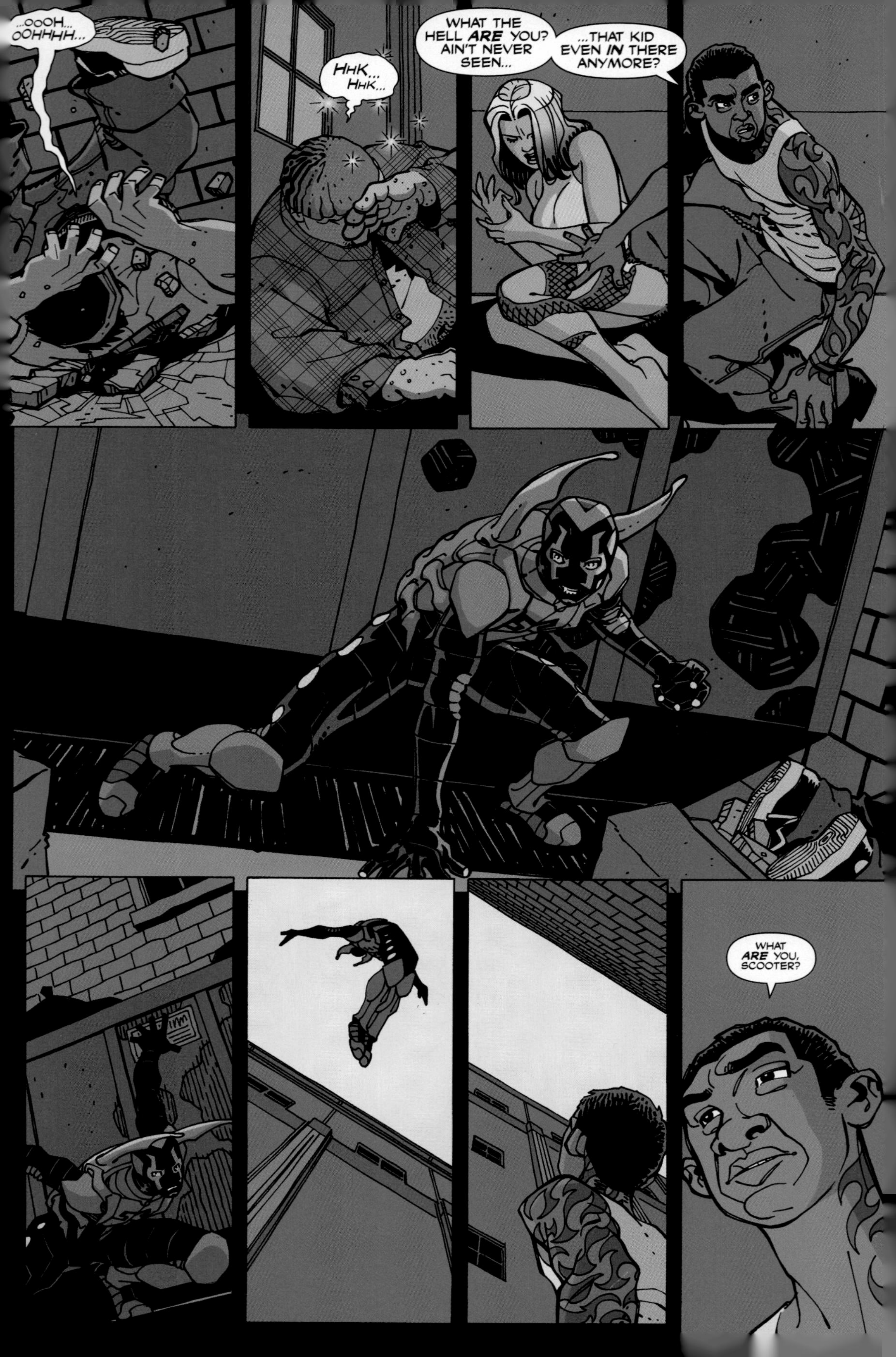
...OOOH... OOHHHH...
HHK... HHK...
WHAT THE HELL ARE YOU? AIN'T NEVER SEEN...
...THAT KID EVEN IN THERE ANYMORE?
WHAT ARE YOU, SCOOTER?

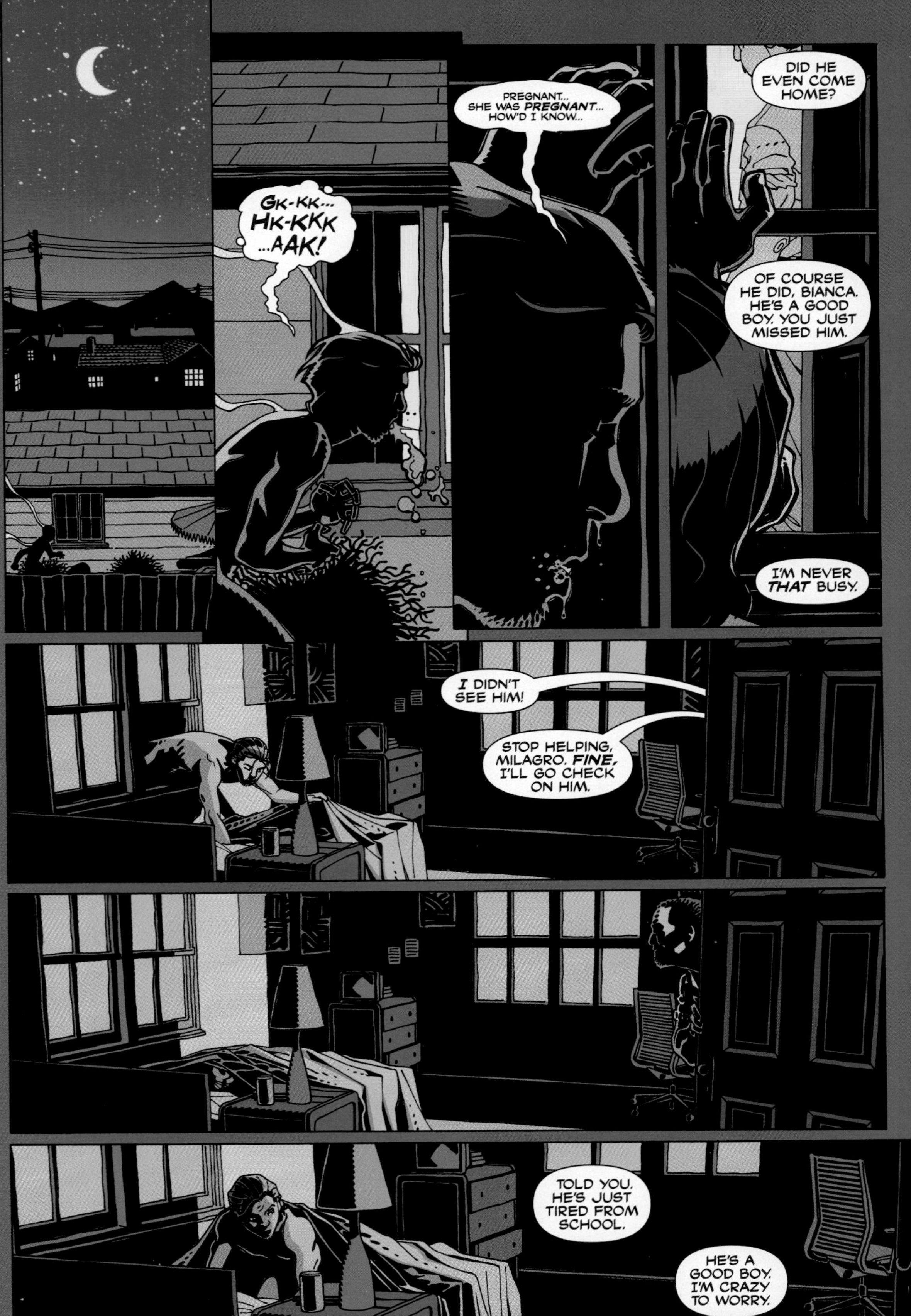
GK-KK...
HK-KKK
...AAK!
PREGNANT...
SHE WAS PREGNANT...
HOW'D I KNOW...
DID HE EVEN COME HOME?
OF COURSE HE DID, BIANCA. HE'S A GOOD BOY. YOU JUST MISSED HIM.
I'M NEVER THAT BUSY.
I DIDN'T SEE HIM!
STOP HELPING, MILAGRO. FINE, I'LL GO CHECK ON HIM.
TOLD YOU. HE'S JUST TIRED FROM SCHOOL.
HE'S A GOOD BOY. I'M CRAZY TO WORRY.

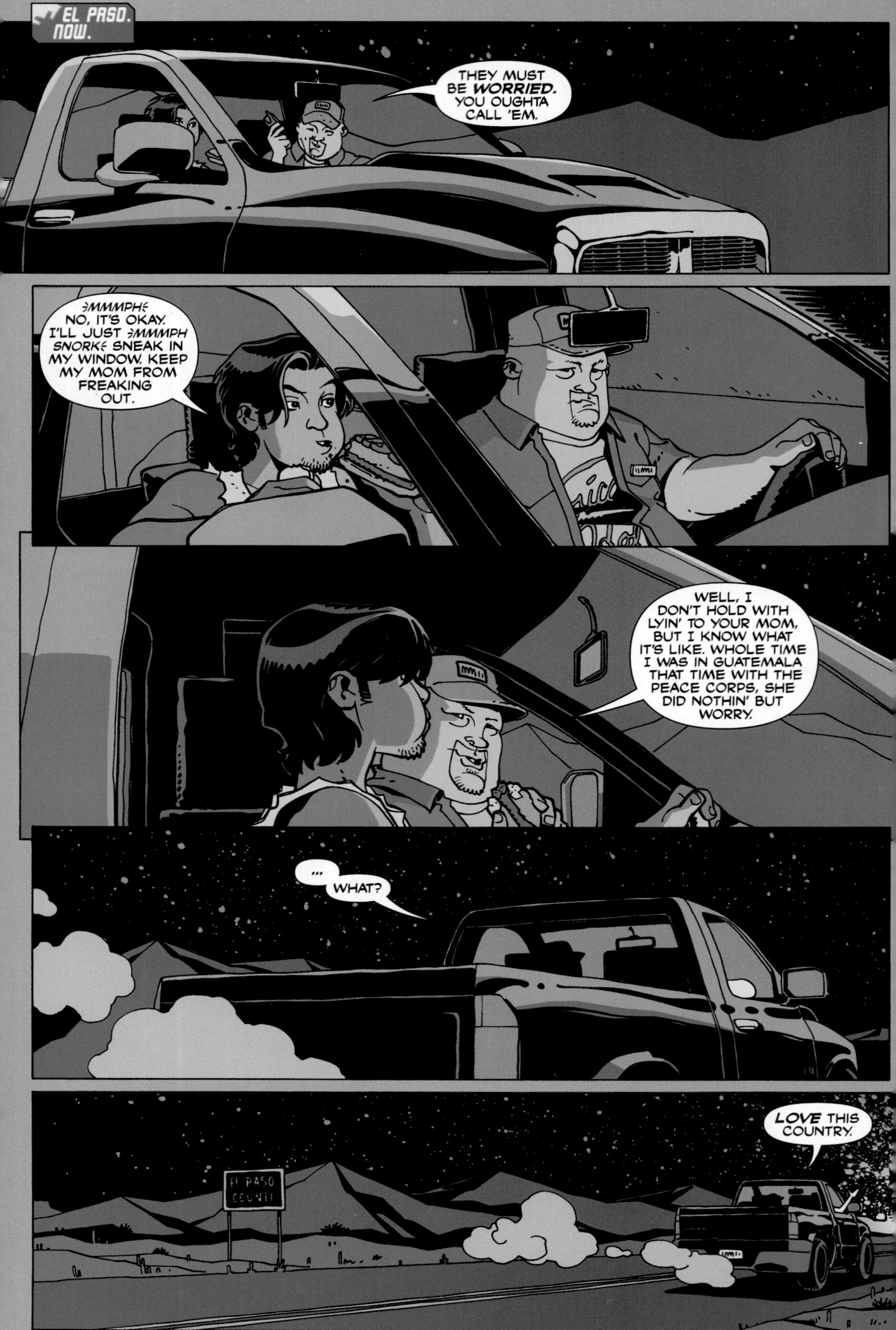
EL PASO. NOW.
THEY MUST BE WORRIED. YOU OUGHTA CALL 'EM.
≥MMMPH≤ NO, IT'S OKAY. I'LL JUST ≥MMMPH SNORK≤ SNEAK IN MY WINDOW. KEEP MY MOM FROM FREAKING OUT.
WELL, I DON'T HOLD WITH LYIN' TO YOUR MOM, BUT I KNOW WHAT IT'S LIKE. WHOLE TIME I WAS IN GUATEMALA THAT TIME WITH THE PEACE CORPS, SHE DID NOTHIN' BUT WORRY.
... WHAT?
EL PASO COUNTY
LOVE THIS COUNTRY.

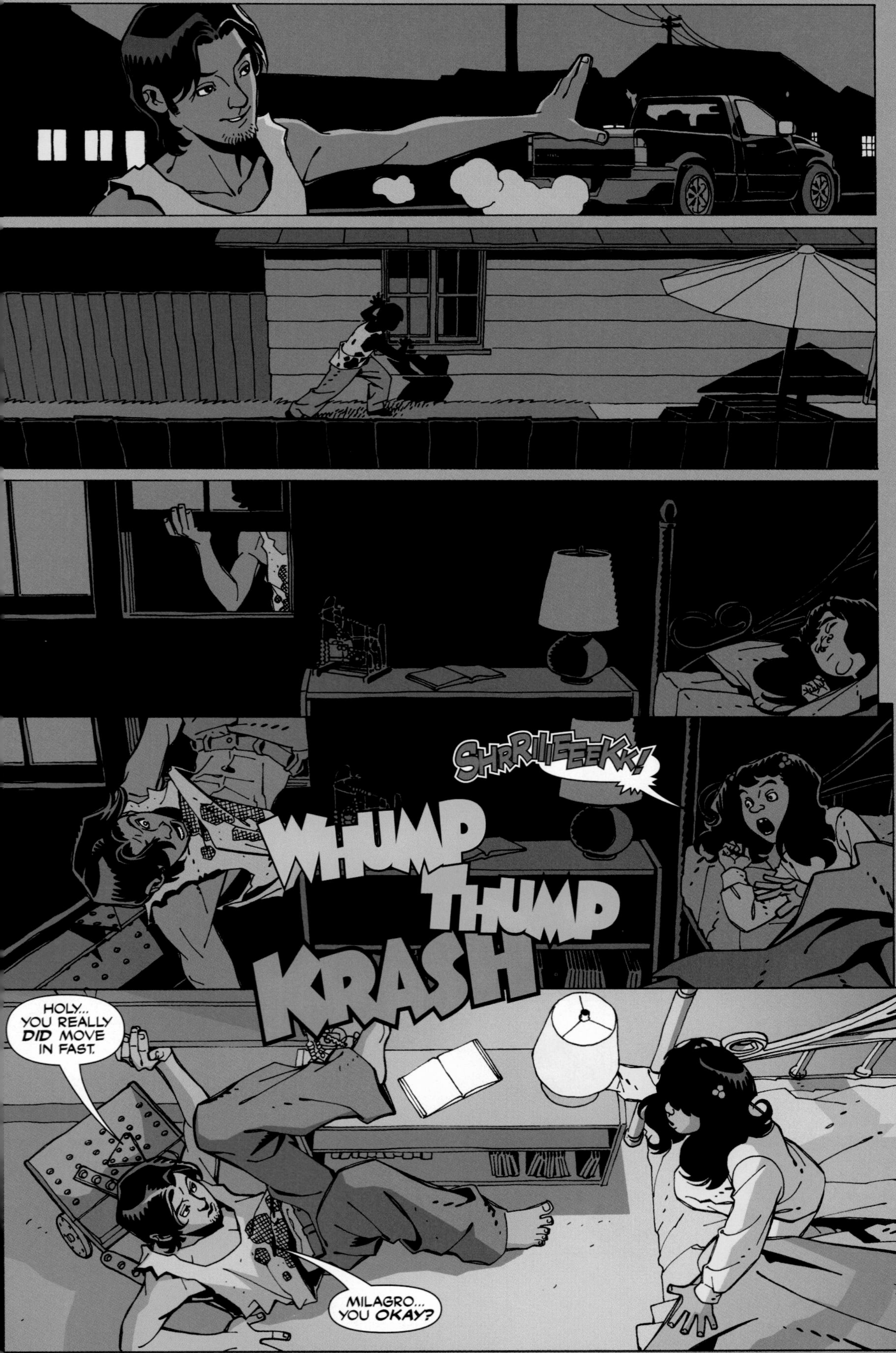

SHRIIIEEEKK!
WHUMP
THUMP
KRASH
HOLY... YOU REALLY DID MOVE IN FAST.
MILAGRO... YOU OKAY?

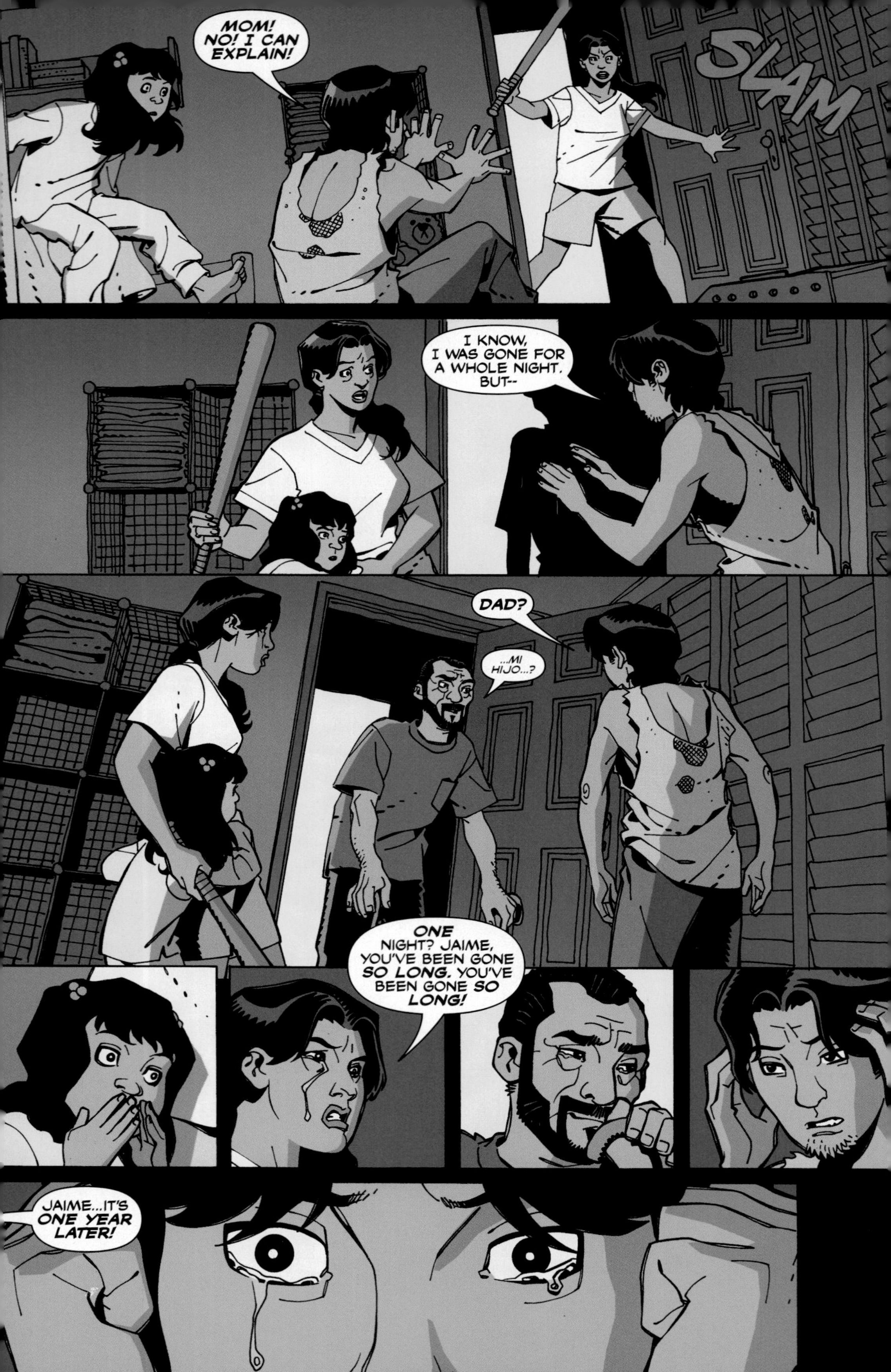
MOM! NO! I CAN EXPLAIN!
SLAM
I KNOW, I WAS GONE FOR A WHOLE NIGHT, BUT--
DAD?
...MI HIJO...?
ONE NIGHT? JAIME, YOU'VE BEEN GONE SO LONG. YOU'VE BEEN GONE SO LONG!
JAIME...IT'S ONE YEAR LATER!

BLUE BEETLE #3
Cover by Duncan Rouleau
Interior art by Cynthia Martin
and Phil Moy

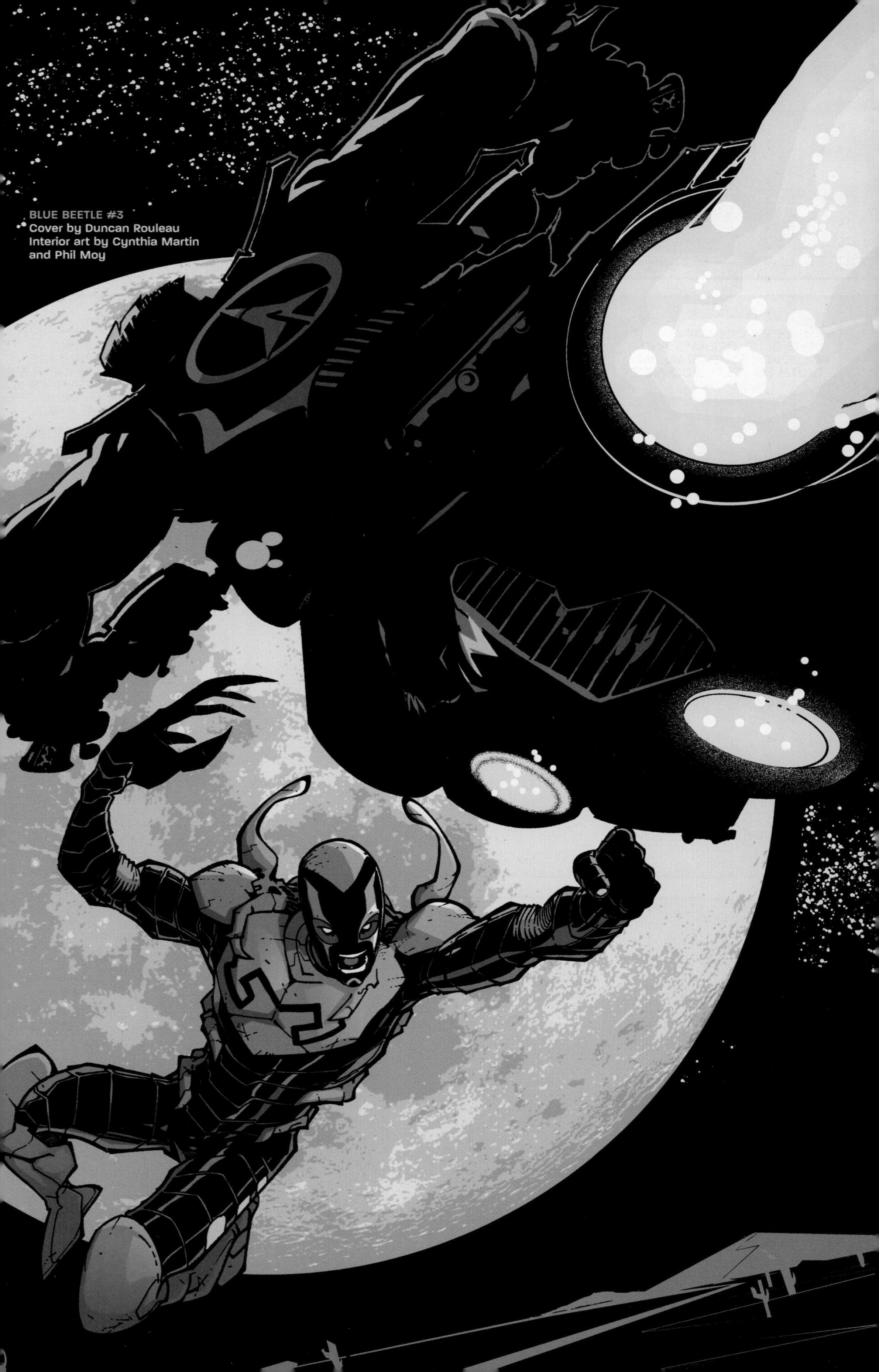

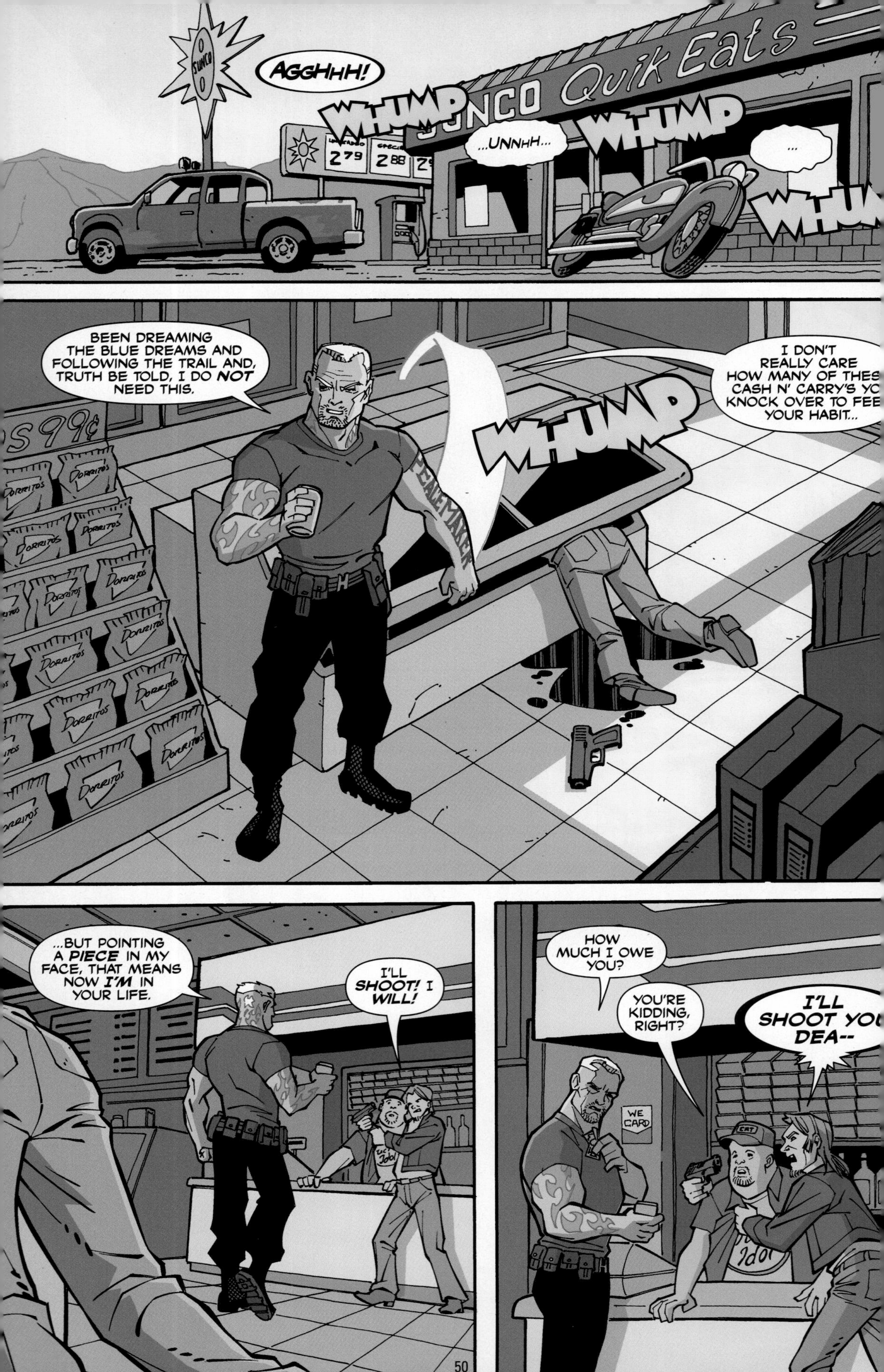
SUNCO
AGGHHH!
WHUMP
SUNCO Quik Eats
...UNNHH...
WHUMP
...
WHUMP
BEEN DREAMING THE BLUE DREAMS AND FOLLOWING THE TRAIL AND, TRUTH BE TOLD, I DO NOT NEED THIS.
I DON'T REALLY CARE HOW MANY OF THES CASH N' CARRY'S YO KNOCK OVER TO FEE YOUR HABIT...
WHUMP
PEACEMAKER
DORRITOS
...BUT POINTING A PIECE IN MY FACE, THAT MEANS NOW I'M IN YOUR LIFE.
I'LL SHOOT! I WILL!
HOW MUCH I OWE YOU?
YOU'RE KIDDING, RIGHT?
I'LL SHOOT YO DEA--
WE CARD

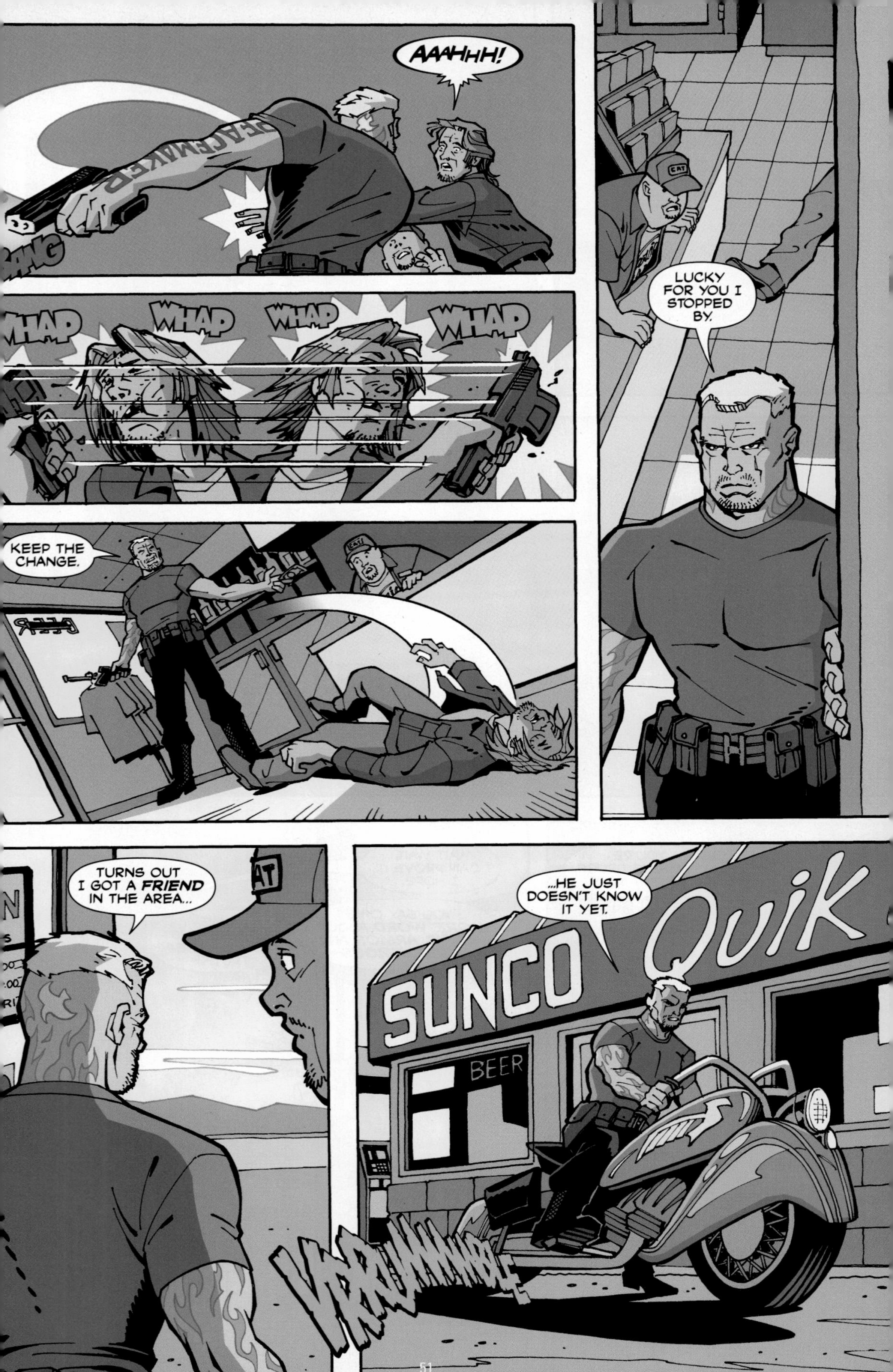

AAAHHH!
PEACEMAKER
BANG
WHAP
WHAP
WHAP
WHAP
LUCKY FOR YOU I STOPPED BY.
KEEP THE CHANGE.
TURNS OUT I GOT A FRIEND IN THE AREA...
...HE JUST DOESN'T KNOW IT YET.
SUNCO
Quik
BEER
VRRUMMMBLE

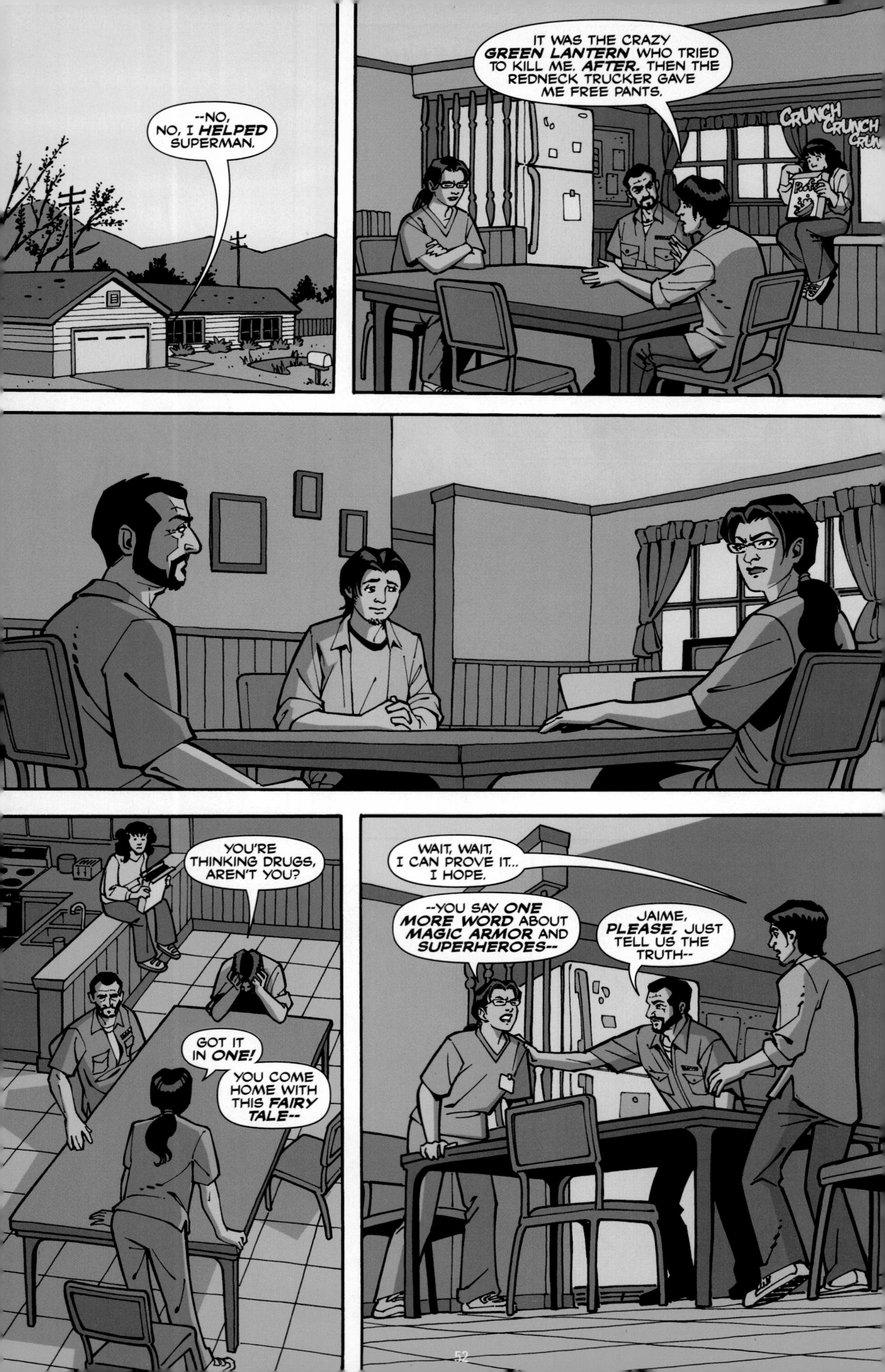
--NO, NO, I **HELPED** SUPERMAN.
IT WAS THE CRAZY **GREEN LANTERN** WHO TRIED TO KILL ME. **AFTER.** THEN THE REDNECK TRUCKER GAVE ME FREE PANTS.
CRUNCH CRUNCH CRUN
YOU'RE THINKING DRUGS, AREN'T YOU?
GOT IT IN **ONE!**
YOU COME HOME WITH THIS **FAIRY TALE--**
WAIT, WAIT, I CAN PROVE IT... I HOPE.
--YOU SAY **ONE MORE WORD** ABOUT **MAGIC ARMOR** AND **SUPERHEROES--**
JAIME, **PLEASE,** JUST TELL US THE TRUTH--

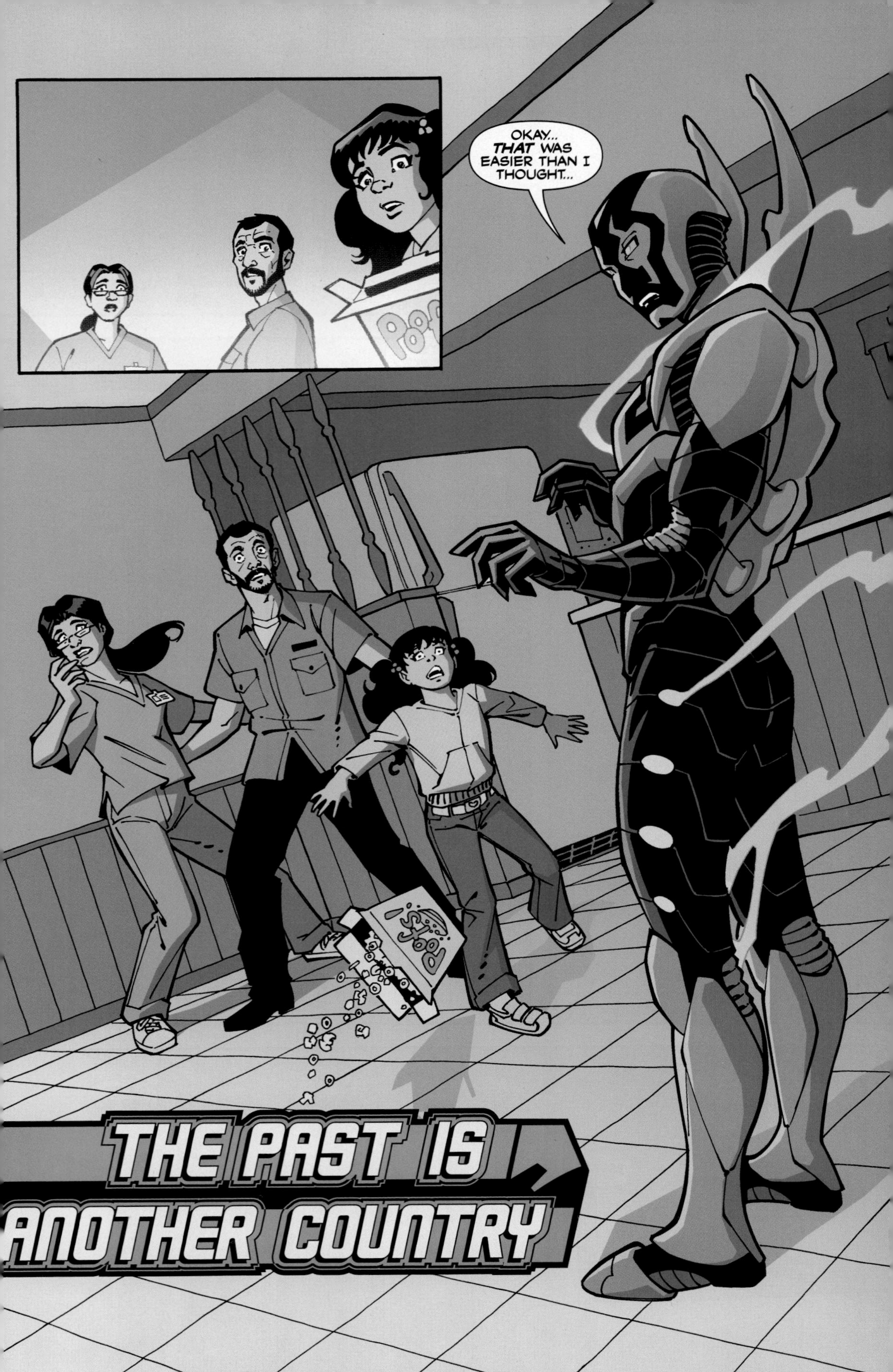
OKAY... *THAT* WAS EASIER THAN I THOUGHT...
THE PAST IS ANOTHER COUNTRY

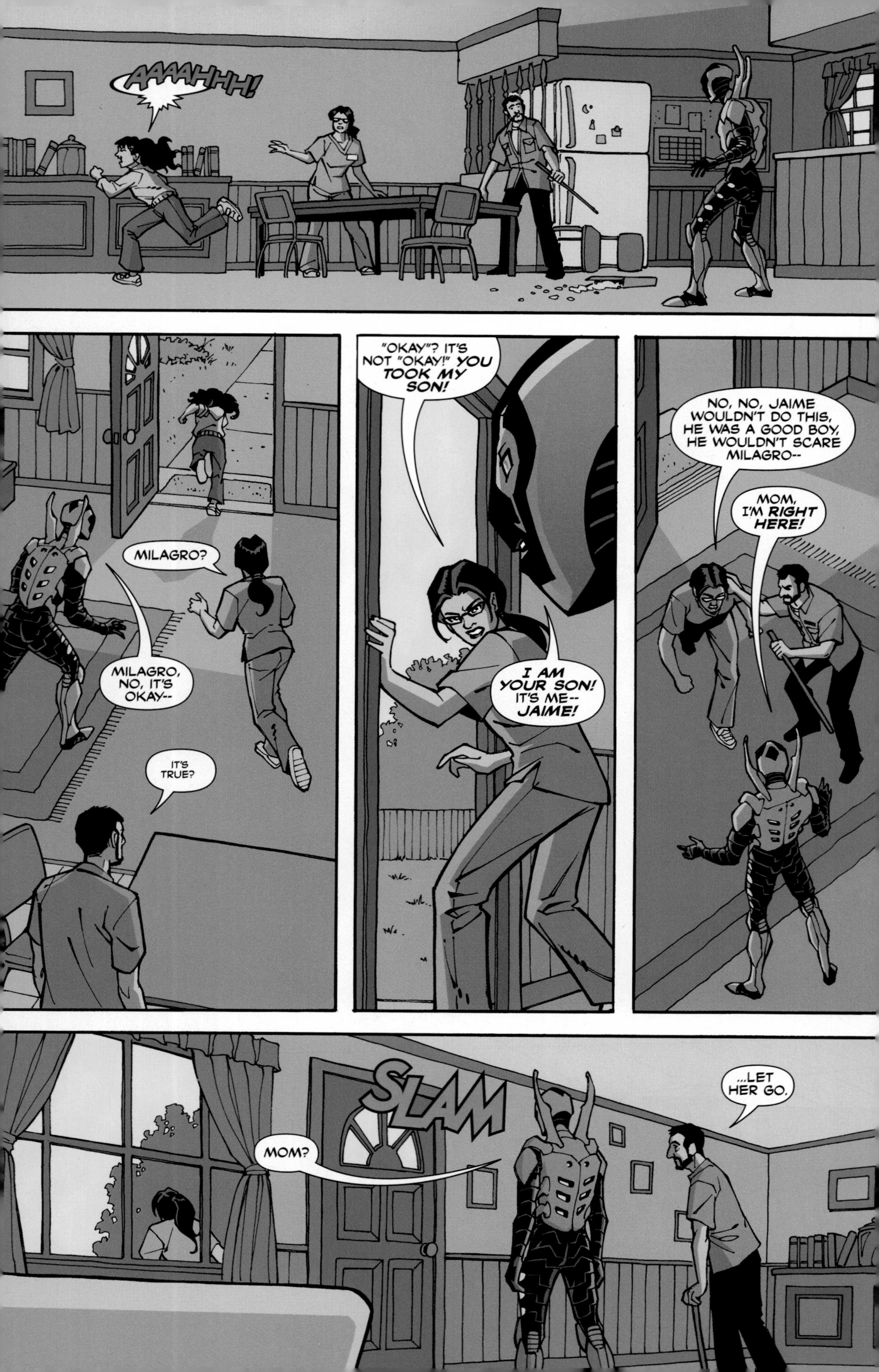
AAAAHHH!
MILAGRO?
MILAGRO, NO, IT'S OKAY--
IT'S TRUE?
"OKAY"? IT'S NOT "OKAY!" YOU TOOK MY SON!
I AM YOUR SON! IT'S ME-- JAIME!
NO, NO, JAIME WOULDN'T DO THIS, HE WAS A GOOD BOY, HE WOULDN'T SCARE MILAGRO--
MOM, I'M RIGHT HERE!
SLAM
MOM?
...LET HER GO.

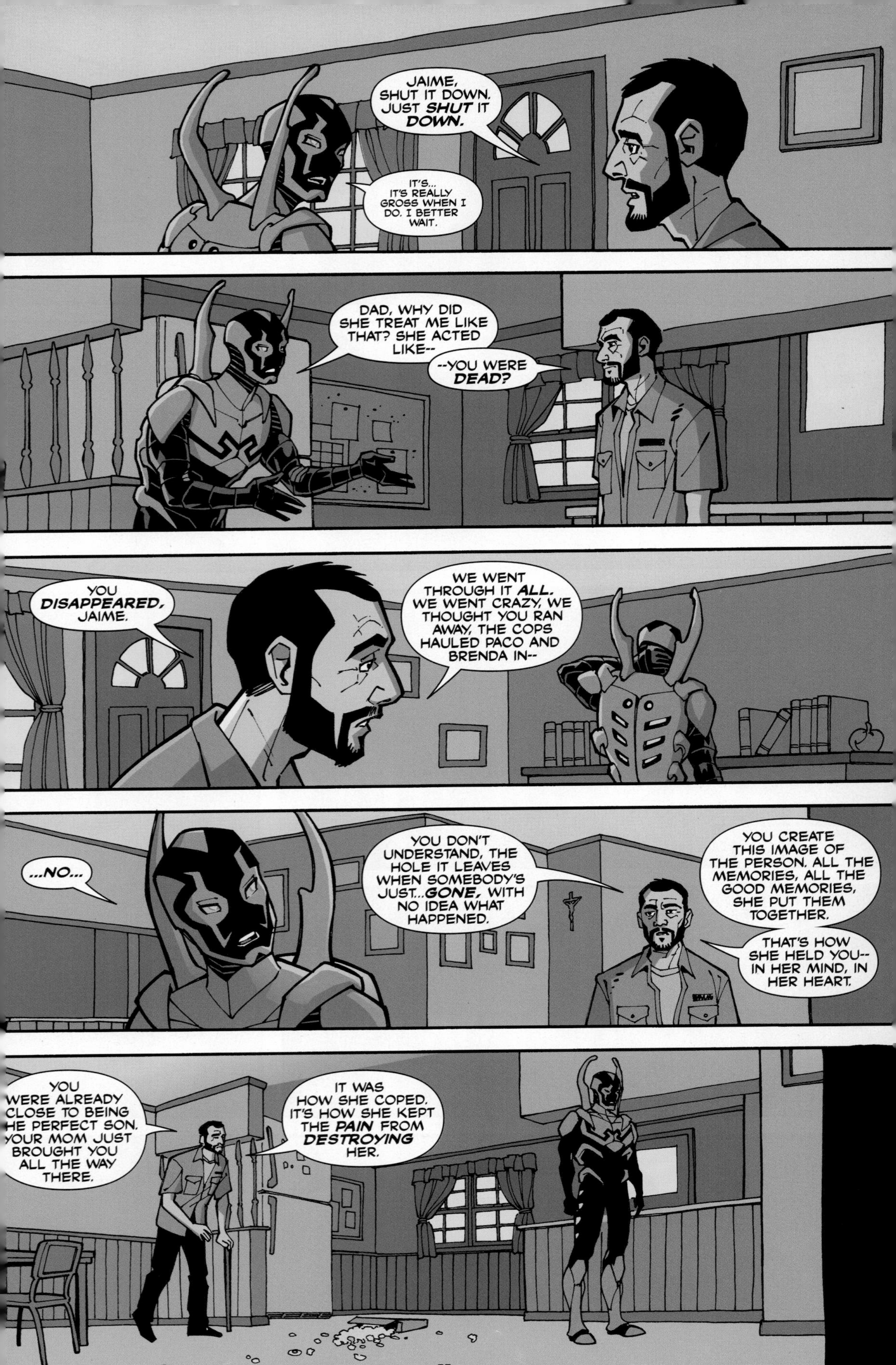
JAIME, SHUT IT DOWN. JUST SHUT IT DOWN.
IT'S... IT'S REALLY GROSS WHEN I DO. I BETTER WAIT.
DAD, WHY DID SHE TREAT ME LIKE THAT? SHE ACTED LIKE--
--YOU WERE DEAD?
YOU DISAPPEARED, JAIME.
WE WENT THROUGH IT ALL. WE WENT CRAZY, WE THOUGHT YOU RAN AWAY, THE COPS HAULED PACO AND BRENDA IN--
...NO...
YOU DON'T UNDERSTAND, THE HOLE IT LEAVES WHEN SOMEBODY'S JUST...GONE, WITH NO IDEA WHAT HAPPENED.
YOU CREATE THIS IMAGE OF THE PERSON, ALL THE MEMORIES, ALL THE GOOD MEMORIES, SHE PUT THEM TOGETHER.
THAT'S HOW SHE HELD YOU-- IN HER MIND, IN HER HEART.
YOU WERE ALREADY CLOSE TO BEING HE PERFECT SON. YOUR MOM JUST BROUGHT YOU ALL THE WAY THERE.
IT WAS HOW SHE COPED. IT'S HOW SHE KEPT THE PAIN FROM DESTROYING HER.

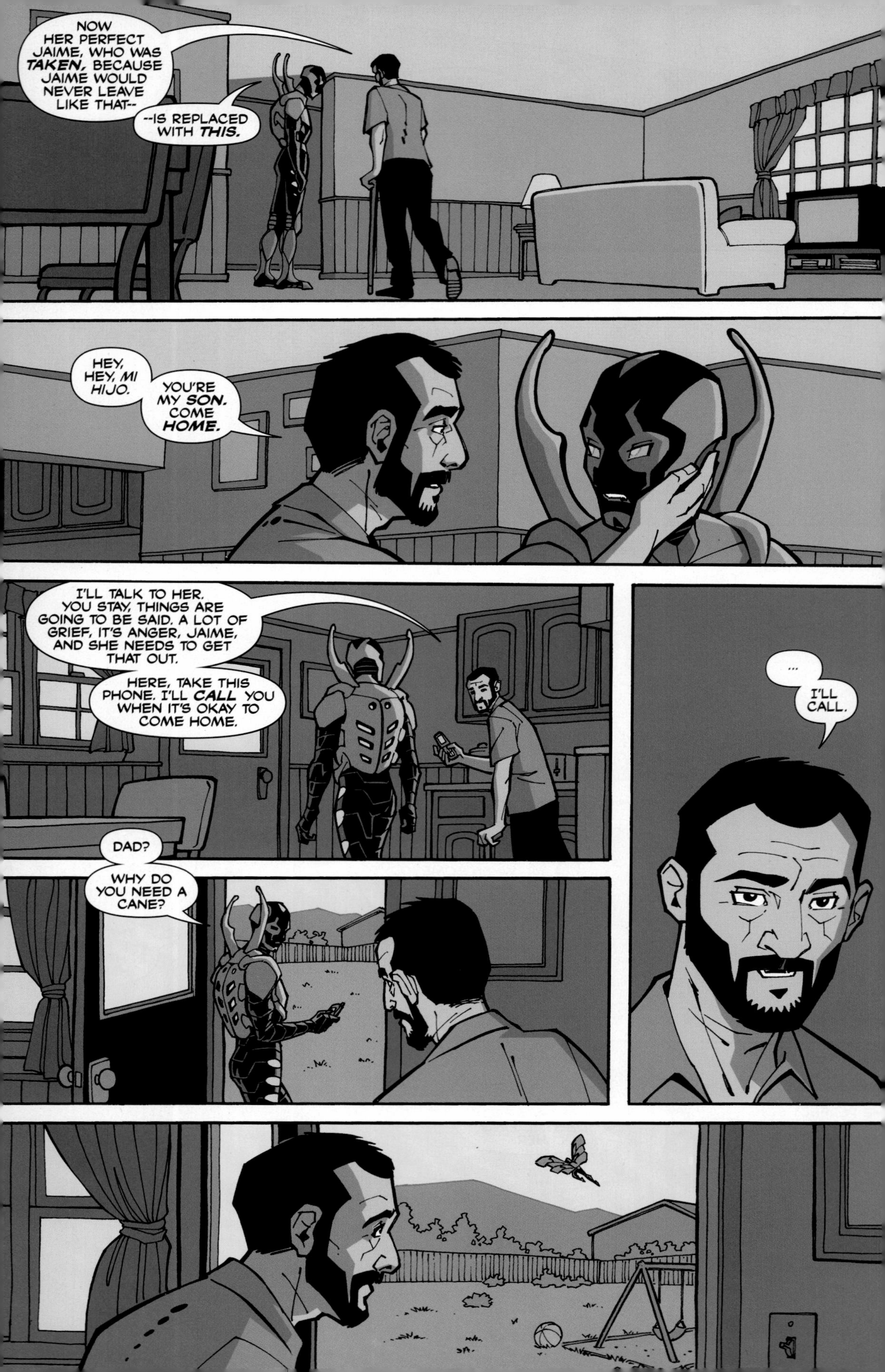
NOW HER PERFECT JAIME, WHO WAS TAKEN, BECAUSE JAIME WOULD NEVER LEAVE LIKE THAT--
--IS REPLACED WITH THIS.
HEY, HEY, MI HIJO.
YOU'RE MY SON. COME HOME.
I'LL TALK TO HER. YOU STAY, THINGS ARE GOING TO BE SAID. A LOT OF GRIEF, IT'S ANGER, JAIME, AND SHE NEEDS TO GET THAT OUT.
HERE, TAKE THIS PHONE. I'LL CALL YOU WHEN IT'S OKAY TO COME HOME.
DAD?
WHY DO YOU NEED A CANE?
...
I'LL CALL.

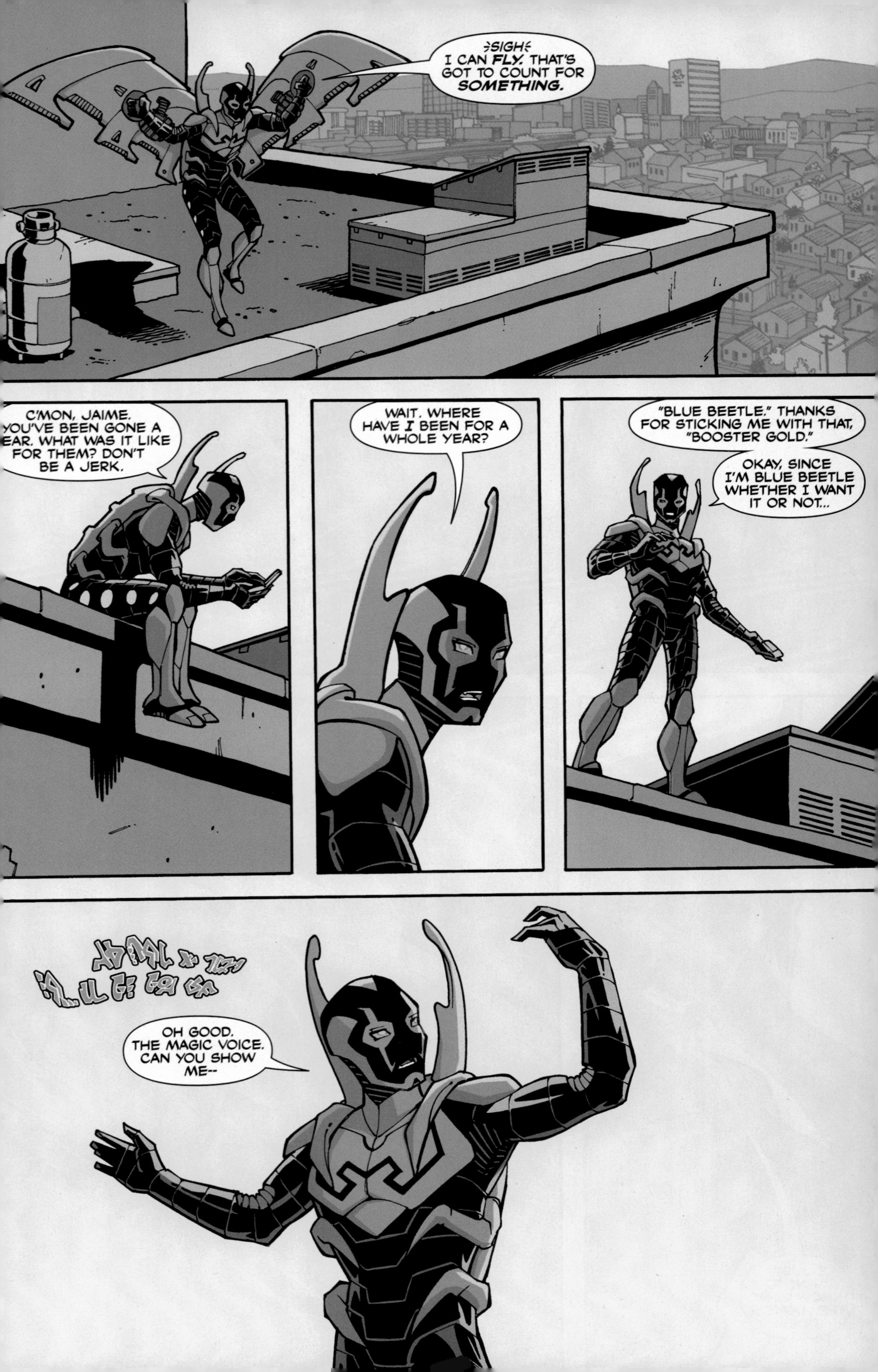

>SIGH< I CAN FLY. THAT'S GOT TO COUNT FOR SOMETHING.
C'MON, JAIME. YOU'VE BEEN GONE A YEAR. WHAT WAS IT LIKE FOR THEM? DON'T BE A JERK.
WAIT. WHERE HAVE I BEEN FOR A WHOLE YEAR?
"BLUE BEETLE." THANKS FOR STICKING ME WITH THAT, "BOOSTER GOLD."
OKAY, SINCE I'M BLUE BEETLE WHETHER I WANT IT OR NOT...
OH GOOD. THE MAGIC VOICE. CAN YOU SHOW ME--

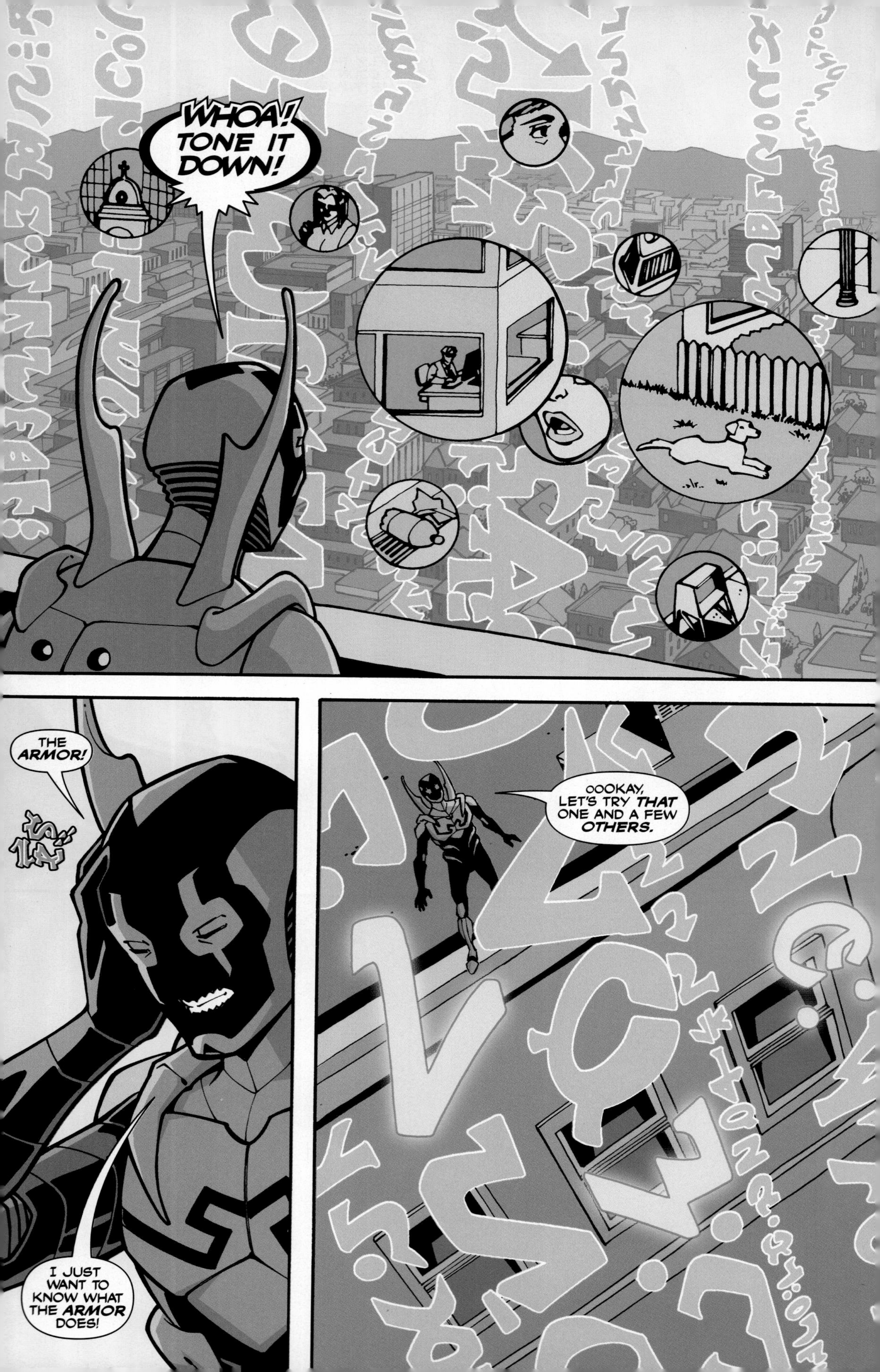

WHOA! TONE IT DOWN!
THE ARMOR!
TSSK
I JUST WANT TO KNOW WHAT THE ARMOR DOES!
OOOKAY, LET'S TRY THAT ONE AND A FEW OTHERS.

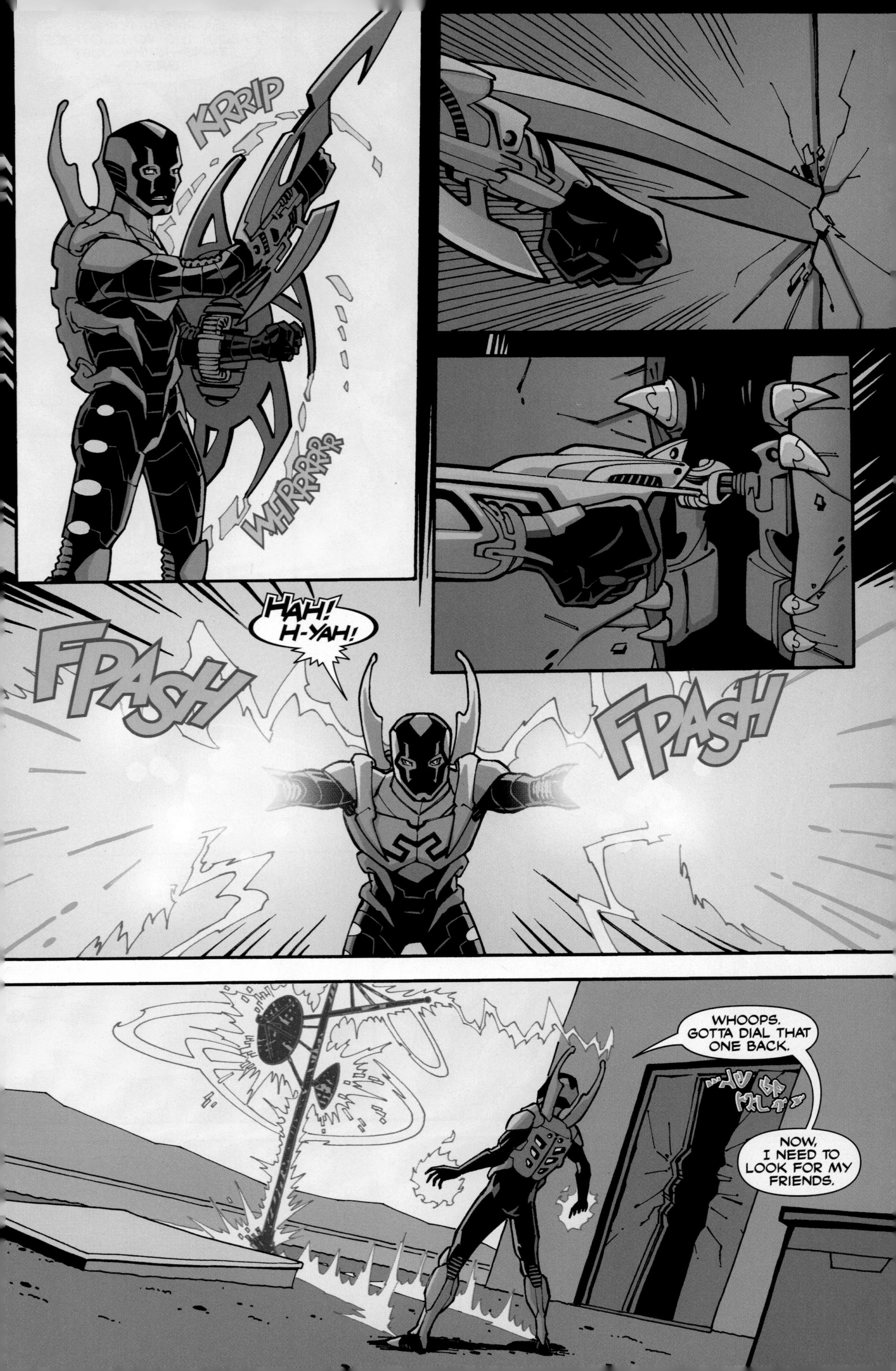
KRRIP
WHRRRRRR
HAH! H-YAH!
FPASH
FPASH
WHOOPS. GOTTA DIAL THAT ONE BACK.
NOW, I NEED TO LOOK FOR MY FRIENDS.

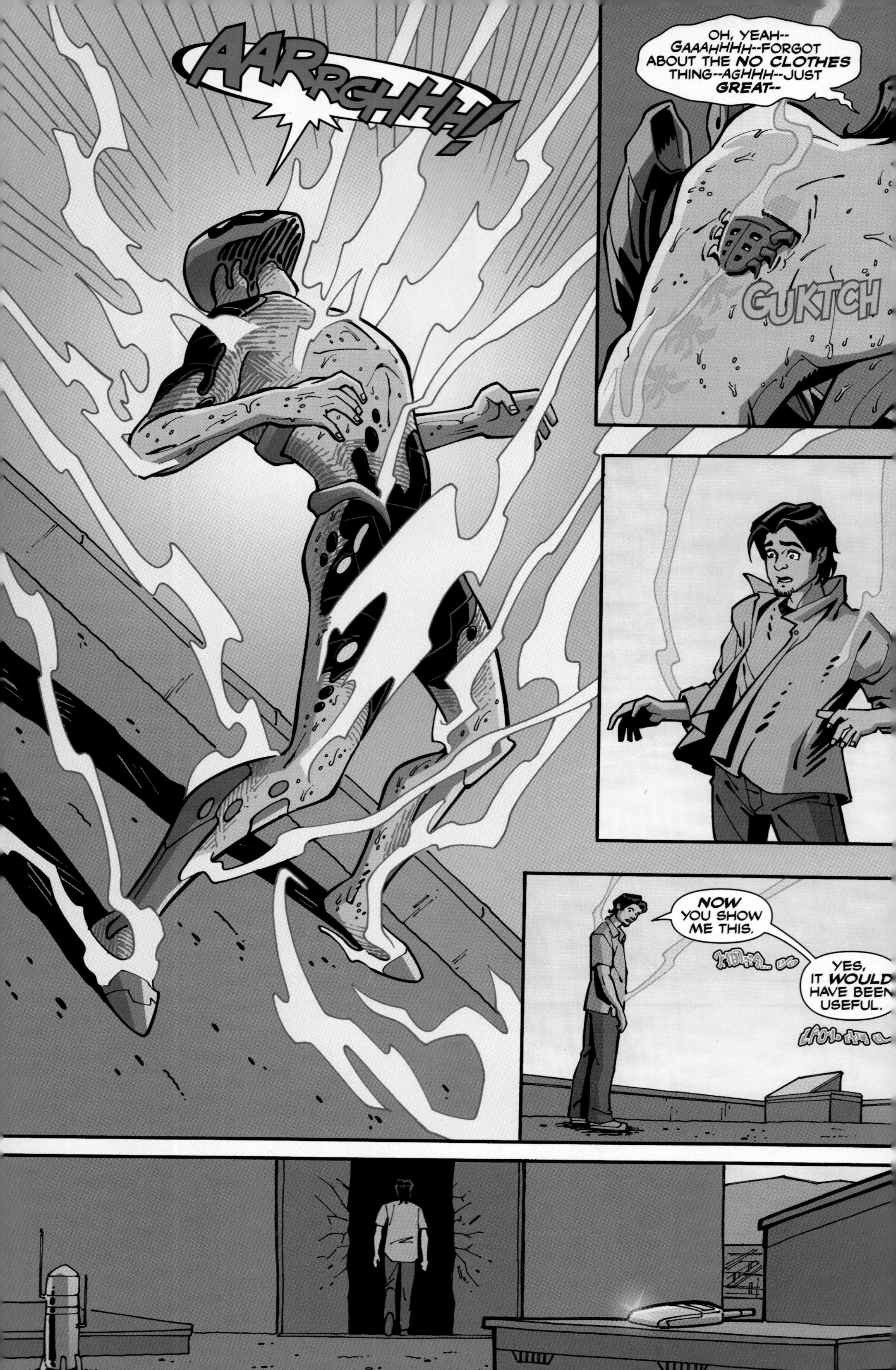
AARRGHHH!
OH, YEAH-- GAAAHHHH--FORGOT ABOUT THE **NO CLOTHES** THING--AGHHH--JUST **GREAT**--
GUKTCH
NOW YOU SHOW ME THIS.
YES, IT **WOULD** HAVE BEEN USEFUL.

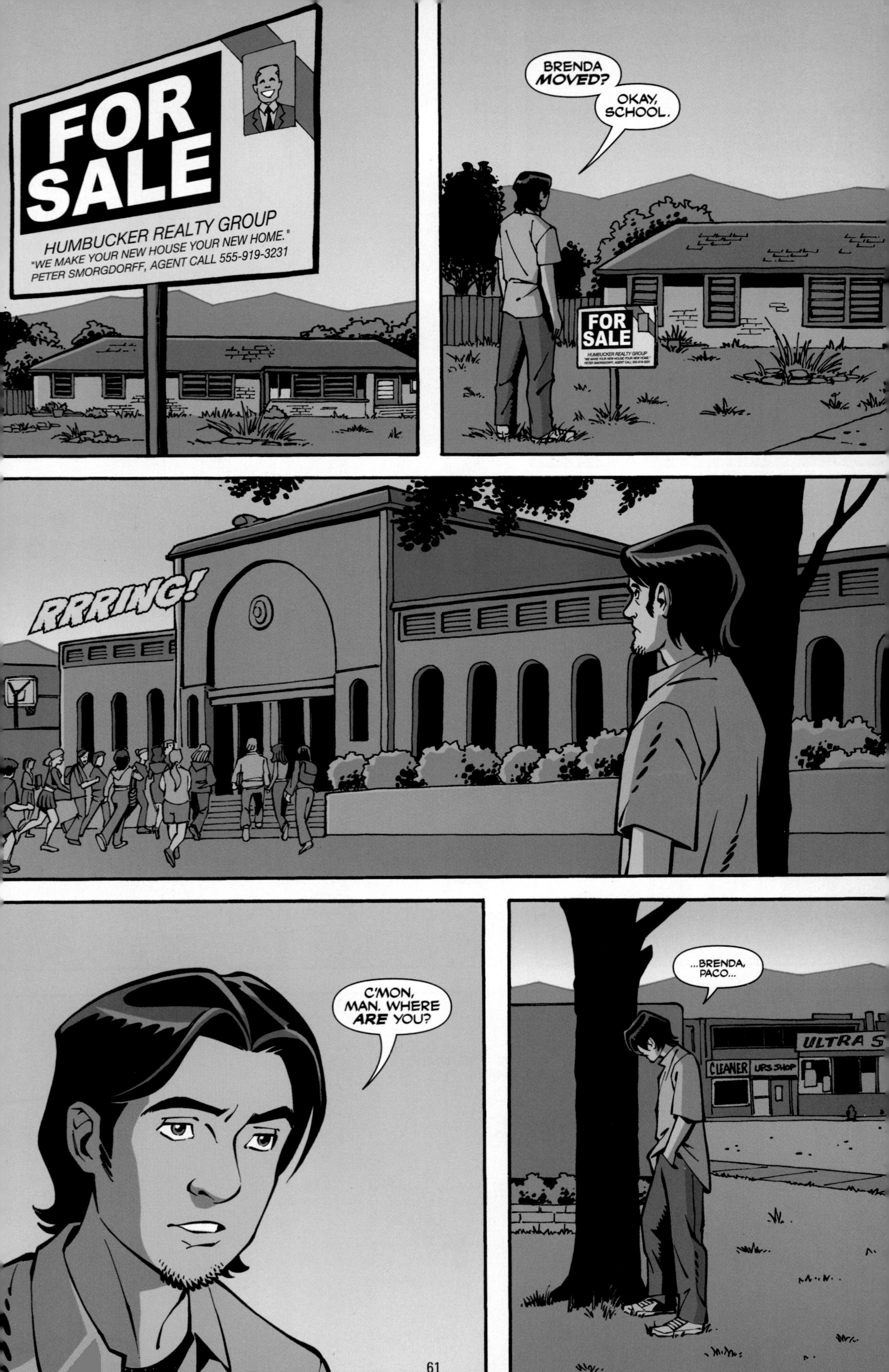
FOR SALE
HUMBUCKER REALTY GROUP
"WE MAKE YOUR NEW HOUSE YOUR NEW HOME."
PETER SMORGDORFF, AGENT CALL 555-919-3231
BRENDA *MOVED?*
OKAY, SCHOOL.
FOR SALE
HUMBUCKER REALTY GROUP
RRRING!
C'MON, MAN. WHERE *ARE* YOU?
...BRENDA, PACO...
CLEANER
UPS SHOP
ULTRA S

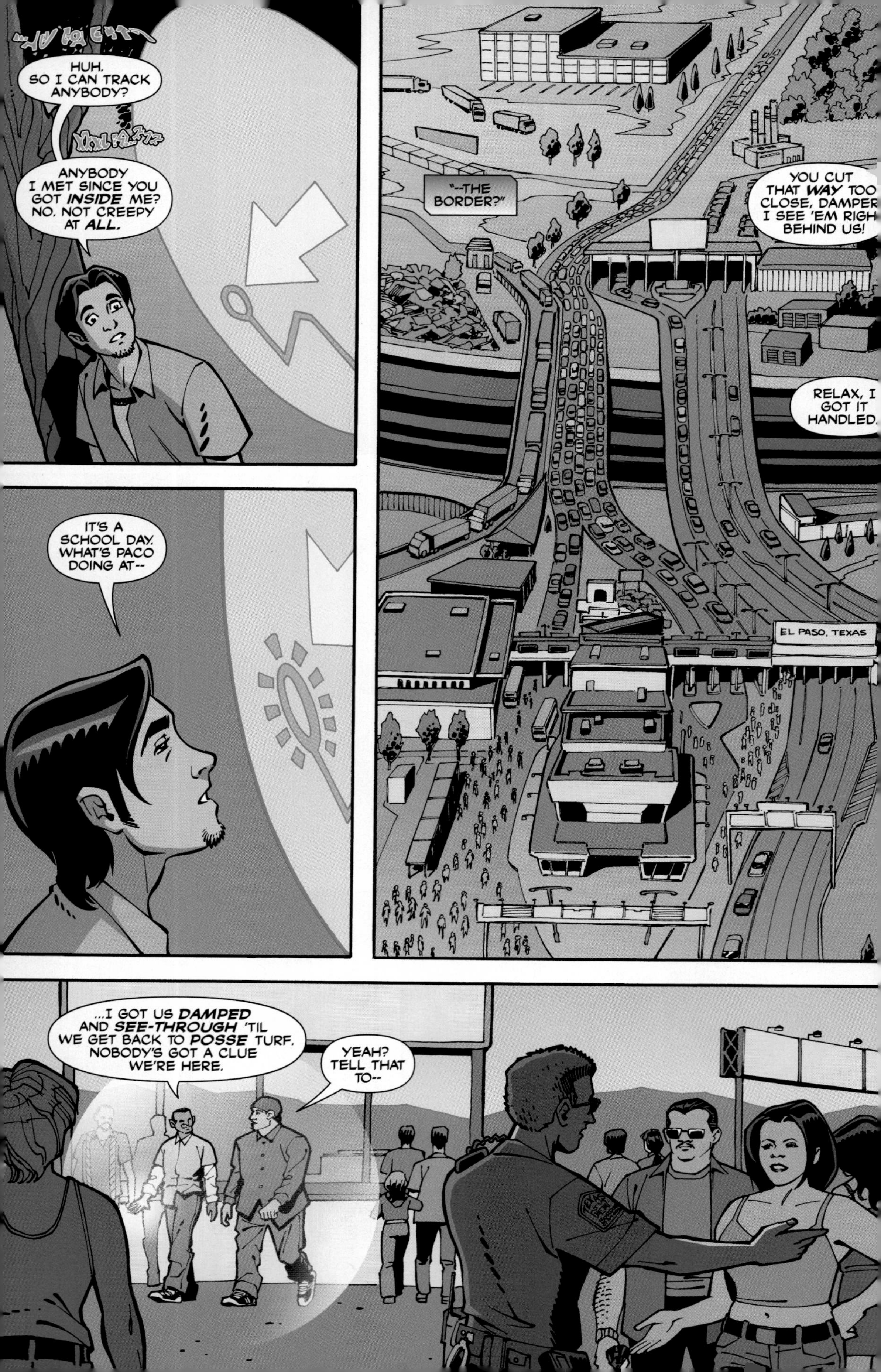
HUH, SO I CAN TRACK ANYBODY?
ANYBODY I MET SINCE YOU GOT INSIDE ME? NO, NOT CREEPY AT ALL.
IT'S A SCHOOL DAY. WHAT'S PACO DOING AT--
"--THE BORDER?"
YOU CUT THAT WAY TOO CLOSE, DAMPER I SEE 'EM RIGH BEHIND US!
RELAX, I GOT IT HANDLED.
EL PASO, TEXAS
...I GOT US DAMPED AND SEE-THROUGH 'TIL WE GET BACK TO POSSE TURF. NOBODY'S GOT A CLUE WE'RE HERE.
YEAH? TELL THAT TO--

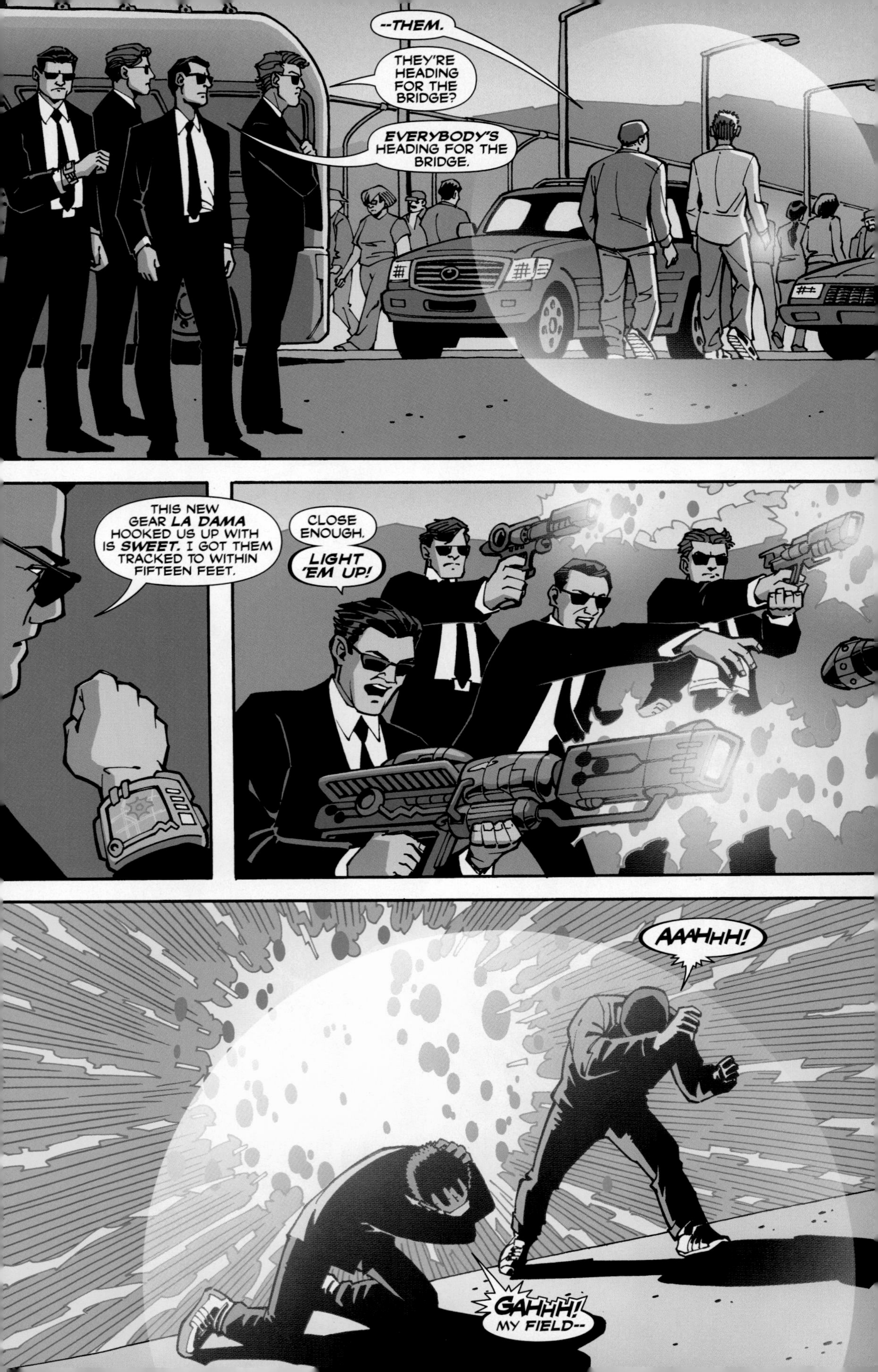
--THEM.
THEY'RE HEADING FOR THE BRIDGE?
EVERYBODY'S HEADING FOR THE BRIDGE.
THIS NEW GEAR LA DAMA HOOKED US UP WITH IS SWEET. I GOT THEM TRACKED TO WITHIN FIFTEEN FEET.
CLOSE ENOUGH.
LIGHT 'EM UP!
AAAHHH!
GAHHH! MY FIELD--

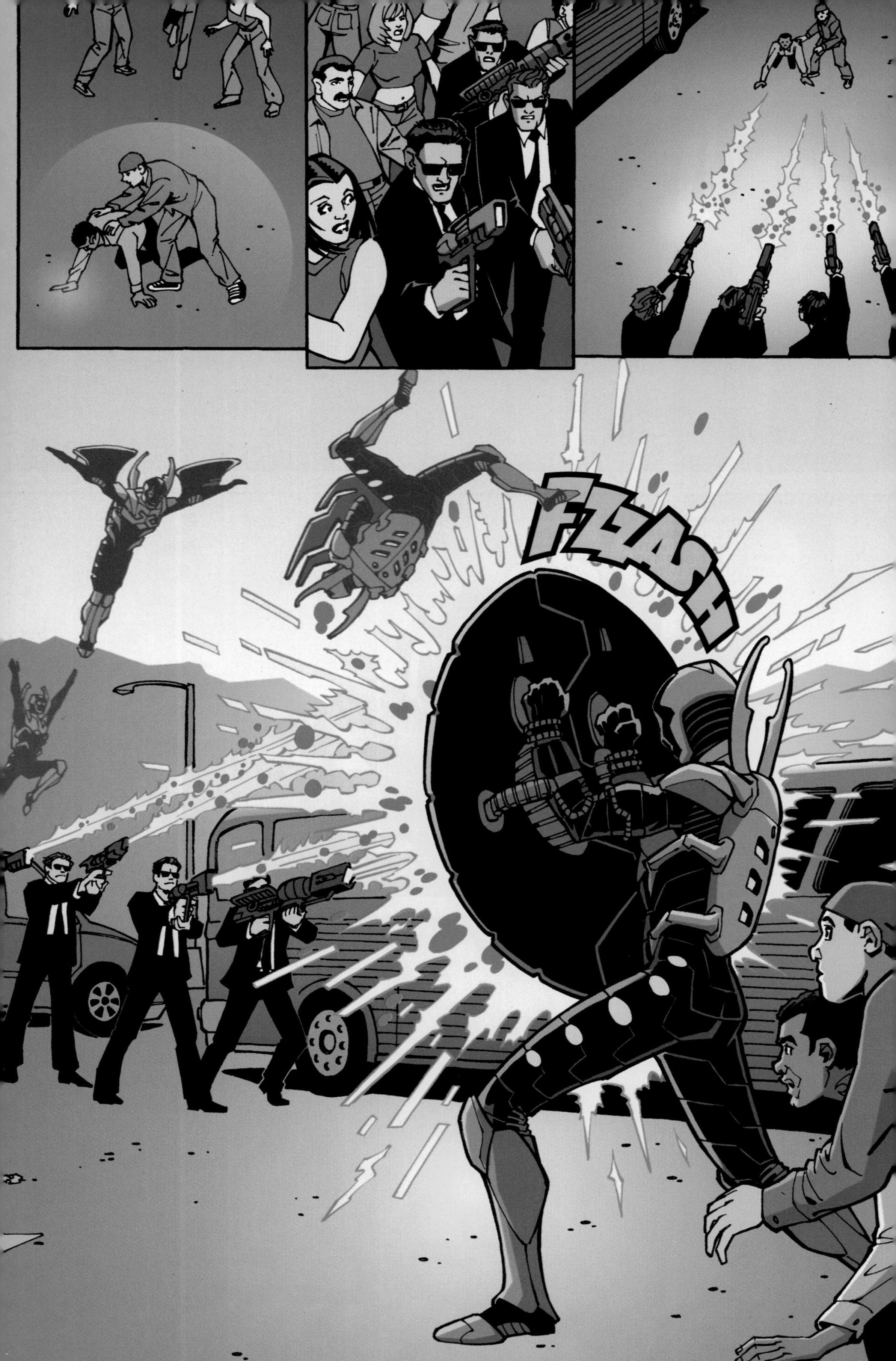
FZASH!

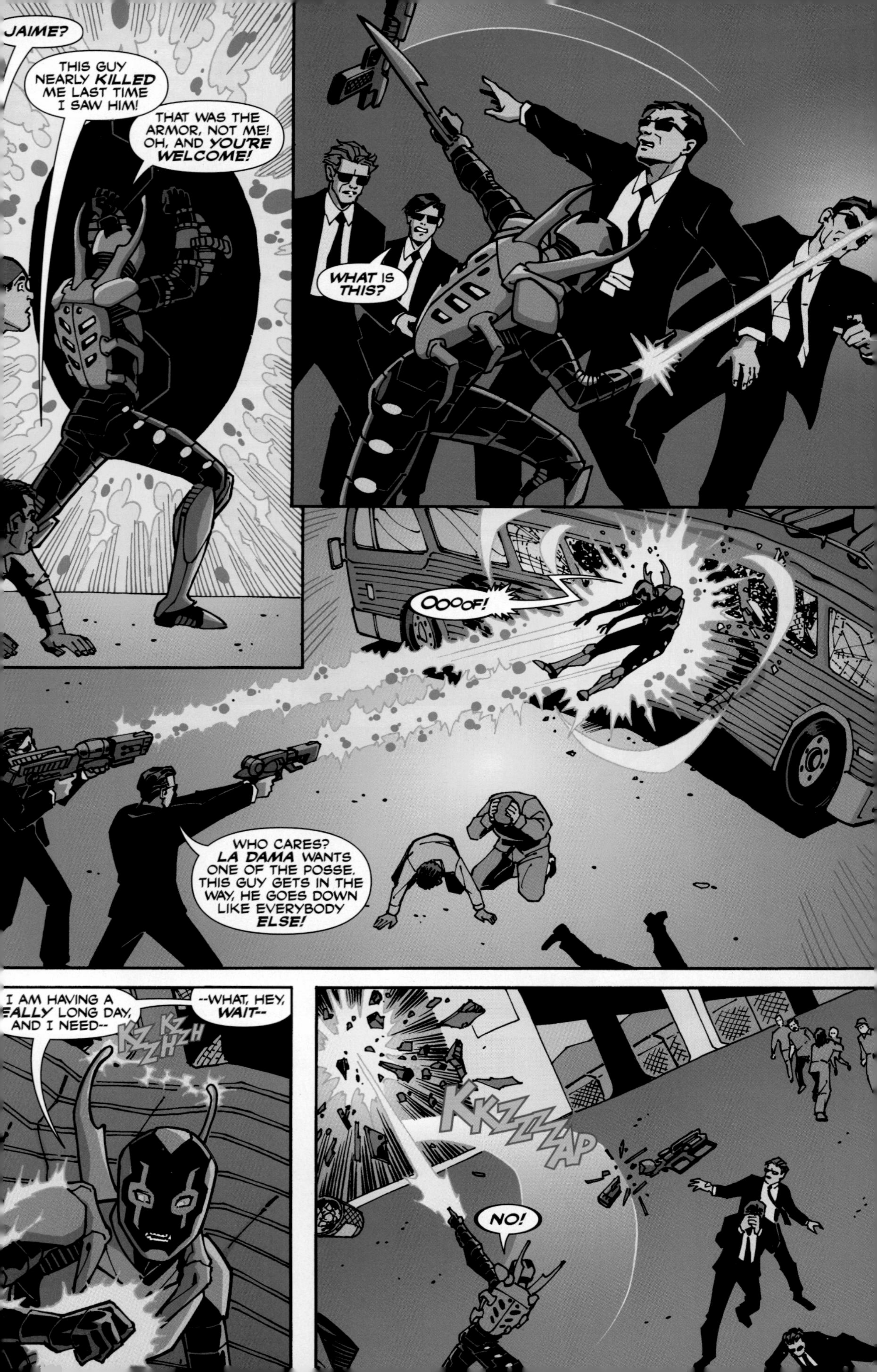
JAIME?
THIS GUY NEARLY KILLED ME LAST TIME I SAW HIM!
THAT WAS THE ARMOR, NOT ME! OH, AND YOU'RE WELCOME!
WHAT IS THIS?
OOOOF!
WHO CARES? LA DAMA WANTS ONE OF THE POSSE. THIS GUY GETS IN THE WAY, HE GOES DOWN LIKE EVERYBODY ELSE!
I AM HAVING A EALLY LONG DAY, AND I NEED--
--WHAT, HEY, WAIT--
KZZ KZHZH
KKZZZZAP
NO!

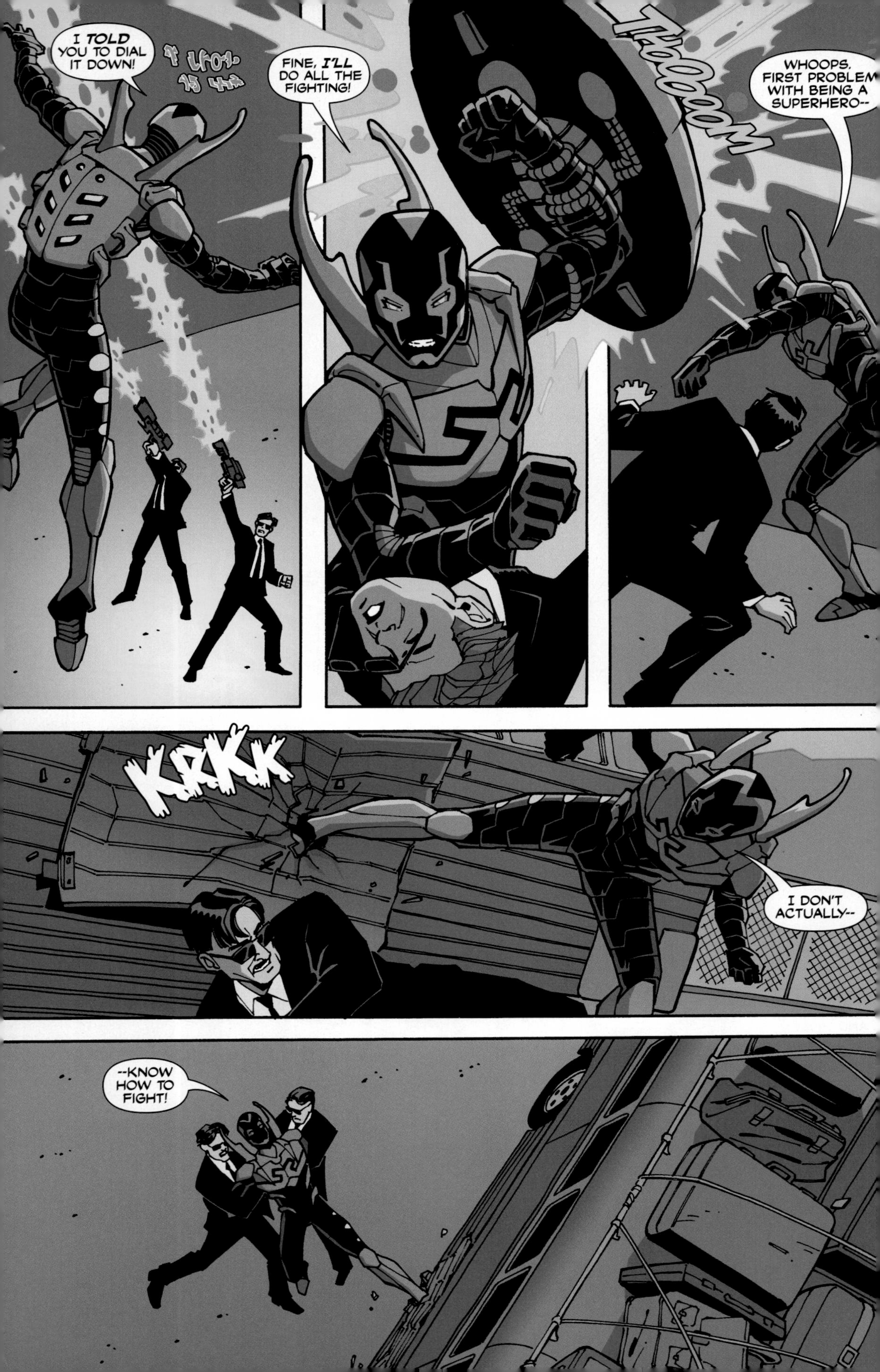
I TOLD YOU TO DIAL IT DOWN!
FINE, I'LL DO ALL THE FIGHTING!
THOOOOOM
WHOOPS. FIRST PROBLEM WITH BEING A SUPERHERO--
KRKK
I DON'T ACTUALLY--
--KNOW HOW TO FIGHT!

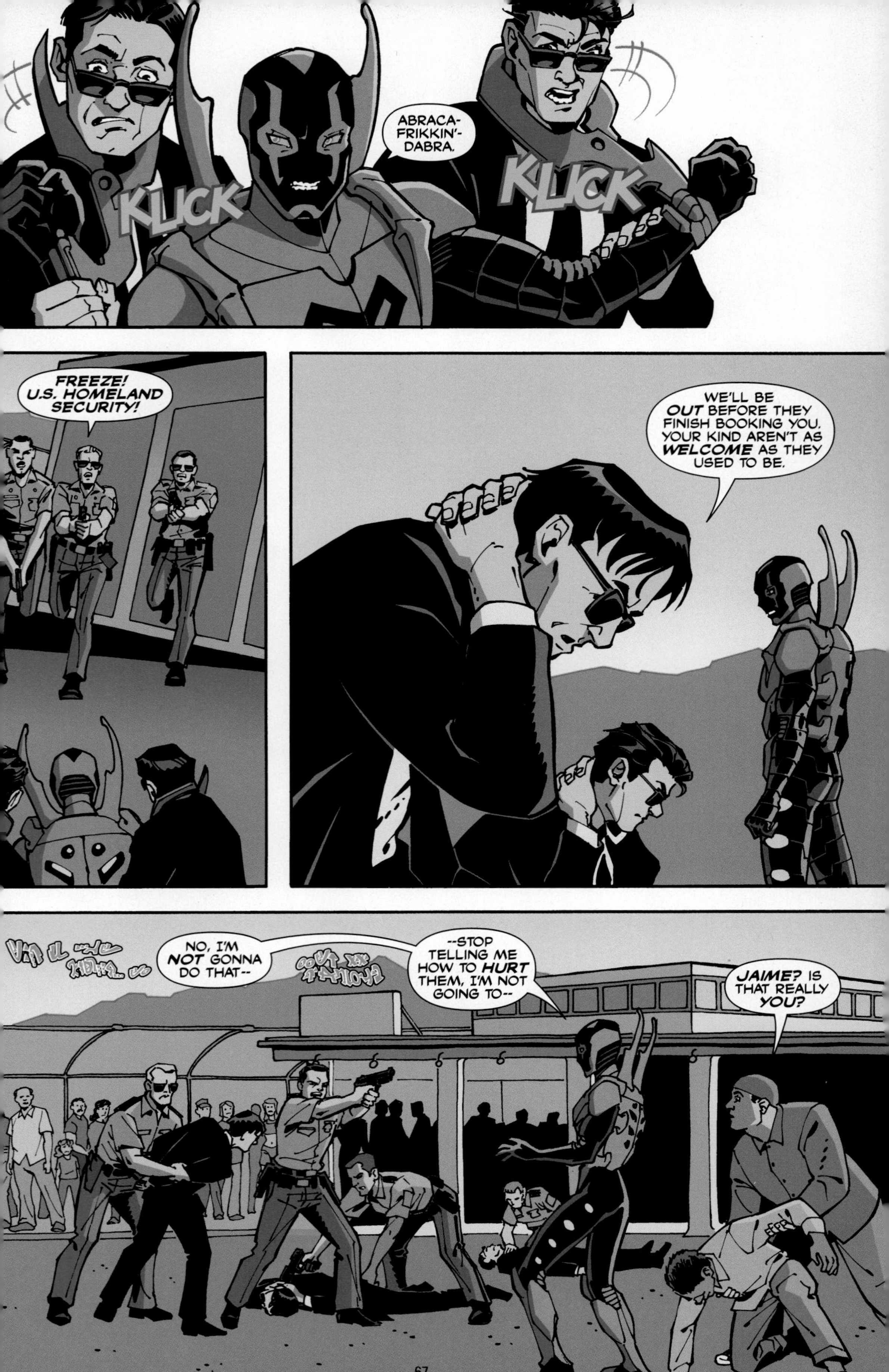
KLICK
ABRACA-FRIKKIN'-DABRA.
KLICK
FREEZE! U.S. HOMELAND SECURITY!
WE'LL BE OUT BEFORE THEY FINISH BOOKING YOU. YOUR KIND AREN'T AS WELCOME AS THEY USED TO BE.
NO, I'M NOT GONNA DO THAT--
--STOP TELLING ME HOW TO HURT THEM, I'M NOT GOING TO--
JAIME? IS THAT REALLY YOU?

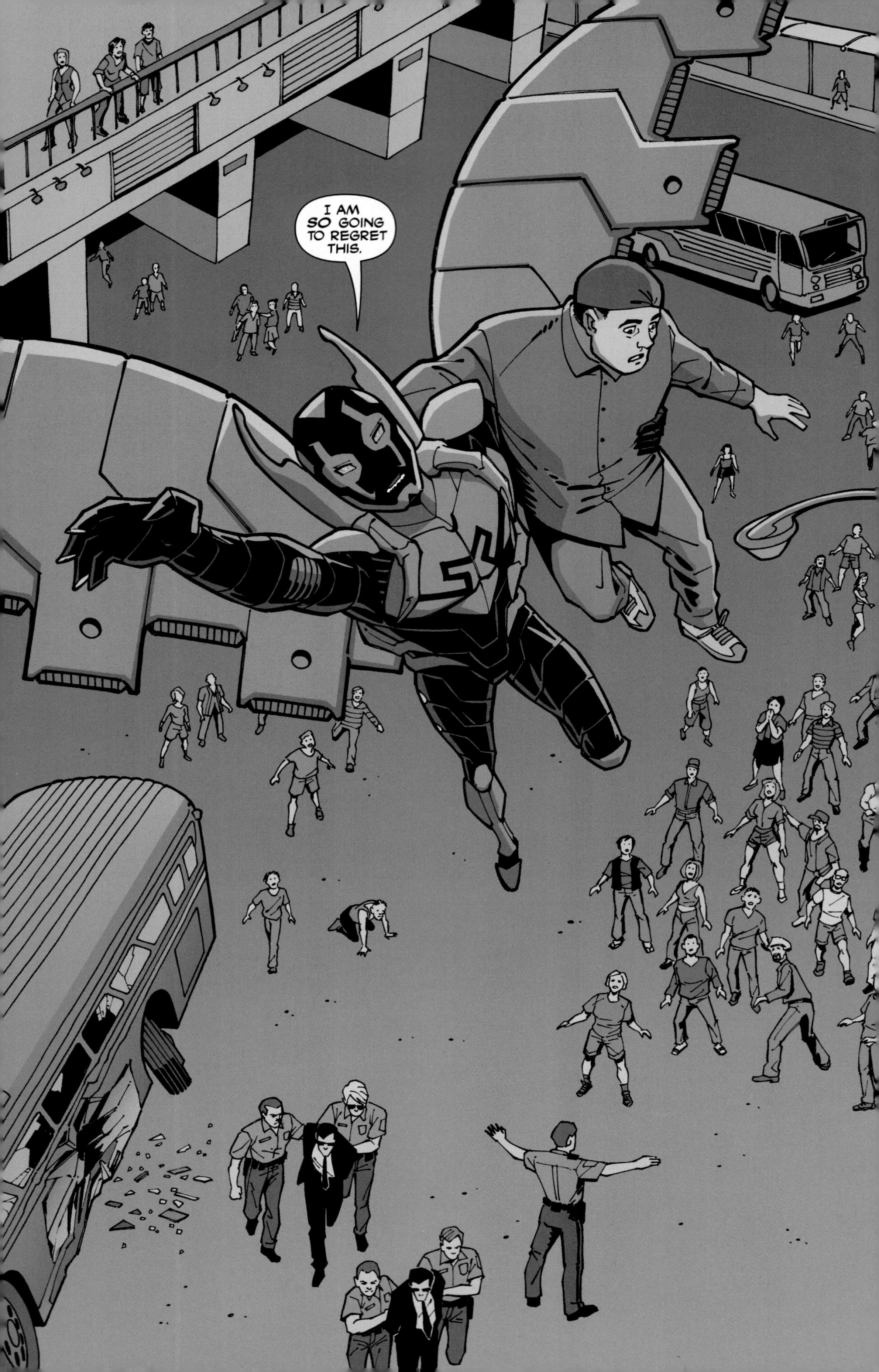
I AM SO GOING TO REGRET THIS.

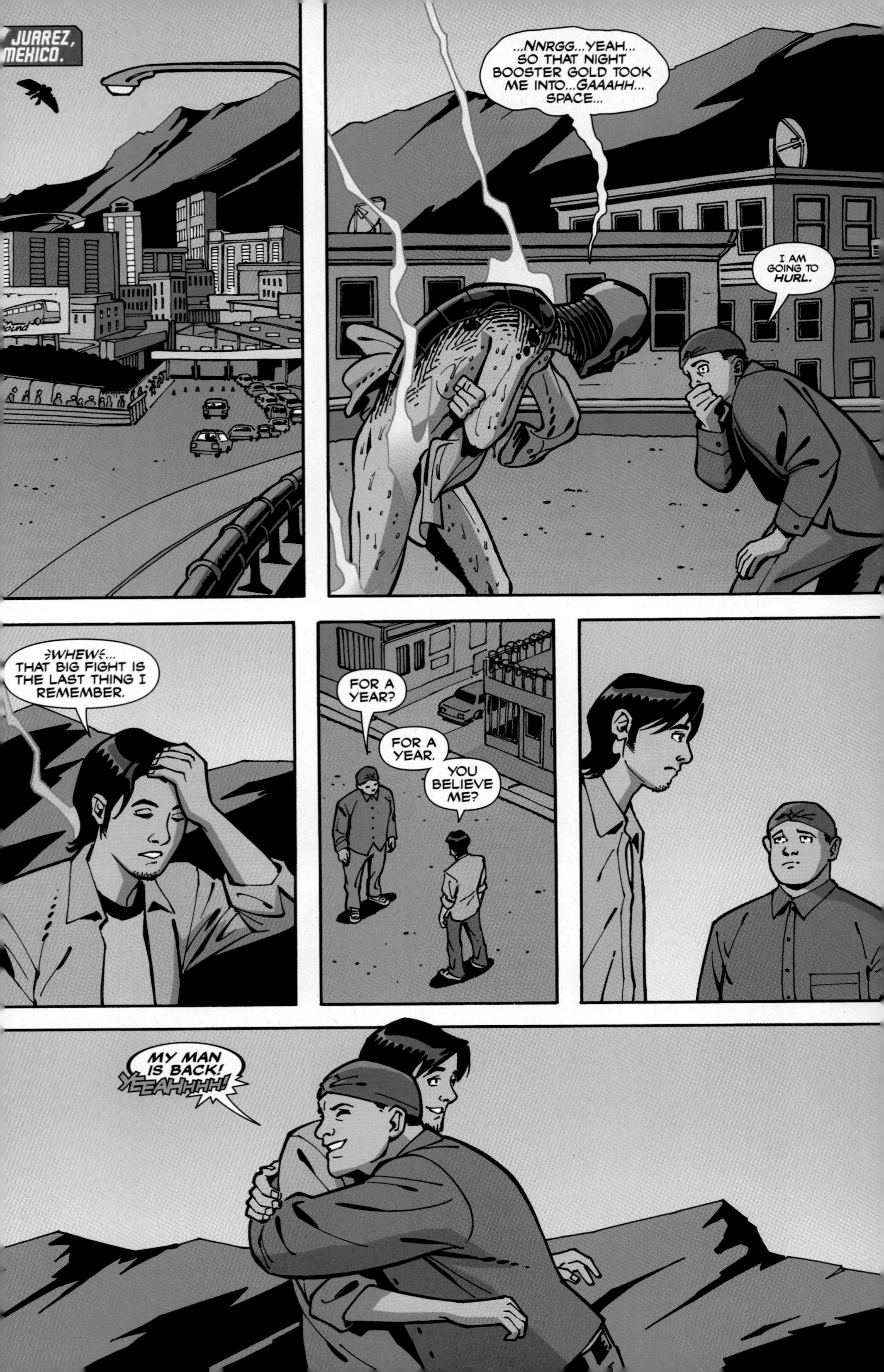
JUAREZ, MEXICO.
...NNRGG...YEAH... SO THAT NIGHT BOOSTER GOLD TOOK ME INTO...GAAAHH... SPACE...
I AM GOING TO HURL.
WHEW... THAT BIG FIGHT IS THE LAST THING I REMEMBER.
FOR A YEAR?
FOR A YEAR.
YOU BELIEVE ME?
MY MAN IS BACK!
YEEAHHHH!

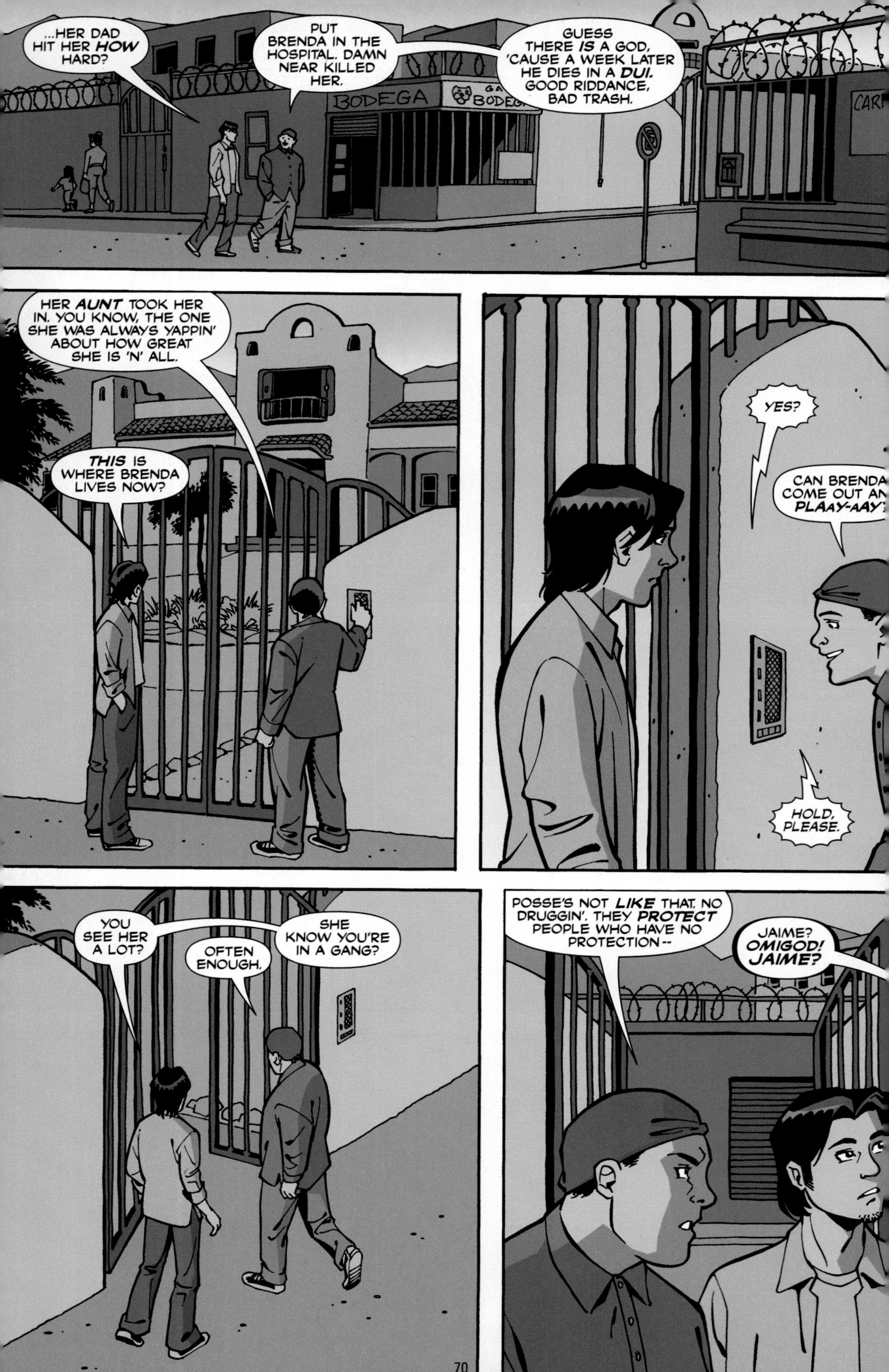

...HER DAD HIT HER HOW HARD?
PUT BRENDA IN THE HOSPITAL. DAMN NEAR KILLED HER.
GUESS THERE IS A GOD, 'CAUSE A WEEK LATER HE DIES IN A DUI. GOOD RIDDANCE, BAD TRASH.
BODEGA
HER AUNT TOOK HER IN. YOU KNOW, THE ONE SHE WAS ALWAYS YAPPIN' ABOUT HOW GREAT SHE IS 'N' ALL.
THIS IS WHERE BRENDA LIVES NOW?
YES?
CAN BRENDA COME OUT AN PLAAY-AAY
HOLD, PLEASE.
YOU SEE HER A LOT?
OFTEN ENOUGH.
SHE KNOW YOU'RE IN A GANG?
POSSE'S NOT LIKE THAT. NO DRUGGIN'. THEY PROTECT PEOPLE WHO HAVE NO PROTECTION --
JAIME? OMIGOD! JAIME?

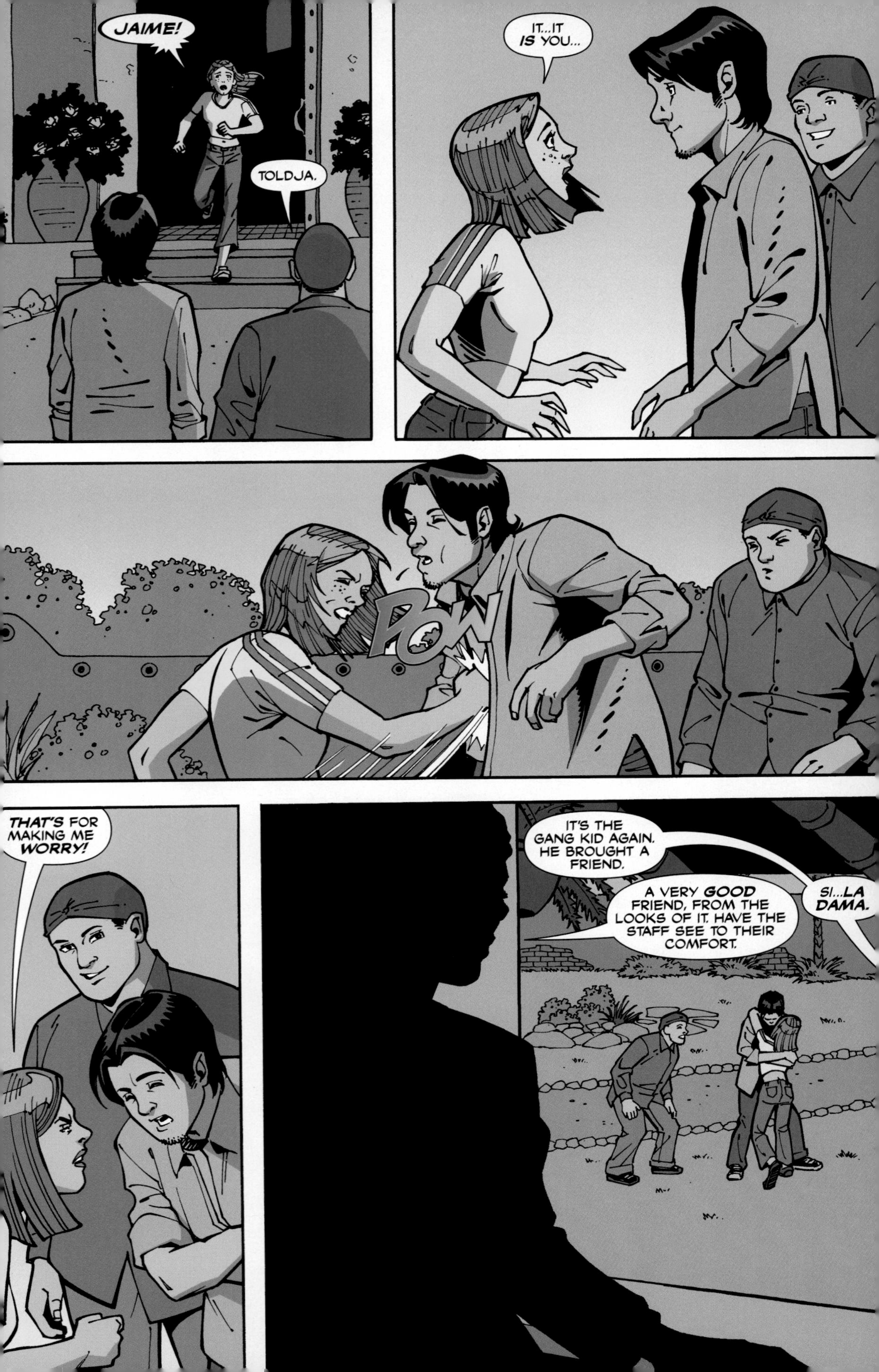
JAIME!
TOLDJA.
IT...IT IS YOU...
POW
THAT'S FOR MAKING ME WORRY!
IT'S THE GANG KID AGAIN. HE BROUGHT A FRIEND.
SI...LA DAMA.
A VERY GOOD FRIEND, FROM THE LOOKS OF IT. HAVE THE STAFF SEE TO THEIR COMFORT.

BLUE BEETLE #4
Cover by Duncan Rouleau
Interior art by Cully Hamner

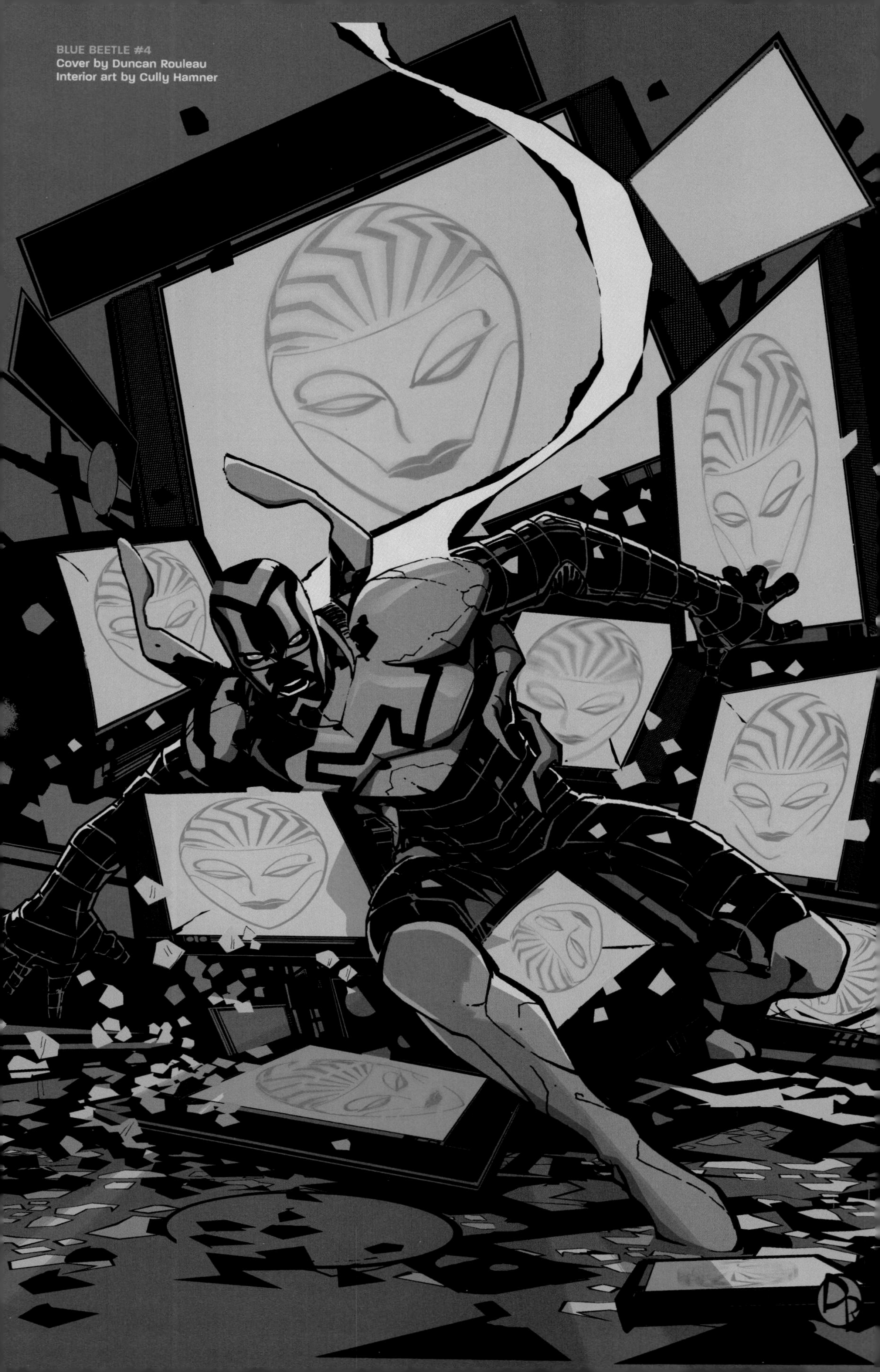

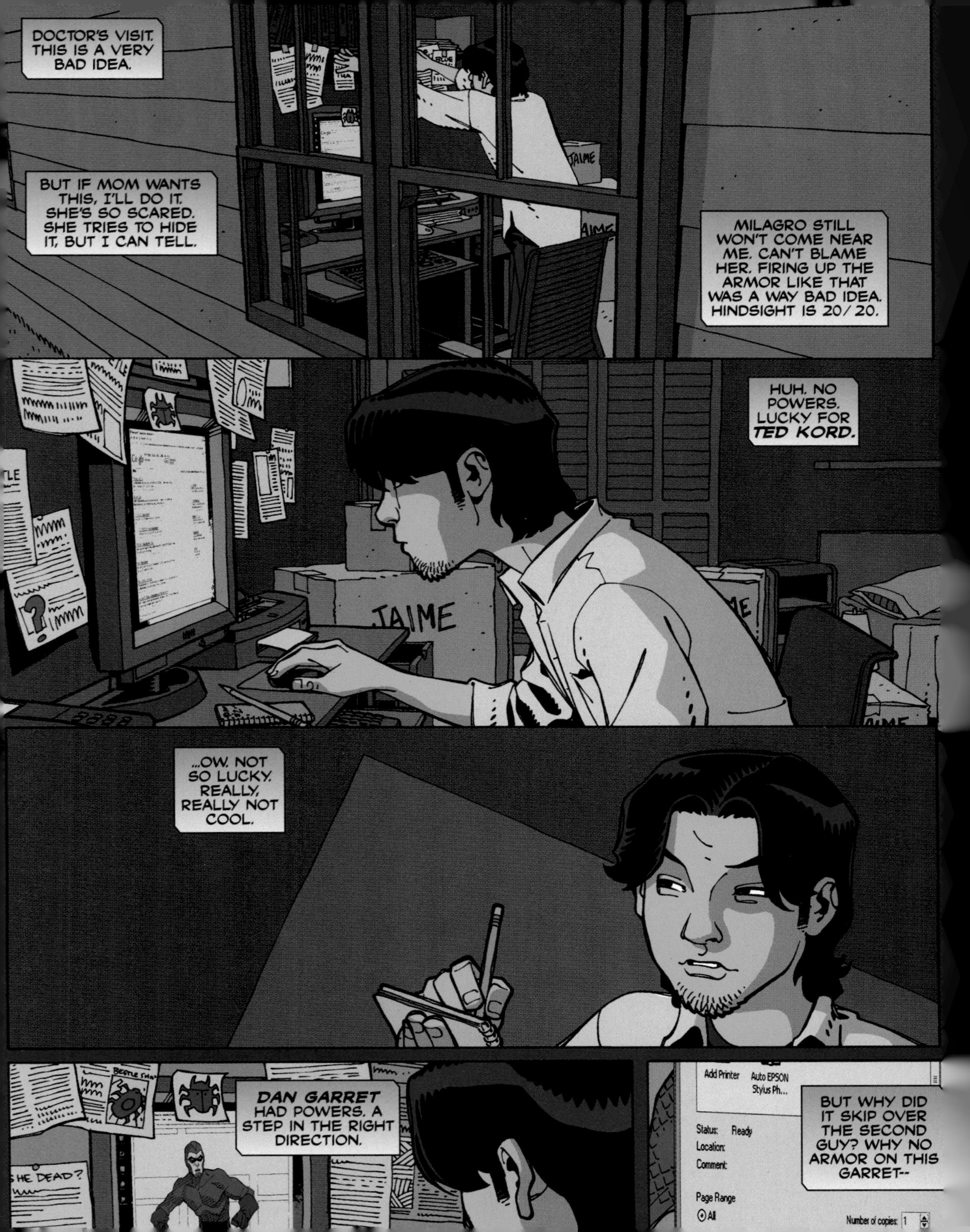
DOCTOR'S VISIT. THIS IS A VERY BAD IDEA.
BUT IF MOM WANTS THIS, I'LL DO IT. SHE'S SO SCARED. SHE TRIES TO HIDE IT, BUT I CAN TELL.
MILAGRO STILL WON'T COME NEAR ME. CAN'T BLAME HER. FIRING UP THE ARMOR LIKE THAT WAS A WAY BAD IDEA. HINDSIGHT IS 20/20.
JAIME
HUH. NO POWERS. LUCKY FOR *TED KORD.*
JAIME
...OW. NOT SO LUCKY. REALLY, REALLY NOT COOL.
DAN GARRET HAD POWERS. A STEP IN THE RIGHT DIRECTION.
HE DEAD?
Add Printer
Auto EPSON Stylus Ph...
Status: Ready
Location:
Comment:
Page Range
All
Number of copies: 1
BUT WHY DID IT SKIP OVER THE SECOND GUY? WHY NO ARMOR ON THIS GARRET--

PERSON OF INTEREST

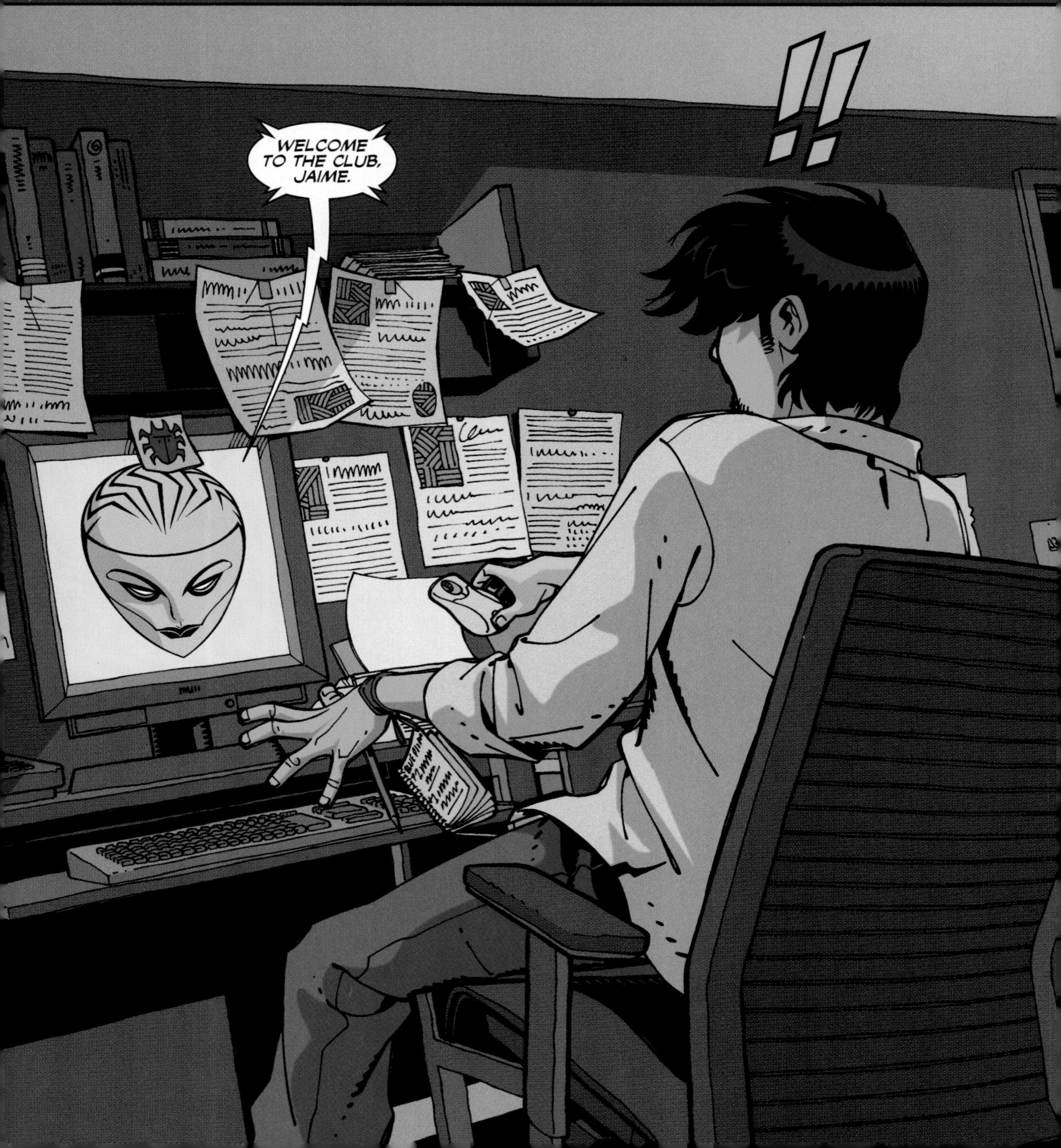
WELCOME TO THE CLUB, JAIME.
!!

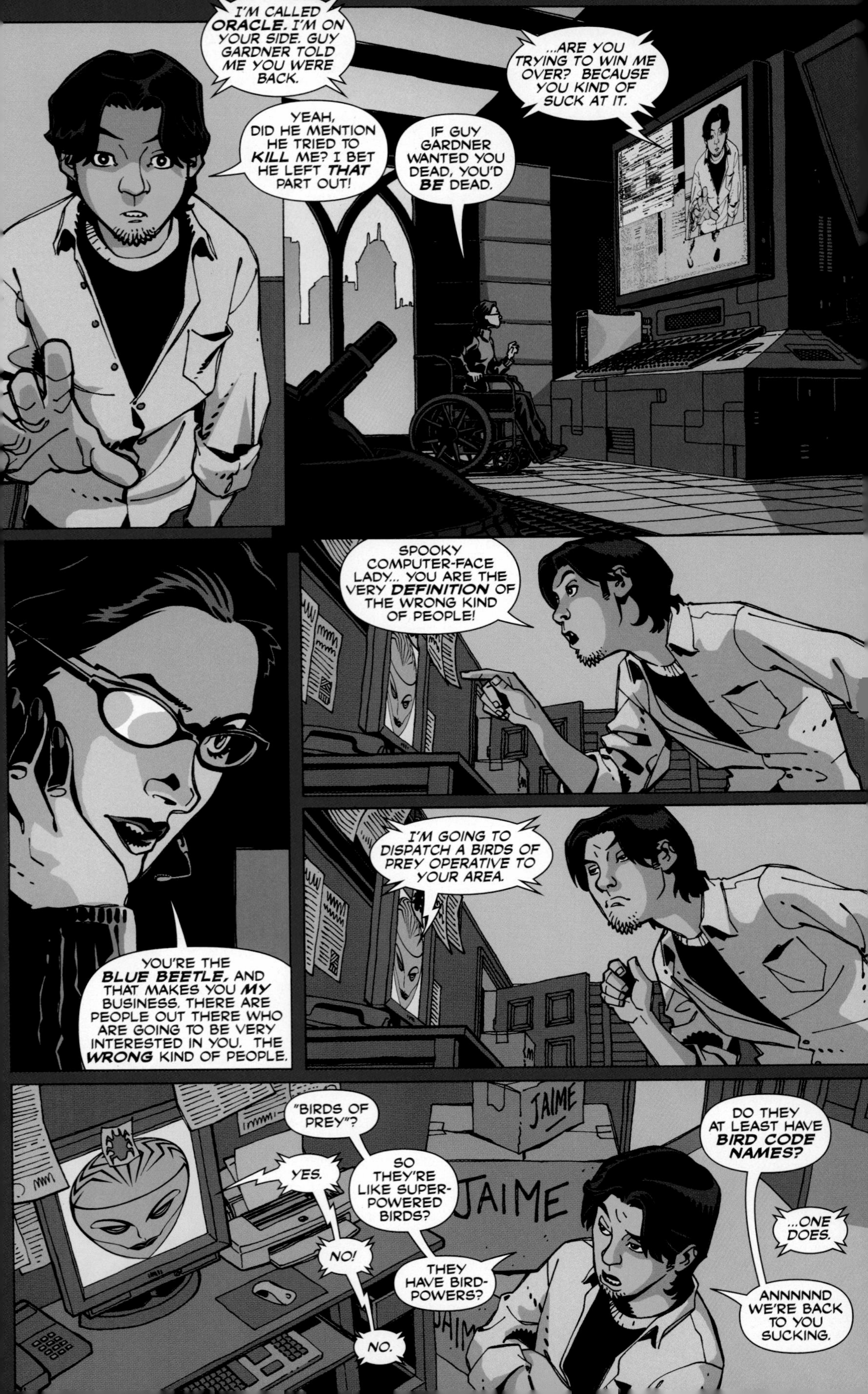

I'M CALLED ORACLE. I'M ON YOUR SIDE. GUY GARDNER TOLD ME YOU WERE BACK.
YEAH, DID HE MENTION HE TRIED TO KILL ME? I BET HE LEFT THAT PART OUT!
IF GUY GARDNER WANTED YOU DEAD, YOU'D BE DEAD.
...ARE YOU TRYING TO WIN ME OVER? BECAUSE YOU KIND OF SUCK AT IT.
YOU'RE THE BLUE BEETLE, AND THAT MAKES YOU MY BUSINESS. THERE ARE PEOPLE OUT THERE WHO ARE GOING TO BE VERY INTERESTED IN YOU. THE WRONG KIND OF PEOPLE.
SPOOKY COMPUTER-FACE LADY... YOU ARE THE VERY DEFINITION OF THE WRONG KIND OF PEOPLE!
I'M GOING TO DISPATCH A BIRDS OF PREY OPERATIVE TO YOUR AREA.
"BIRDS OF PREY"?
YES.
SO THEY'RE LIKE SUPER-POWERED BIRDS?
NO!
THEY HAVE BIRD-POWERS?
NO.
DO THEY AT LEAST HAVE BIRD CODE NAMES?
...ONE DOES.
ANNNNND WE'RE BACK TO YOU SUCKING.
JAIME
JAIME

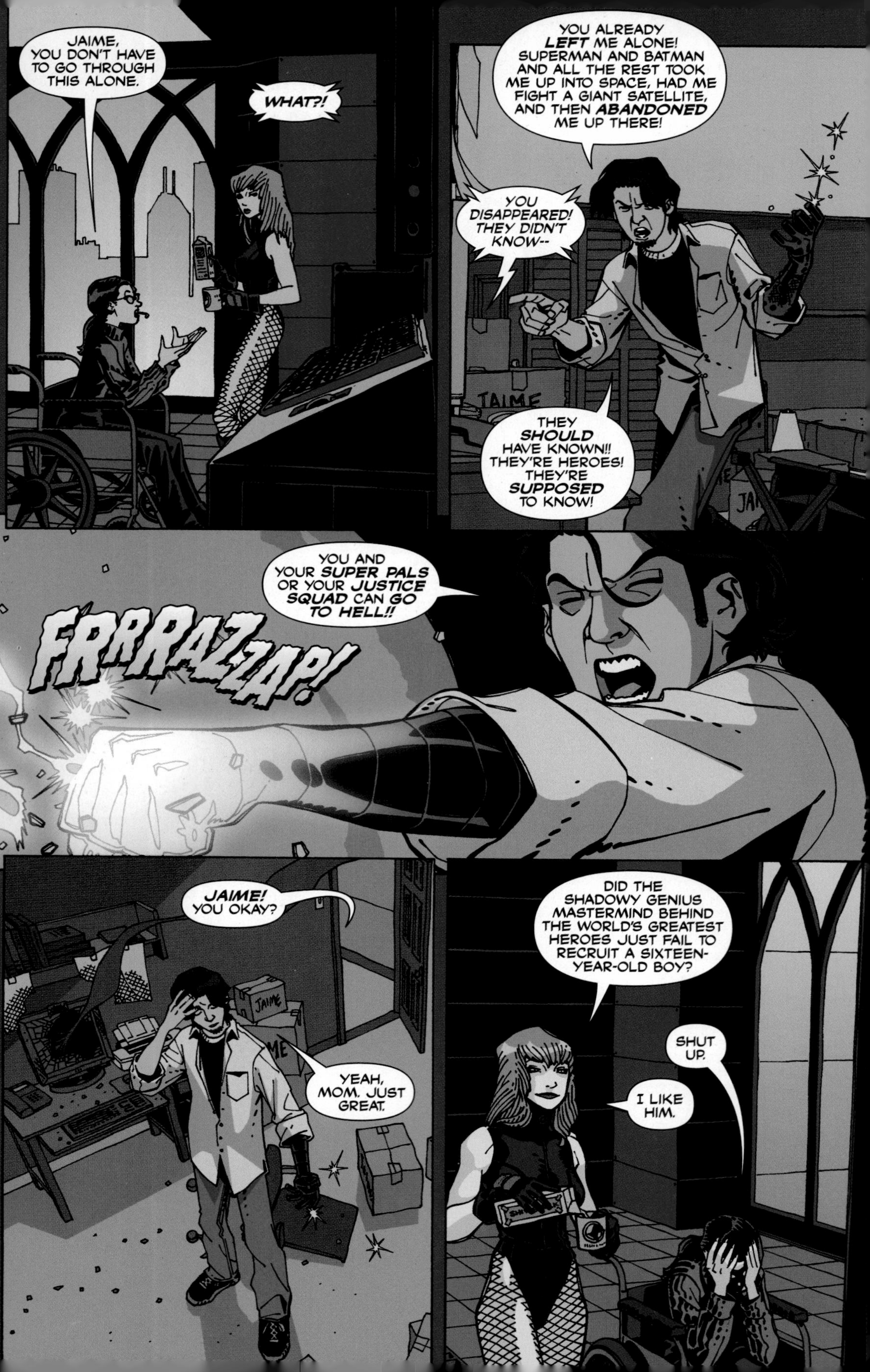
JAIME, YOU DON'T HAVE TO GO THROUGH THIS ALONE.
WHAT?!
YOU ALREADY LEFT ME ALONE! SUPERMAN AND BATMAN AND ALL THE REST TOOK ME UP INTO SPACE, HAD ME FIGHT A GIANT SATELLITE, AND THEN ABANDONED ME UP THERE!
YOU DISAPPEARED! THEY DIDN'T KNOW--
THEY SHOULD HAVE KNOWN!! THEY'RE HEROES! THEY'RE SUPPOSED TO KNOW!
JAIME
YOU AND YOUR SUPER PALS OR YOUR JUSTICE SQUAD CAN GO TO HELL!!
FRRRAZZAP!
JAIME! YOU OKAY?
JAIME
YEAH, MOM. JUST GREAT.
DID THE SHADOWY GENIUS MASTERMIND BEHIND THE WORLD'S GREATEST HEROES JUST FAIL TO RECRUIT A SIXTEEN-YEAR-OLD BOY?
SHUT UP.
I LIKE HIM.

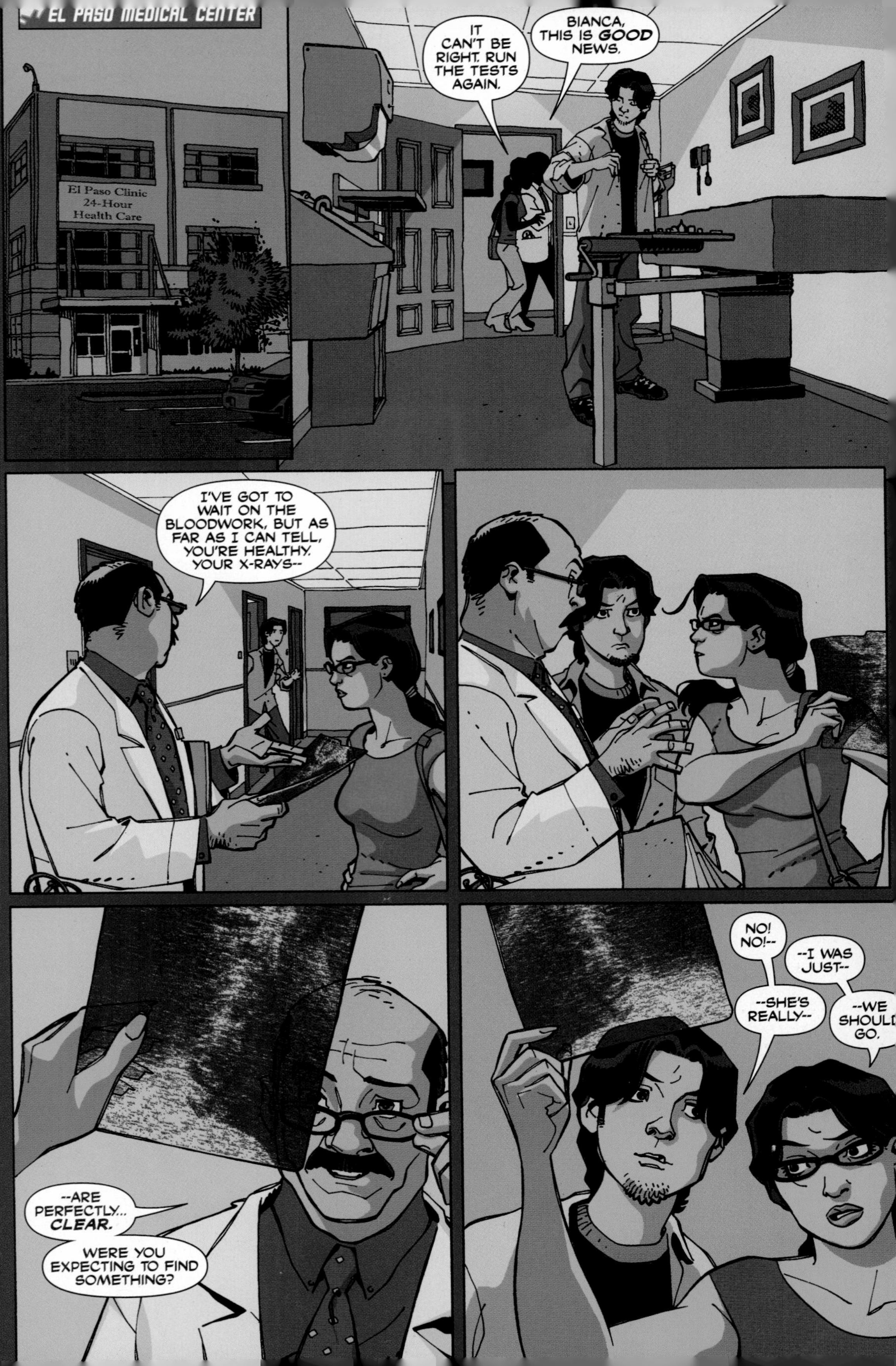
EL PASO MEDICAL CENTER
El Paso Clinic
24-Hour
Health Care
IT CAN'T BE RIGHT. RUN THE TESTS AGAIN.
BIANCA, THIS IS GOOD NEWS.
I'VE GOT TO WAIT ON THE BLOODWORK, BUT AS FAR AS I CAN TELL, YOU'RE HEALTHY. YOUR X-RAYS--
--ARE PERFECTLY... CLEAR.
WERE YOU EXPECTING TO FIND SOMETHING?
NO! NO!--
--SHE'S REALLY--
--I WAS JUST--
--WE SHOULD GO.

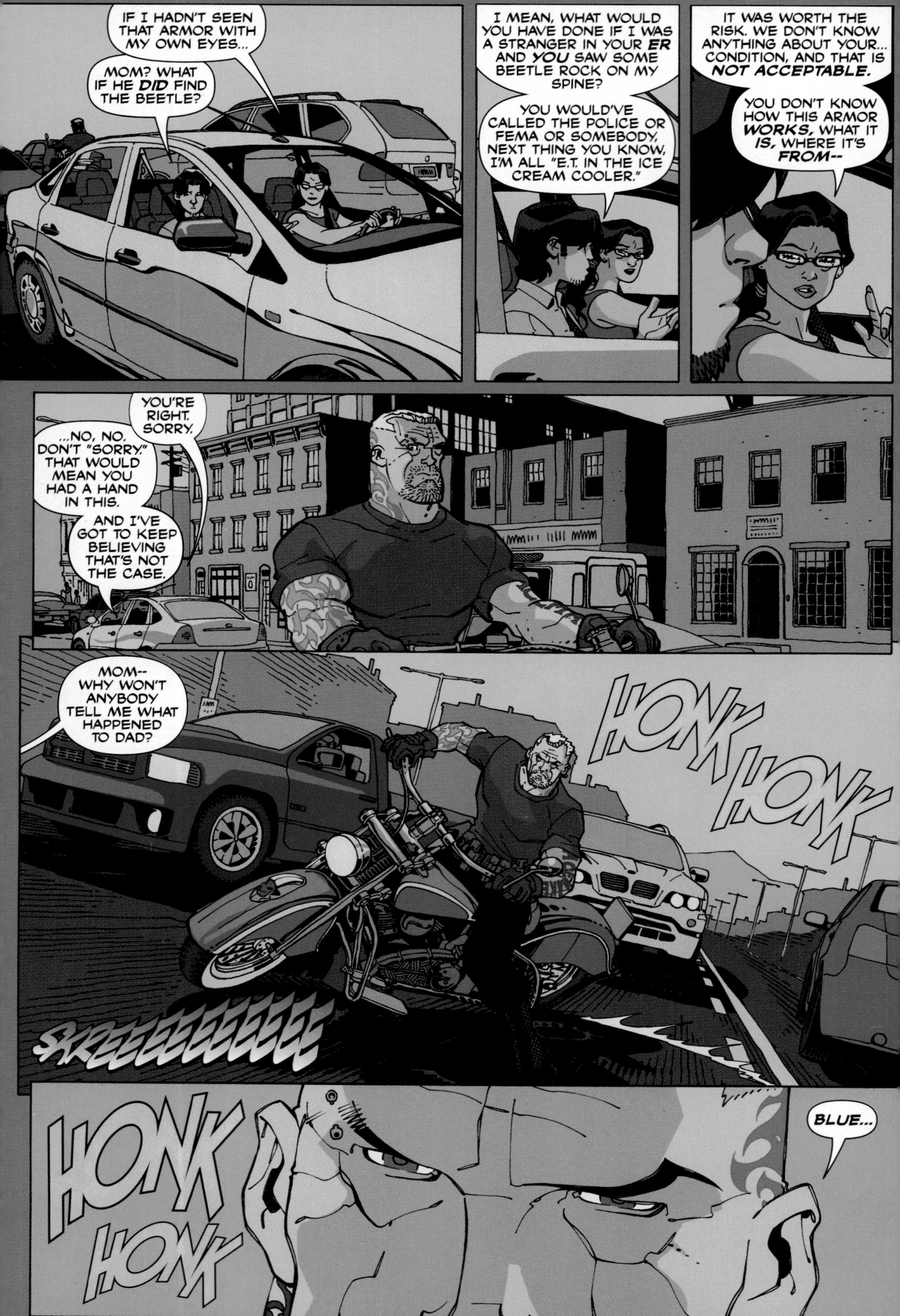
IF I HADN'T SEEN THAT ARMOR WITH MY OWN EYES...
MOM? WHAT IF HE DID FIND THE BEETLE?
I MEAN, WHAT WOULD YOU HAVE DONE IF I WAS A STRANGER IN YOUR ER AND YOU SAW SOME BEETLE ROCK ON MY SPINE?
YOU WOULD'VE CALLED THE POLICE OR FEMA OR SOMEBODY, NEXT THING YOU KNOW, I'M ALL "E.T. IN THE ICE CREAM COOLER."
IT WAS WORTH THE RISK. WE DON'T KNOW ANYTHING ABOUT YOUR... CONDITION, AND THAT IS NOT ACCEPTABLE.
YOU DON'T KNOW HOW THIS ARMOR WORKS, WHAT IT IS, WHERE IT'S FROM--
YOU'RE RIGHT. SORRY.
...NO, NO. DON'T "SORRY." THAT WOULD MEAN YOU HAD A HAND IN THIS.
AND I'VE GOT TO KEEP BELIEVING THAT'S NOT THE CASE.
MOM-- WHY WON'T ANYBODY TELL ME WHAT HAPPENED TO DAD?
HONK HONK
SKREEEEEEEEEEE
HONK HONK
BLUE...

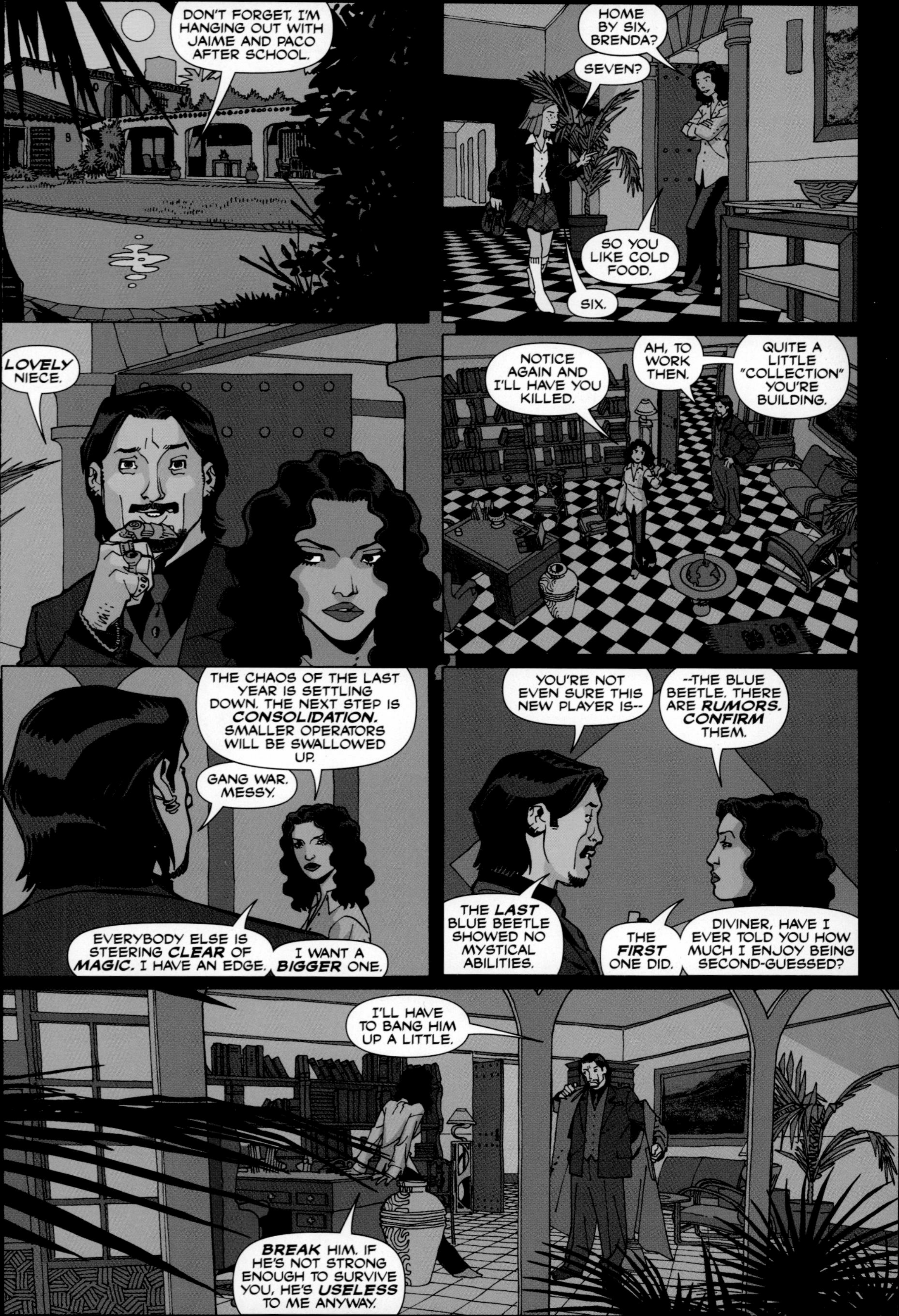
DON'T FORGET, I'M HANGING OUT WITH JAIME AND PACO AFTER SCHOOL.
HOME BY SIX, BRENDA?
SEVEN?
SO YOU LIKE COLD FOOD.
SIX.
LOVELY NIECE.
NOTICE AGAIN AND I'LL HAVE YOU KILLED.
AH, TO WORK THEN.
QUITE A LITTLE "COLLECTION" YOU'RE BUILDING.
THE CHAOS OF THE LAST YEAR IS SETTLING DOWN. THE NEXT STEP IS CONSOLIDATION. SMALLER OPERATORS WILL BE SWALLOWED UP.
GANG WAR. MESSY.
EVERYBODY ELSE IS STEERING CLEAR OF MAGIC. I HAVE AN EDGE.
I WANT A BIGGER ONE.
YOU'RE NOT EVEN SURE THIS NEW PLAYER IS--
--THE BLUE BEETLE. THERE ARE RUMORS. CONFIRM THEM.
THE LAST BLUE BEETLE SHOWED NO MYSTICAL ABILITIES.
THE FIRST ONE DID.
DINER, HAVE I EVER TOLD YOU HOW MUCH I ENJOY BEING SECOND-GUESSED?
I'LL HAVE TO BANG HIM UP A LITTLE.
BREAK HIM. IF HE'S NOT STRONG ENOUGH TO SURVIVE YOU, HE'S USELESS TO ME ANYWAY.

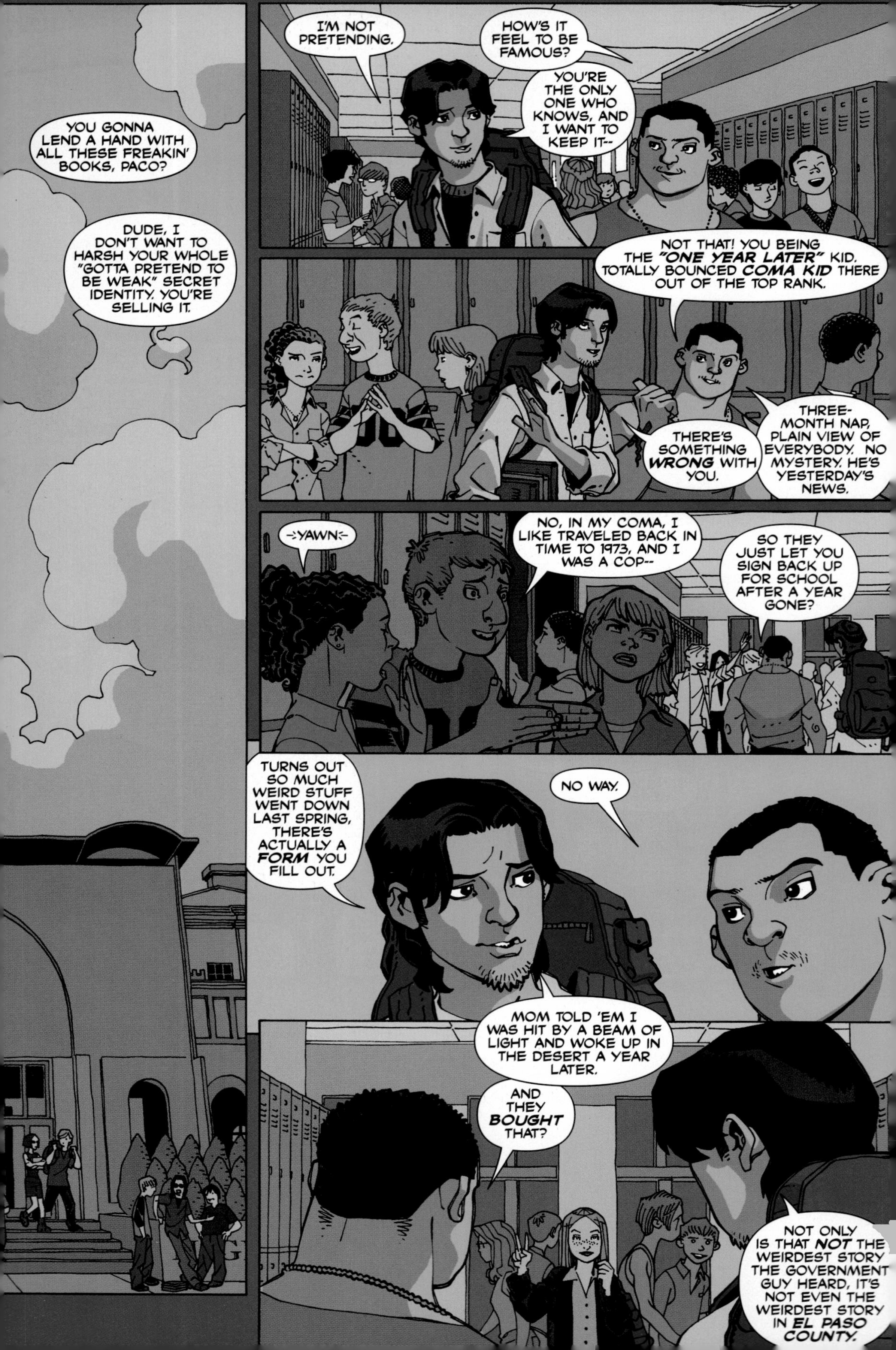
YOU GONNA LEND A HAND WITH ALL THESE FREAKIN' BOOKS, PACO?
DUDE, I DON'T WANT TO HARSH YOUR WHOLE "GOTTA PRETEND TO BE WEAK" SECRET IDENTITY. YOU'RE SELLING IT.
I'M NOT PRETENDING.
HOW'S IT FEEL TO BE FAMOUS?
YOU'RE THE ONLY ONE WHO KNOWS, AND I WANT TO KEEP IT--
NOT THAT! YOU BEING THE *"ONE YEAR LATER"* KID. TOTALLY BOUNCED *COMA KID* THERE OUT OF THE TOP RANK.
THERE'S SOMETHING *WRONG* WITH YOU.
THREE-MONTH NAP, PLAIN VIEW OF EVERYBODY. NO MYSTERY. HE'S YESTERDAY'S NEWS.
-YAWN-
NO, IN MY COMA, I LIKE TRAVELED BACK IN TIME TO 1973, AND I WAS A COP--
SO THEY JUST LET YOU SIGN BACK UP FOR SCHOOL AFTER A YEAR GONE?
TURNS OUT SO MUCH WEIRD STUFF WENT DOWN LAST SPRING, THERE'S ACTUALLY A *FORM* YOU FILL OUT.
NO WAY.
MOM TOLD 'EM I WAS HIT BY A BEAM OF LIGHT AND WOKE UP IN THE DESERT A YEAR LATER.
AND THEY *BOUGHT* THAT?
NOT ONLY IS THAT *NOT* THE WEIRDEST STORY THE GOVERNMENT GUY HEARD, IT'S NOT EVEN THE WEIRDEST STORY IN *EL PASO COUNTY.*

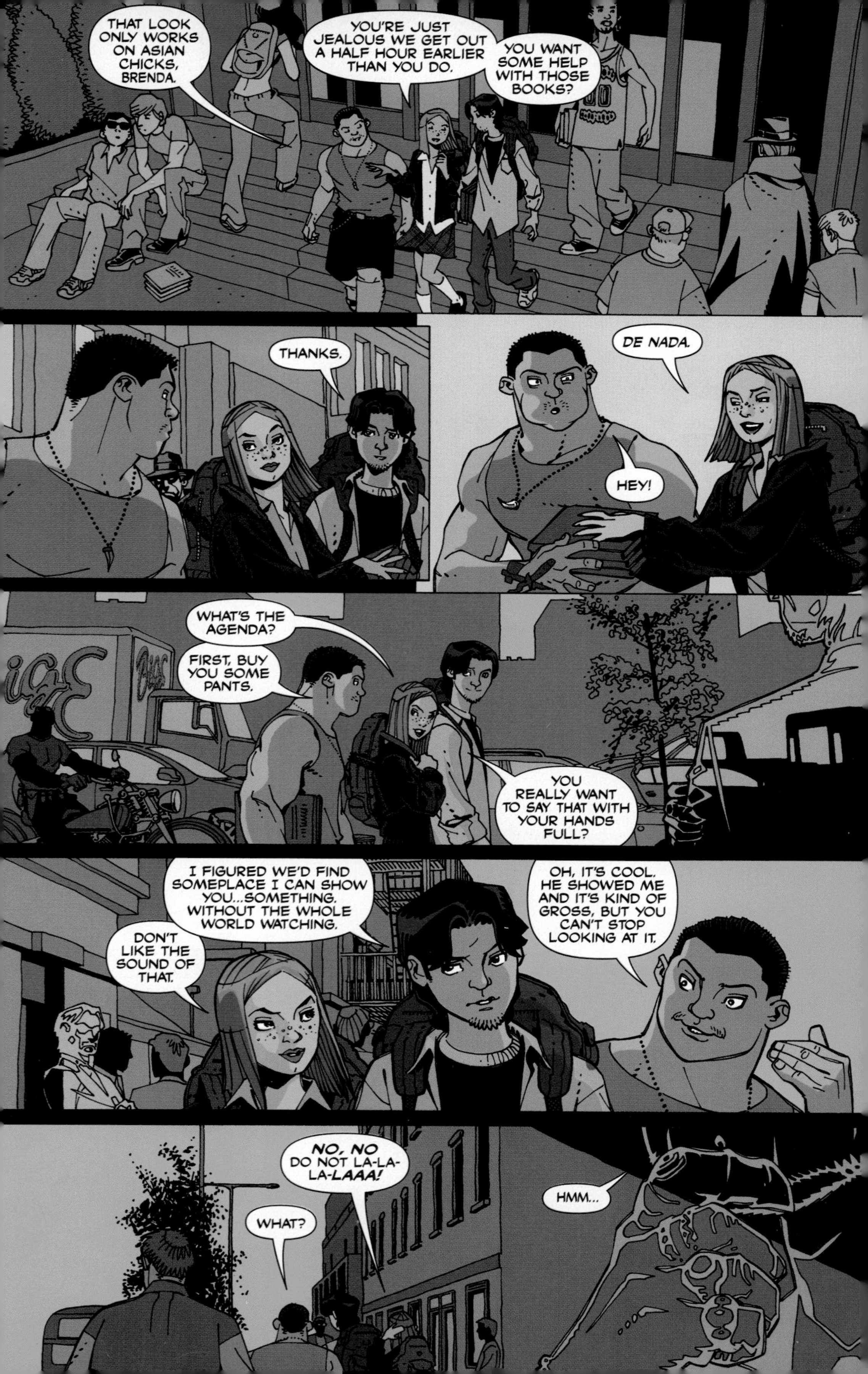
THAT LOOK ONLY WORKS ON ASIAN CHICKS, BRENDA.
YOU'RE JUST JEALOUS WE GET OUT A HALF HOUR EARLIER THAN YOU DO.
YOU WANT SOME HELP WITH THOSE BOOKS?
THANKS.
DE NADA.
HEY!
WHAT'S THE AGENDA?
FIRST, BUY YOU SOME PANTS.
YOU REALLY WANT TO SAY THAT WITH YOUR HANDS FULL?
I FIGURED WE'D FIND SOMEPLACE I CAN SHOW YOU...SOMETHING. WITHOUT THE WHOLE WORLD WATCHING.
DON'T LIKE THE SOUND OF THAT.
OH, IT'S COOL. HE SHOWED ME AND IT'S KIND OF GROSS, BUT YOU CAN'T STOP LOOKING AT IT.
WHAT?
NO, NO DO NOT LA-LA-LA-LAAA!
HMM...

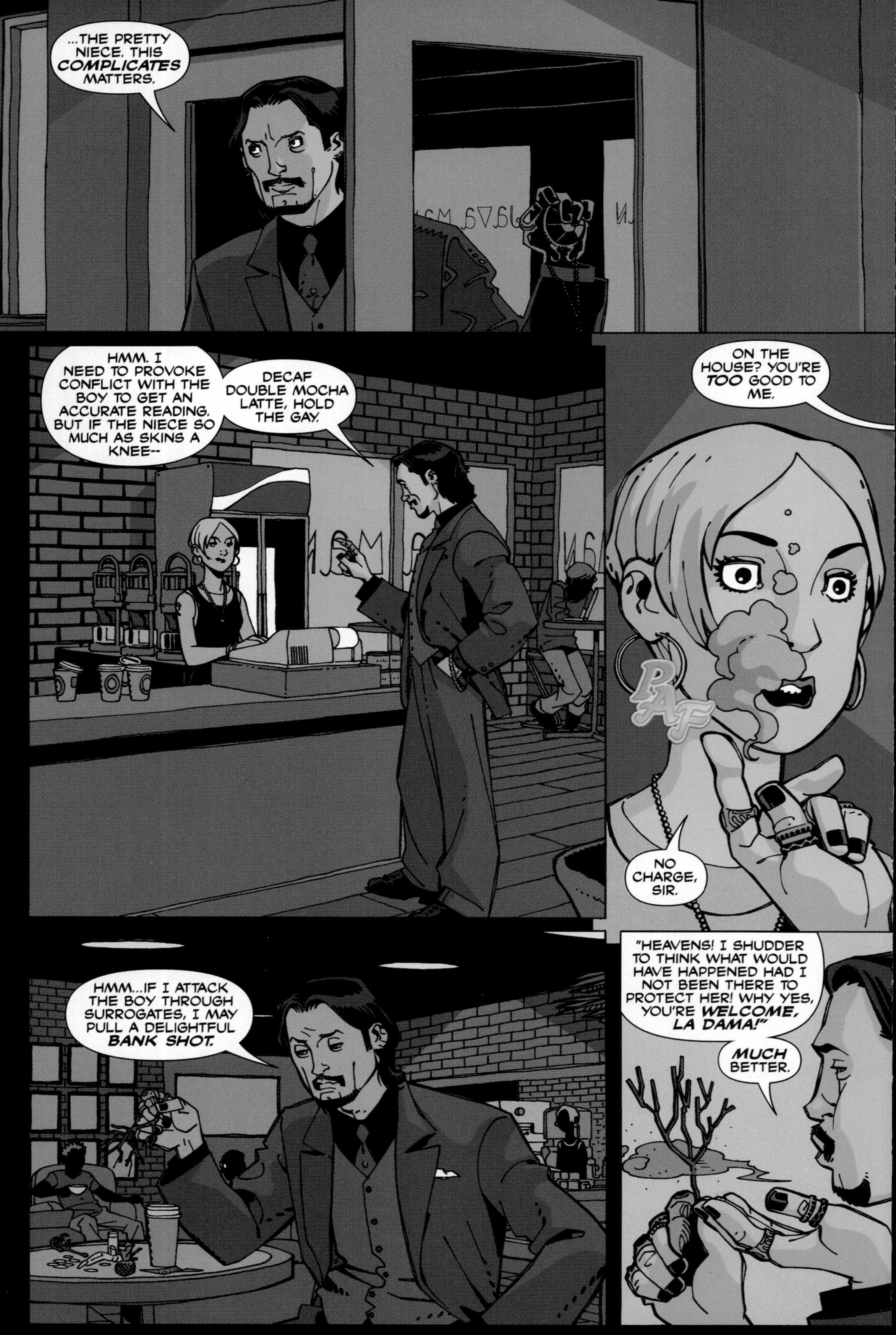

...THE PRETTY NIECE. THIS COMPLICATES MATTERS.
HMM. I NEED TO PROVOKE CONFLICT WITH THE BOY TO GET AN ACCURATE READING. BUT IF THE NIECE SO MUCH AS SKINS A KNEE--
DECAF DOUBLE MOCHA LATTE, HOLD THE GAY.
ON THE HOUSE? YOU'RE TOO GOOD TO ME.
PAF
NO CHARGE, SIR.
HMM...IF I ATTACK THE BOY THROUGH SURROGATES, I MAY PULL A DELIGHTFUL BANK SHOT.
"HEAVENS! I SHUDDER TO THINK WHAT WOULD HAVE HAPPENED HAD I NOT BEEN THERE TO PROTECT HER! WHY YES, YOU'RE WELCOME, LA DAMA!"
MUCH BETTER.

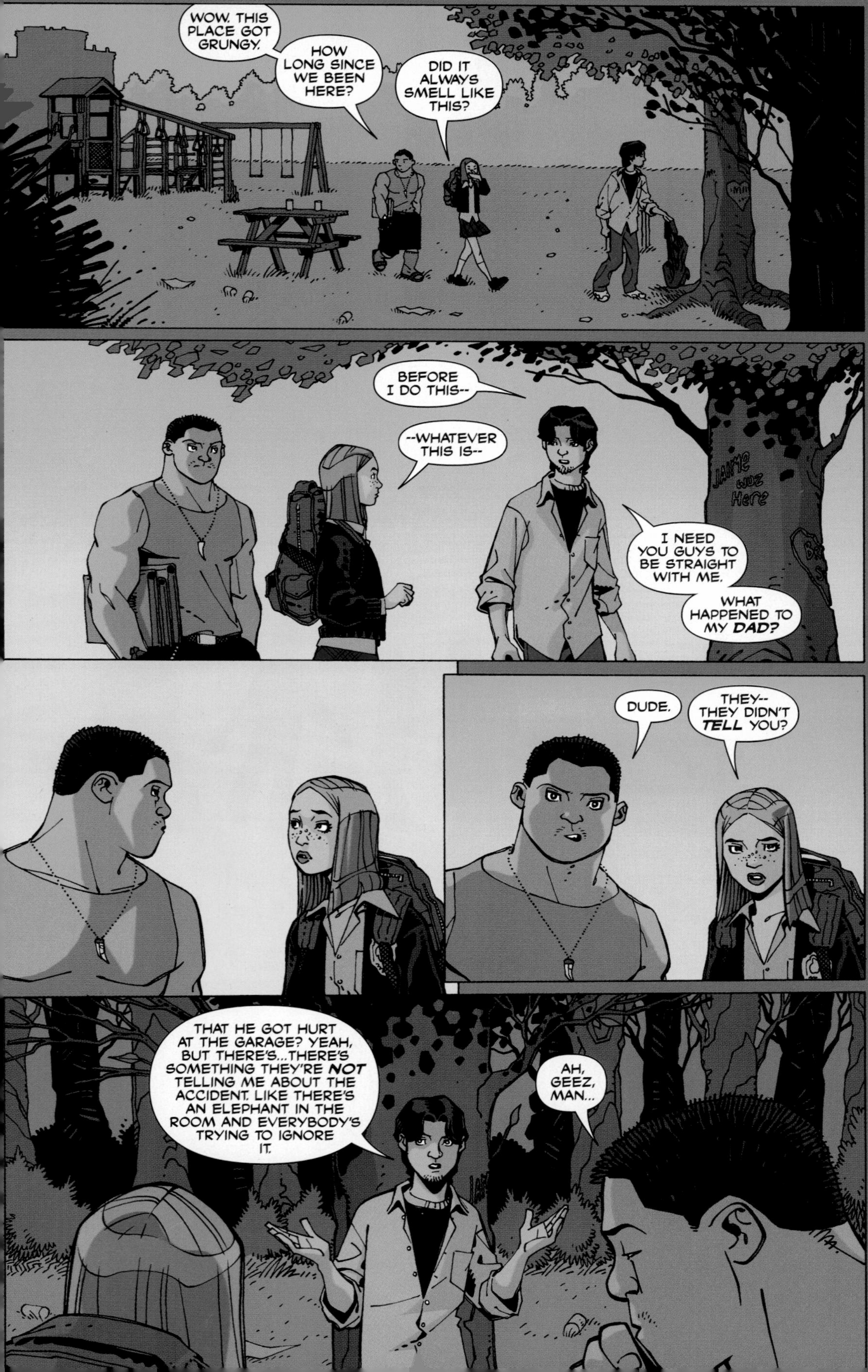
WOW. THIS PLACE GOT GRUNGY.
HOW LONG SINCE WE BEEN HERE?
DID IT ALWAYS SMELL LIKE THIS?
BEFORE I DO THIS--
--WHATEVER THIS IS--
JAIME WUZ HERE
I NEED YOU GUYS TO BE STRAIGHT WITH ME.
WHAT HAPPENED TO MY **DAD?**
DUDE.
THEY-- THEY DIDN'T **TELL** YOU?
THAT HE GOT HURT AT THE GARAGE? YEAH, BUT THERE'S...THERE'S SOMETHING THEY'RE **NOT** TELLING ME ABOUT THE ACCIDENT. LIKE THERE'S AN ELEPHANT IN THE ROOM AND EVERYBODY'S TRYING TO IGNORE IT.
AH, GEEZ, MAN...

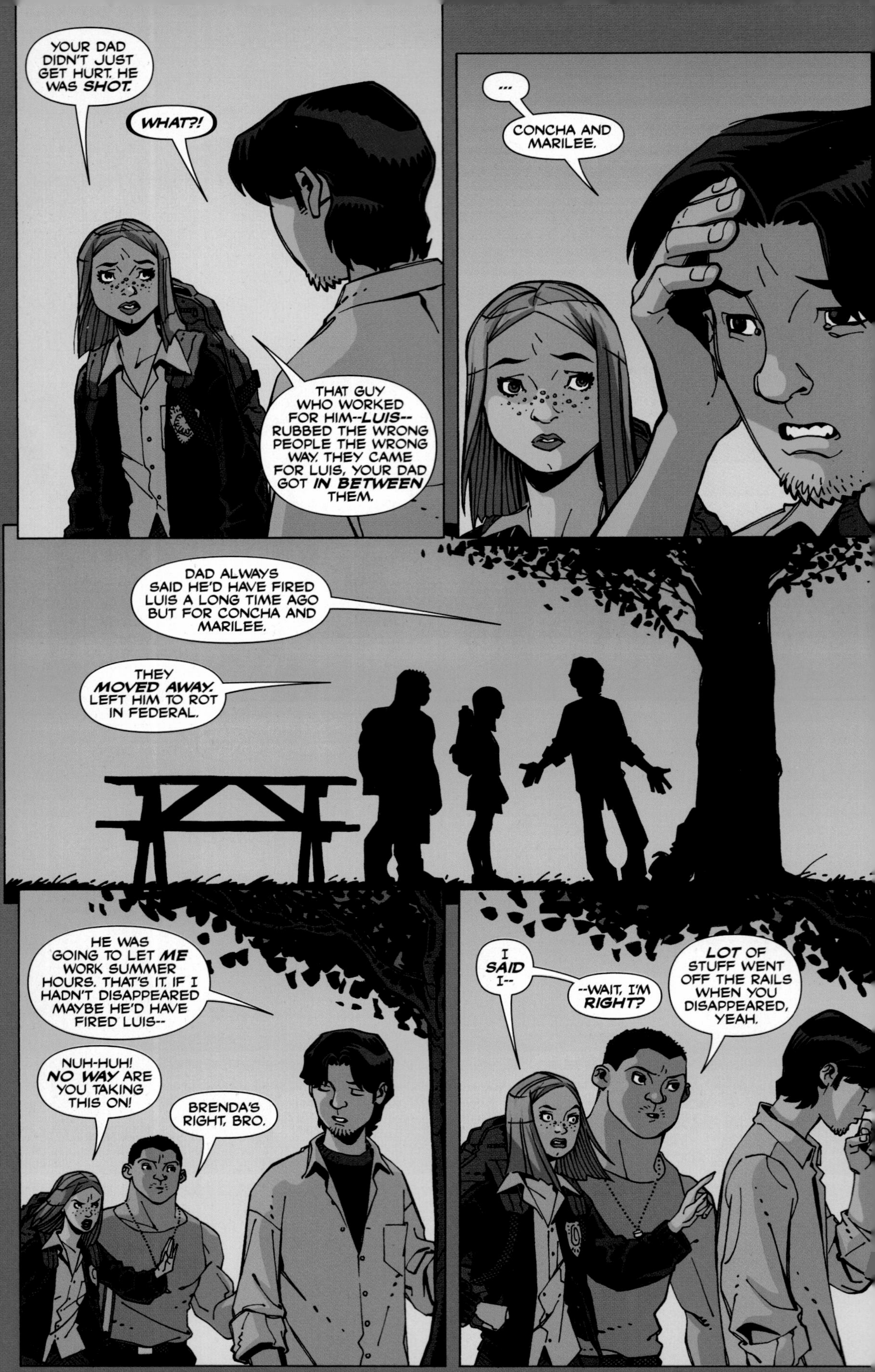
YOUR DAD DIDN'T JUST GET HURT. HE WAS SHOT.
WHAT?!
THAT GUY WHO WORKED FOR HIM--LUIS--RUBBED THE WRONG PEOPLE THE WRONG WAY. THEY CAME FOR LUIS, YOUR DAD GOT IN BETWEEN THEM.
...
CONCHA AND MARILEE.
DAD ALWAYS SAID HE'D HAVE FIRED LUIS A LONG TIME AGO BUT FOR CONCHA AND MARILEE.
THEY MOVED AWAY. LEFT HIM TO ROT IN FEDERAL.
HE WAS GOING TO LET ME WORK SUMMER HOURS. THAT'S IT. IF I HADN'T DISAPPEARED MAYBE HE'D HAVE FIRED LUIS--
NUH-HUH! NO WAY ARE YOU TAKING THIS ON!
BRENDA'S RIGHT, BRO.
I SAID I--
--WAIT, I'M RIGHT?
LOT OF STUFF WENT OFF THE RAILS WHEN YOU DISAPPEARED, YEAH.

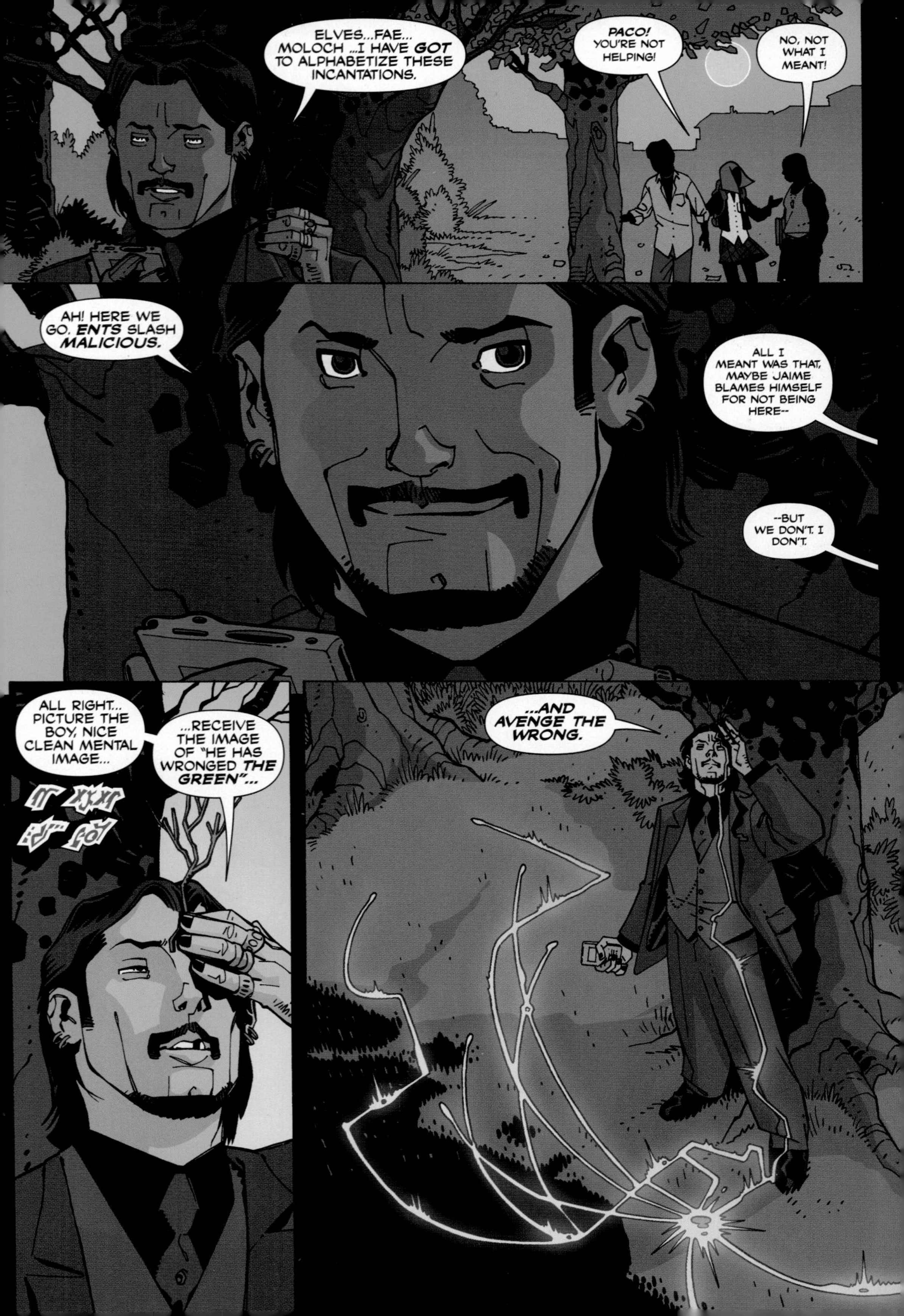
ELVES...FAE... MOLOCH ...I HAVE GOT TO ALPHABETIZE THESE INCANTATIONS.
PACO! YOU'RE NOT HELPING!
NO, NOT WHAT I MEANT!
AH! HERE WE GO. ENTS SLASH MALICIOUS.
ALL I MEANT WAS THAT, MAYBE JAIME BLAMES HIMSELF FOR NOT BEING HERE--
--BUT WE DON'T. I DON'T.
ALL RIGHT... PICTURE THE BOY, NICE CLEAN MENTAL IMAGE...
...RECEIVE THE IMAGE OF "HE HAS WRONGED THE GREEN"...
...AND AVENGE THE WRONG.

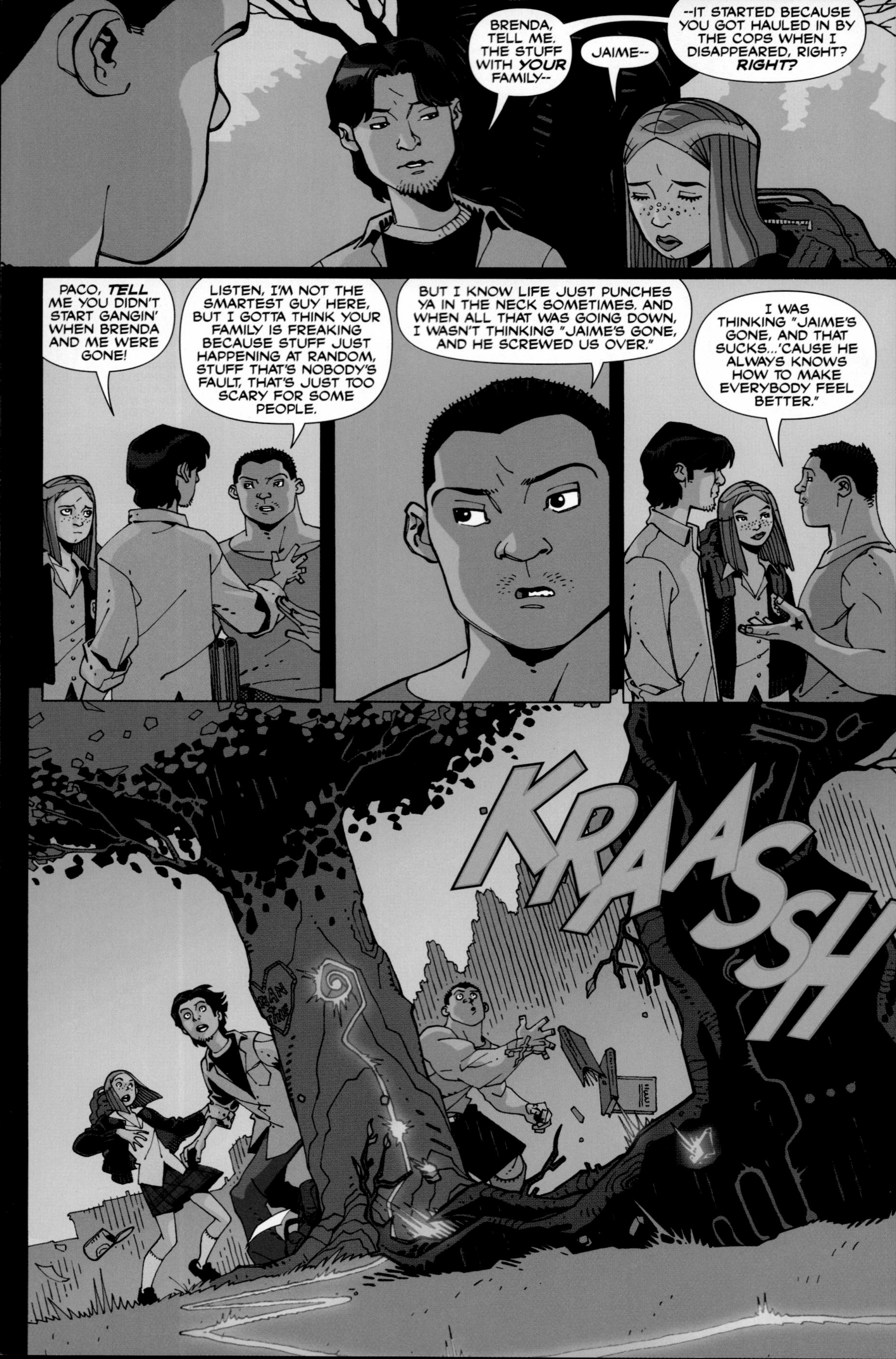
BRENDA, TELL ME. THE STUFF WITH *YOUR* FAMILY--
JAIME--
--IT STARTED BECAUSE YOU GOT HAULED IN BY THE COPS WHEN I DISAPPEARED, RIGHT? ***RIGHT?***
PACO, ***TELL*** ME YOU DIDN'T START GANGIN' WHEN BRENDA AND ME WERE GONE!
LISTEN, I'M NOT THE SMARTEST GUY HERE, BUT I GOTTA THINK YOUR FAMILY IS FREAKING BECAUSE STUFF JUST HAPPENING AT RANDOM, STUFF THAT'S NOBODY'S FAULT, THAT'S JUST TOO SCARY FOR SOME PEOPLE.
BUT I KNOW LIFE JUST PUNCHES YA IN THE NECK SOMETIMES. AND WHEN ALL THAT WAS GOING DOWN, I WASN'T THINKING "JAIME'S GONE, AND HE SCREWED US OVER."
I WAS THINKING "JAIME'S GONE, AND THAT SUCKS...'CAUSE HE ALWAYS KNOWS HOW TO MAKE EVERYBODY FEEL BETTER."
KRAASSH

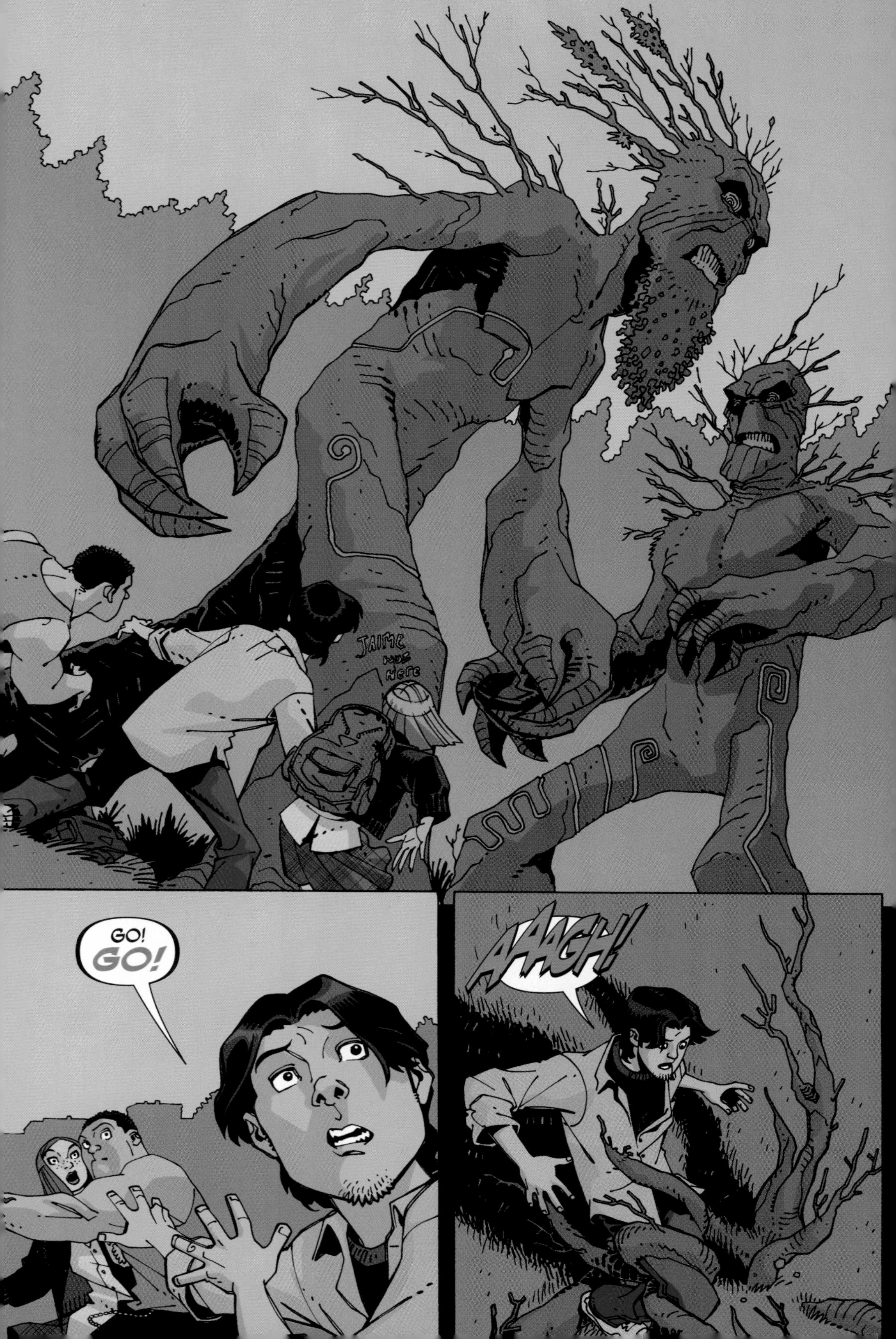
JAIME
was
here
GO!
GO!
AAAGH!

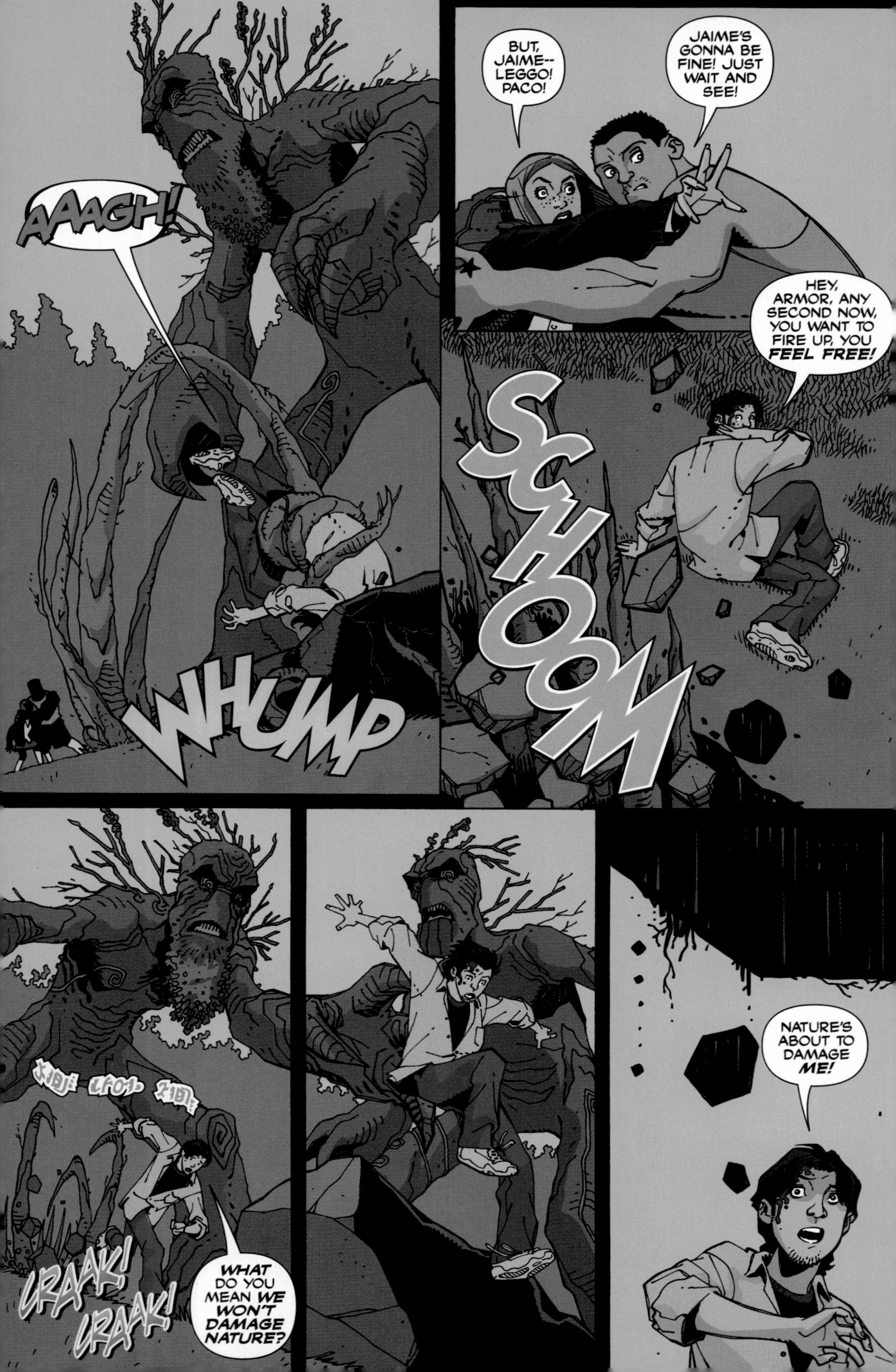
AAAGH!
WHUMP
BUT, JAIME-- LEGGO! PACO!
JAIME'S GONNA BE FINE! JUST WAIT AND SEE!
HEY, ARMOR, ANY SECOND NOW, YOU WANT TO FIRE UP, YOU *FEEL FREE!*
SCHOOOM
CRAAK! CRAAK!
WHAT DO YOU MEAN *WE WON'T DAMAGE* NATURE?
NATURE'S ABOUT TO DAMAGE *ME!*

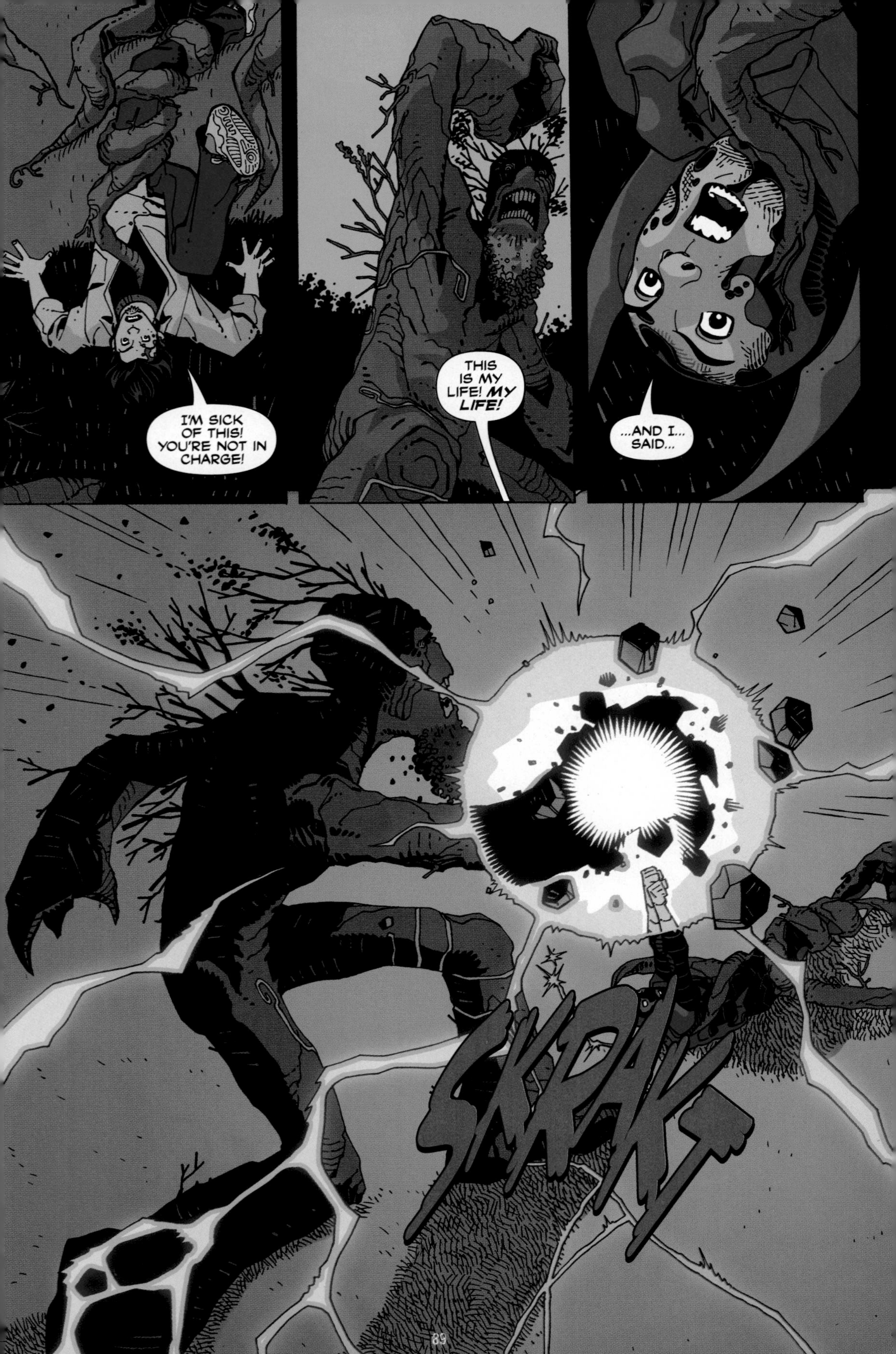
I'M SICK OF THIS! YOU'RE NOT IN CHARGE!
THIS IS MY LIFE! MY LIFE!
...AND I... SAID...
SKRAK

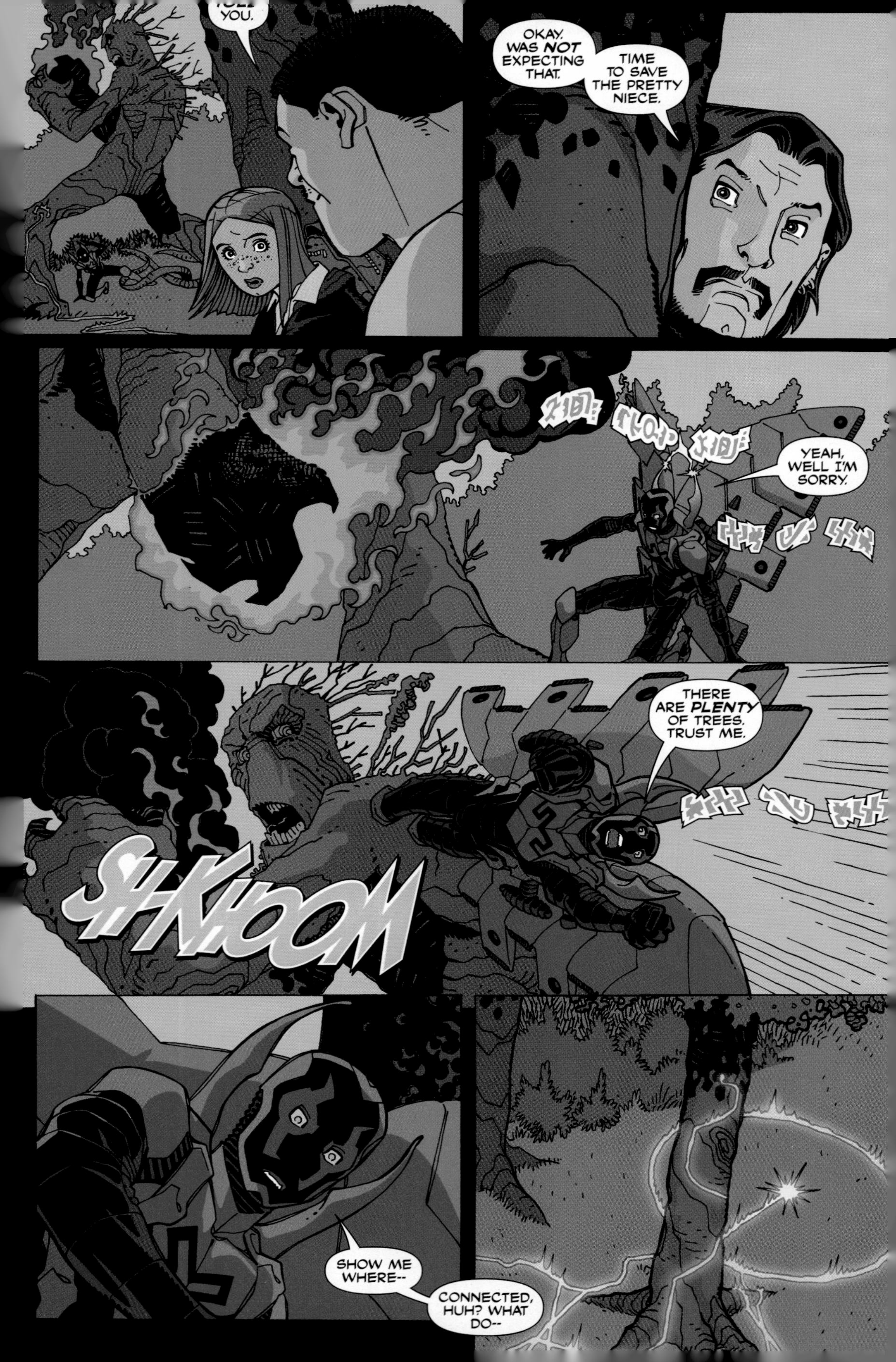
YOU.
OKAY. WAS NOT EXPECTING THAT.
TIME TO SAVE THE PRETTY NIECE.
YEAH, WELL I'M SORRY.
THERE ARE PLENTY OF TREES. TRUST ME.
SH-KHOOM
SHOW ME WHERE--
CONNECTED, HUH? WHAT DO--

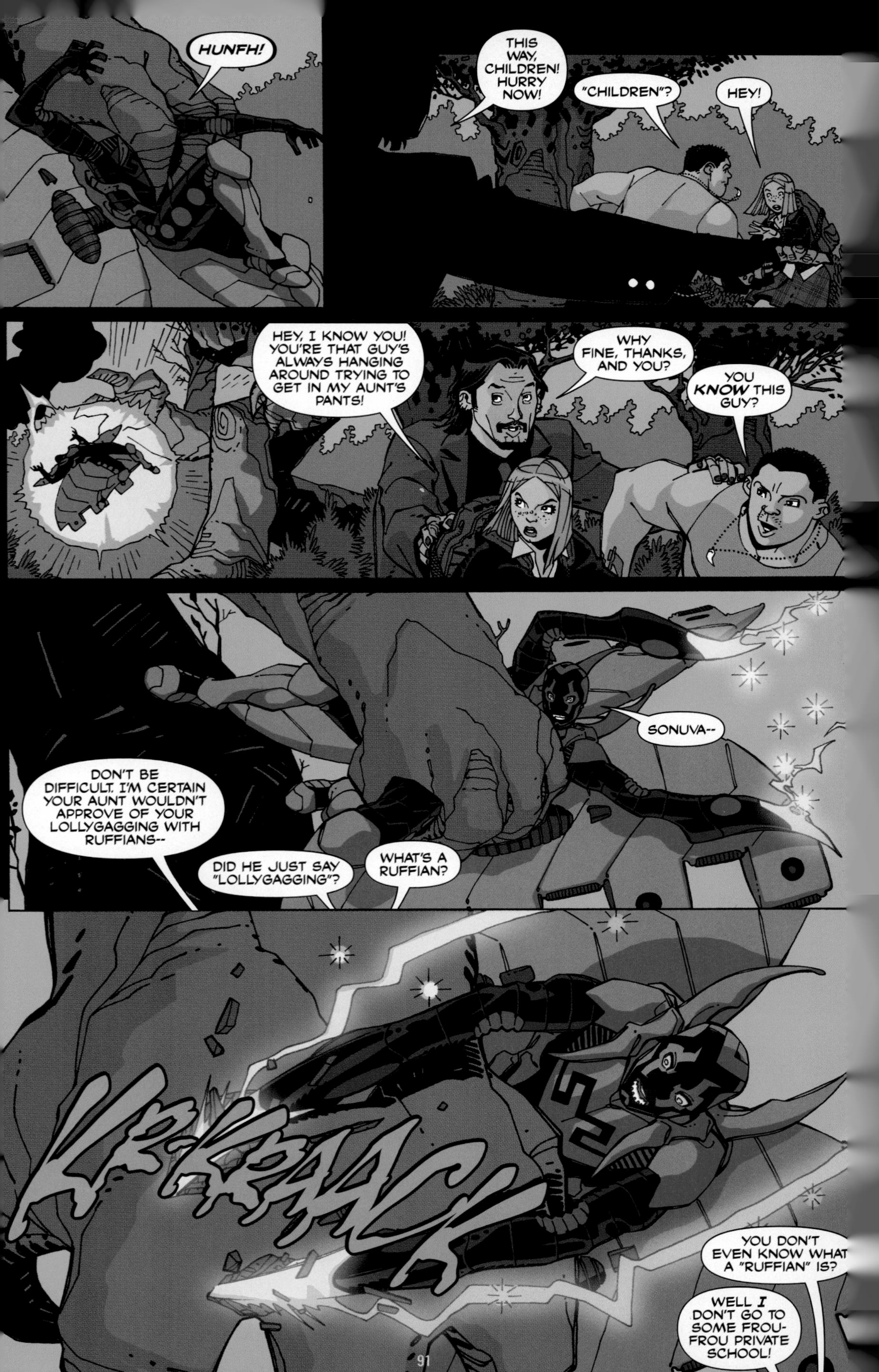
HUNFH!
THIS WAY, CHILDREN! HURRY NOW!
"CHILDREN"?
HEY!
HEY, I KNOW YOU! YOU'RE THAT GUY'S ALWAYS HANGING AROUND TRYING TO GET IN MY AUNT'S PANTS!
WHY FINE, THANKS, AND YOU?
YOU KNOW THIS GUY?
SONUVA--
DON'T BE DIFFICULT. I'M CERTAIN YOUR AUNT WOULDN'T APPROVE OF YOUR LOLLYGAGGING WITH RUFFIANS--
DID HE JUST SAY "LOLLYGAGGING"?
WHAT'S A RUFFIAN?
KR-KRAACK
YOU DON'T EVEN KNOW WHAT A "RUFFIAN" IS?
WELL I DON'T GO TO SOME FROU-FROU PRIVATE SCHOOL!

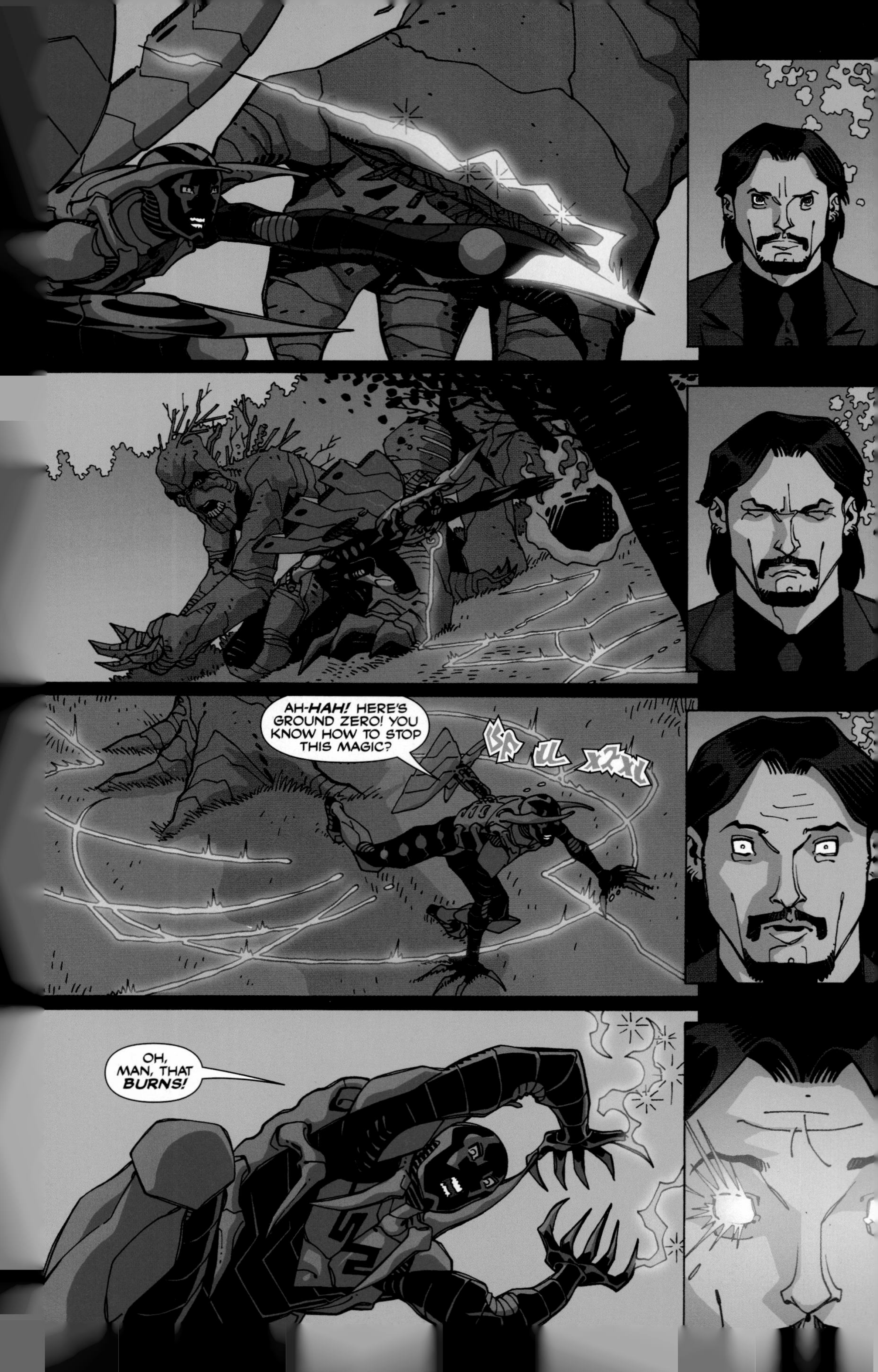
AH-*HAH!* HERE'S GROUND ZERO! YOU KNOW HOW TO STOP THIS MAGIC?
OH, MAN, THAT *BURNS!*

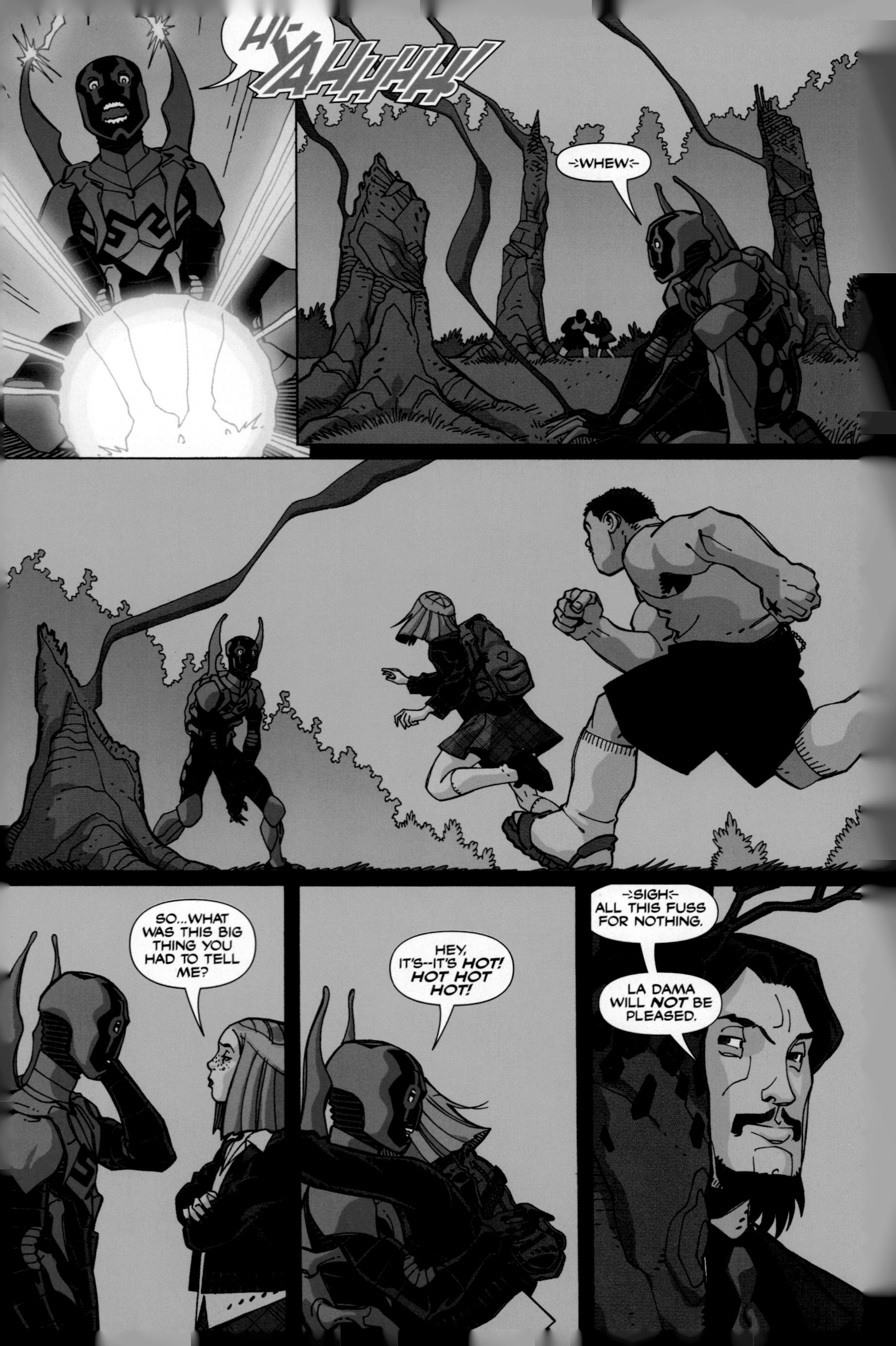
HI-YAHHHH!
-WHEW-
SO...WHAT WAS THIS BIG THING YOU HAD TO TELL ME?
HEY, IT'S--IT'S *HOT!* *HOT HOT HOT!*
-SIGH- ALL THIS FUSS FOR NOTHING.
LA DAMA WILL *NOT* BE PLEASED.

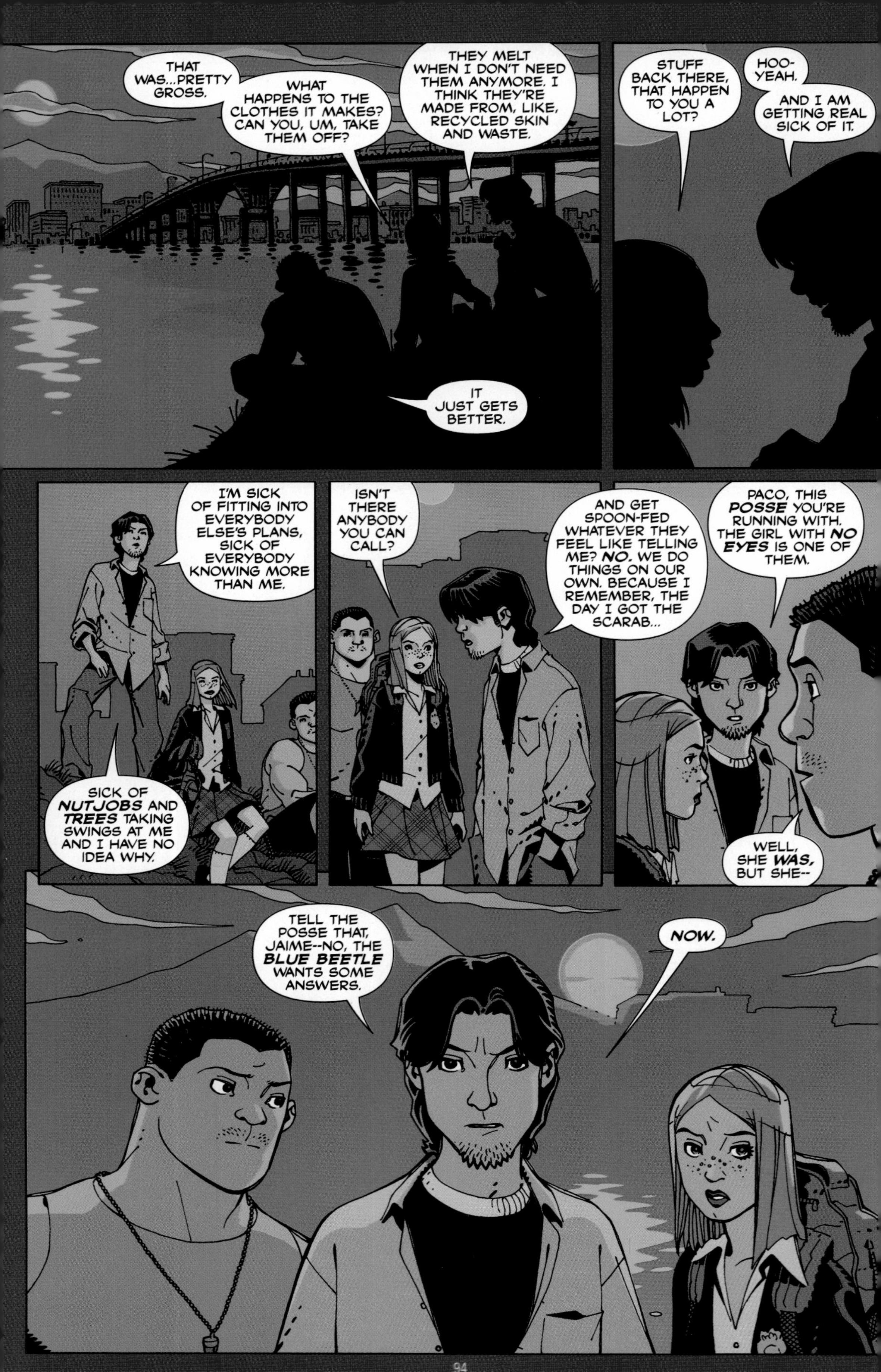
THAT WAS...PRETTY GROSS.
WHAT HAPPENS TO THE CLOTHES IT MAKES? CAN YOU, UM, TAKE THEM OFF?
THEY MELT WHEN I DON'T NEED THEM ANYMORE. I THINK THEY'RE MADE FROM, LIKE, RECYCLED SKIN AND WASTE.
IT JUST GETS BETTER.
STUFF BACK THERE, THAT HAPPEN TO YOU A LOT?
HOO-YEAH.
AND I AM GETTING REAL SICK OF IT.
I'M SICK OF FITTING INTO EVERYBODY ELSE'S PLANS, SICK OF EVERYBODY KNOWING MORE THAN ME.
SICK OF **NUTJOBS** AND **TREES** TAKING SWINGS AT ME AND I HAVE NO IDEA WHY.
ISN'T THERE ANYBODY YOU CAN CALL?
AND GET SPOON-FED WHATEVER THEY FEEL LIKE TELLING ME? **NO.** WE DO THINGS ON OUR OWN. BECAUSE I REMEMBER, THE DAY I GOT THE SCARAB...
PACO, THIS **POSSE** YOU'RE RUNNING WITH. THE GIRL WITH **NO EYES** IS ONE OF THEM.
WELL, SHE **WAS,** BUT SHE--
TELL THE POSSE THAT, JAIME--NO, THE **BLUE BEETLE** WANTS SOME ANSWERS.
NOW.

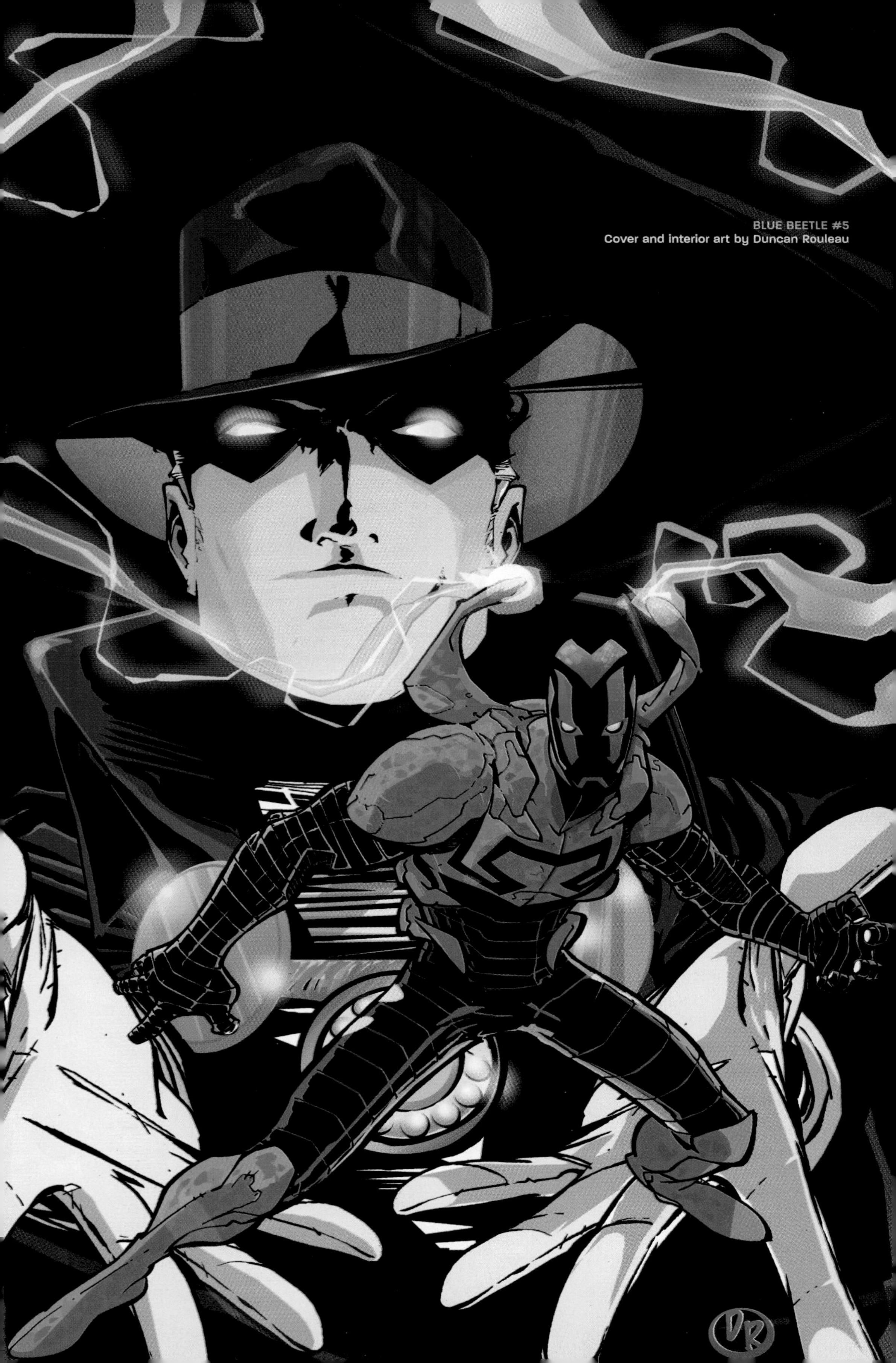

BLUE BEETLE #5
Cover and interior art by Duncan Rouleau

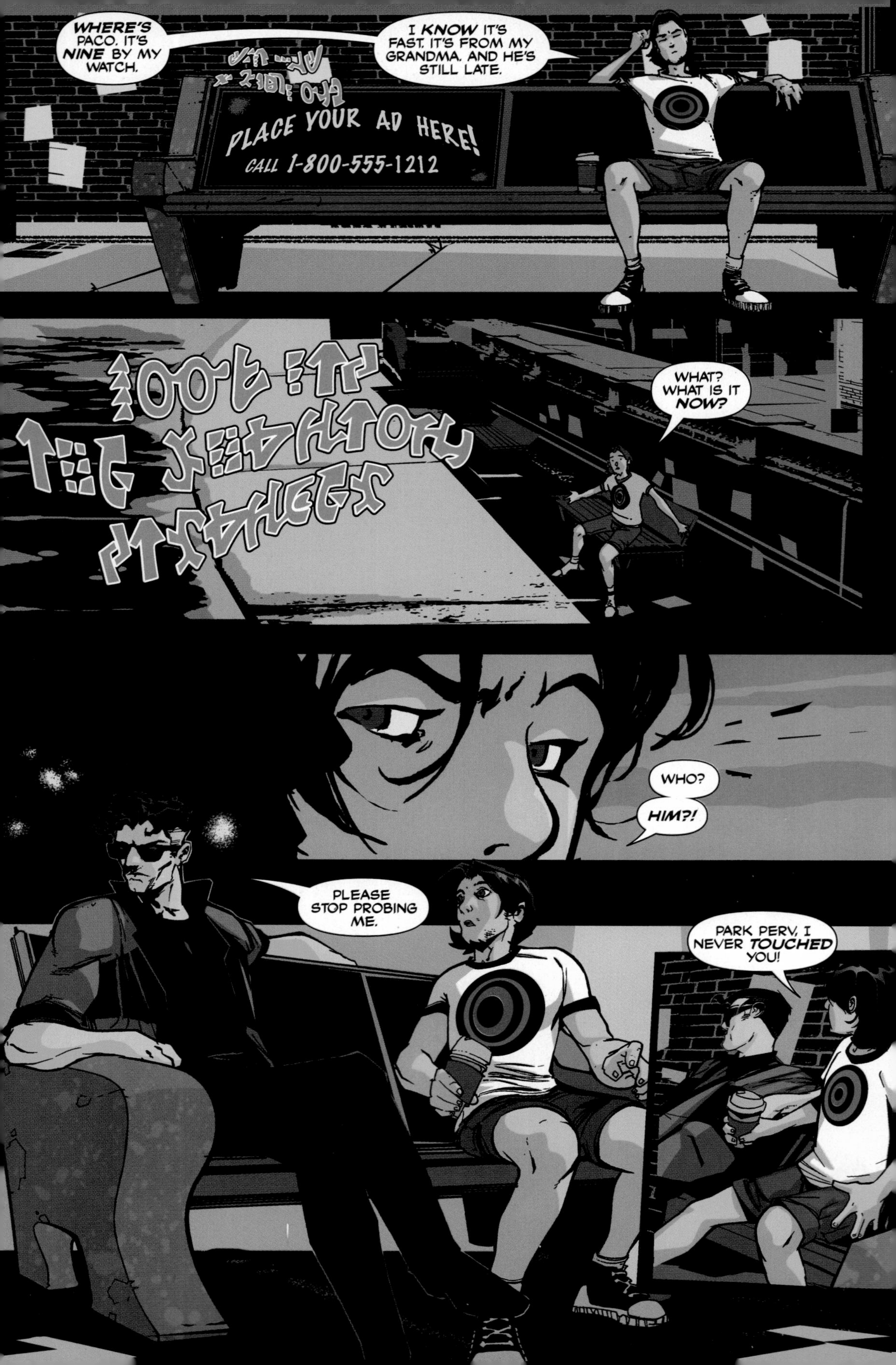
WHERE'S PACO. IT'S NINE BY MY WATCH.
I KNOW IT'S FAST. IT'S FROM MY GRANDMA. AND HE'S STILL LATE.
PLACE YOUR AD HERE!
CALL 1-800-555-1212
WHAT? WHAT IS IT NOW?
WHO?
HIM?!
PLEASE STOP PROBING ME.
PARK PERV, I NEVER TOUCHED YOU!

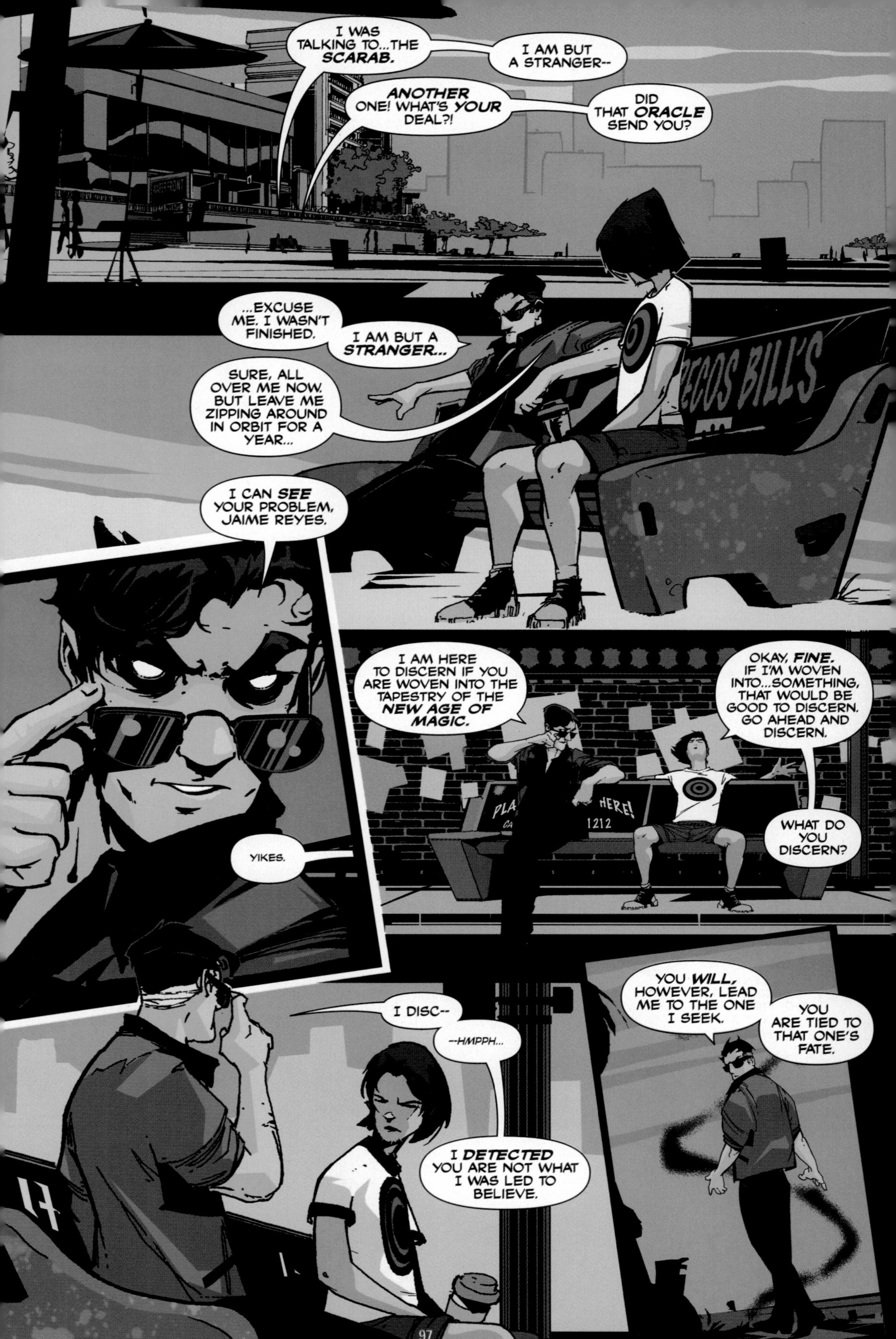
I WAS TALKING TO...THE SCARAB.
I AM BUT A STRANGER--
ANOTHER ONE! WHAT'S YOUR DEAL?!
DID THAT ORACLE SEND YOU?
...EXCUSE ME. I WASN'T FINISHED.
I AM BUT A STRANGER...
SURE, ALL OVER ME NOW. BUT LEAVE ME ZIPPING AROUND IN ORBIT FOR A YEAR...
PECOS BILL'S
I CAN SEE YOUR PROBLEM, JAIME REYES.
YIKES.
I AM HERE TO DISCERN IF YOU ARE WOVEN INTO THE TAPESTRY OF THE NEW AGE OF MAGIC.
OKAY, FINE. IF I'M WOVEN INTO...SOMETHING, THAT WOULD BE GOOD TO DISCERN. GO AHEAD AND DISCERN.
WHAT DO YOU DISCERN?
I DISC--
--HMPPH...
I DETECTED YOU ARE NOT WHAT I WAS LED TO BELIEVE.
YOU WILL, HOWEVER, LEAD ME TO THE ONE I SEEK.
YOU ARE TIED TO THAT ONE'S FATE.

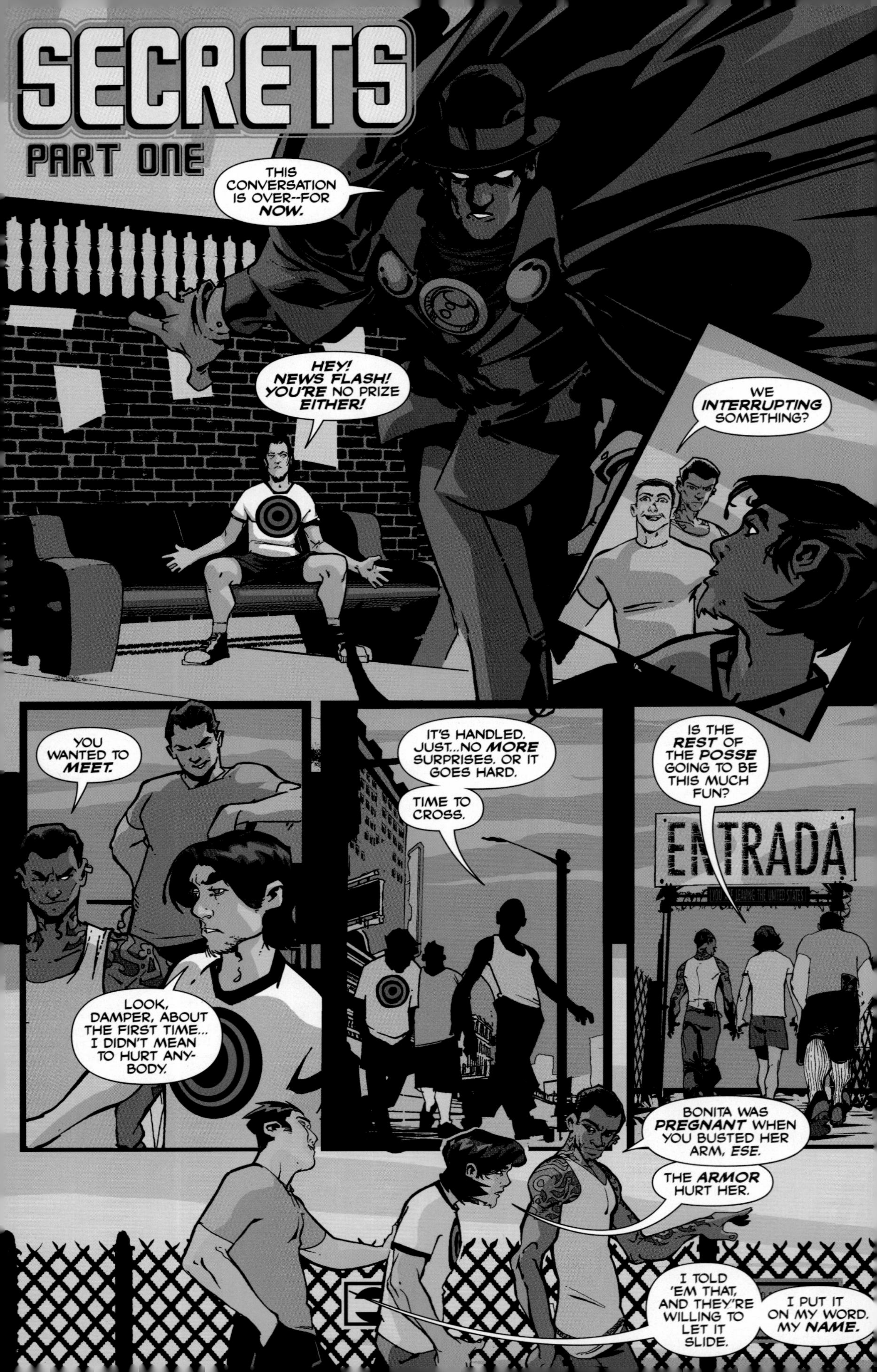
SECRETS
PART ONE
THIS CONVERSATION IS OVER--FOR NOW.
HEY! NEWS FLASH! YOU'RE NO PRIZE EITHER!
WE INTERRUPTING SOMETHING?
YOU WANTED TO MEET.
LOOK, DAMPER, ABOUT THE FIRST TIME... I DIDN'T MEAN TO HURT ANY-BODY.
IT'S HANDLED. JUST...NO MORE SURPRISES, OR IT GOES HARD.
TIME TO CROSS.
IS THE REST OF THE POSSE GOING TO BE THIS MUCH FUN?
ENTRADA
BONITA WAS PREGNANT WHEN YOU BUSTED HER ARM, ESE.
THE ARMOR HURT HER.
I TOLD 'EM THAT, AND THEY'RE WILLING TO LET IT SLIDE.
I PUT IT ON MY WORD. MY NAME.

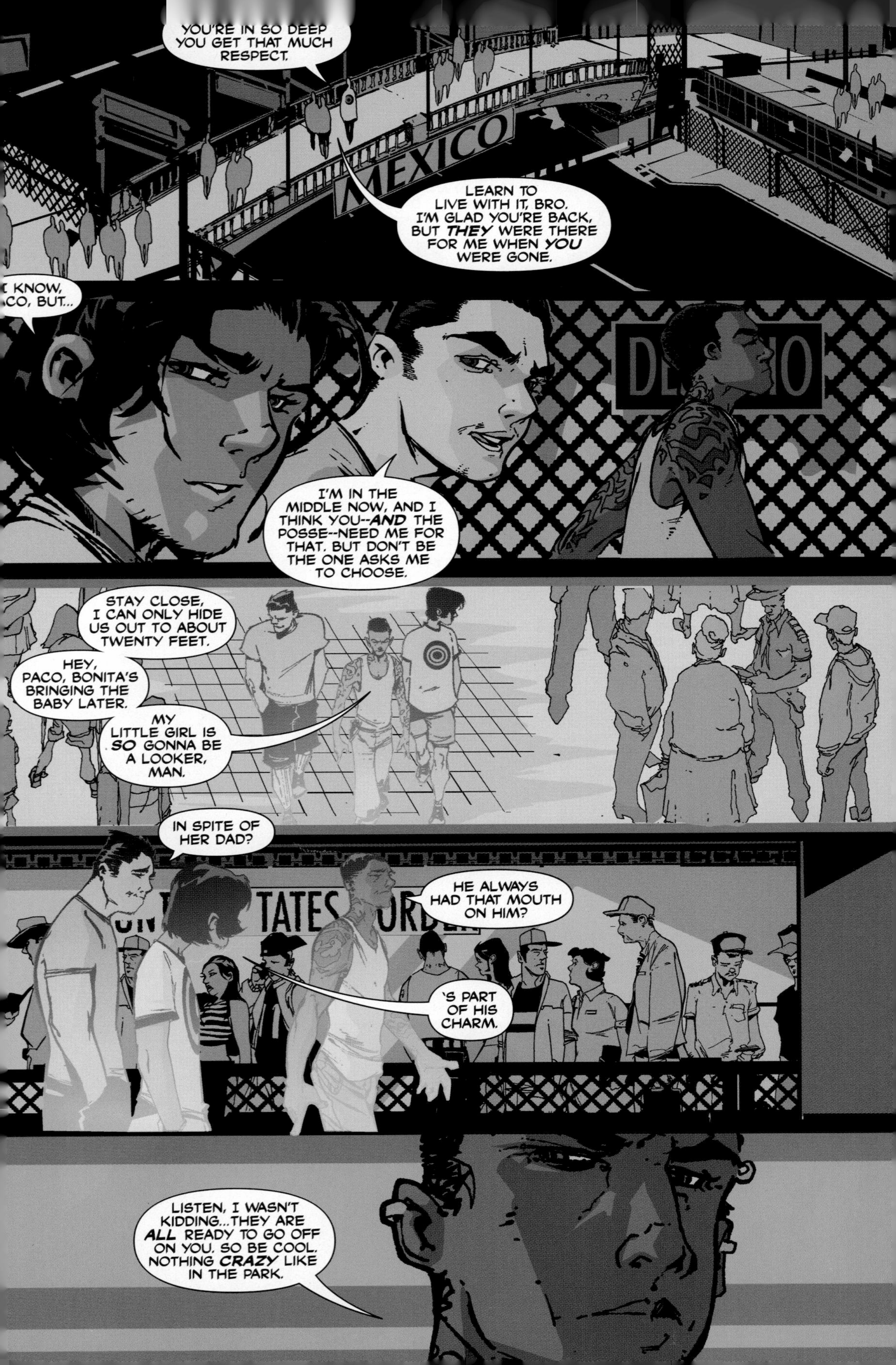
YOU'RE IN SO DEEP YOU GET THAT MUCH RESPECT.
LEARN TO LIVE WITH IT, BRO. I'M GLAD YOU'RE BACK, BUT THEY WERE THERE FOR ME WHEN YOU WERE GONE.
MEXICO
KNOW, CO, BUT...
I'M IN THE MIDDLE NOW, AND I THINK YOU--AND THE POSSE--NEED ME FOR THAT. BUT DON'T BE THE ONE ASKS ME TO CHOOSE.
STAY CLOSE, I CAN ONLY HIDE US OUT TO ABOUT TWENTY FEET.
HEY, PACO, BONITA'S BRINGING THE BABY LATER.
MY LITTLE GIRL IS SO GONNA BE A LOOKER, MAN.
IN SPITE OF HER DAD?
HE ALWAYS HAD THAT MOUTH ON HIM?
'S PART OF HIS CHARM.
LISTEN, I WASN'T KIDDING...THEY ARE ALL READY TO GO OFF ON YOU. SO BE COOL. NOTHING CRAZY LIKE IN THE PARK.

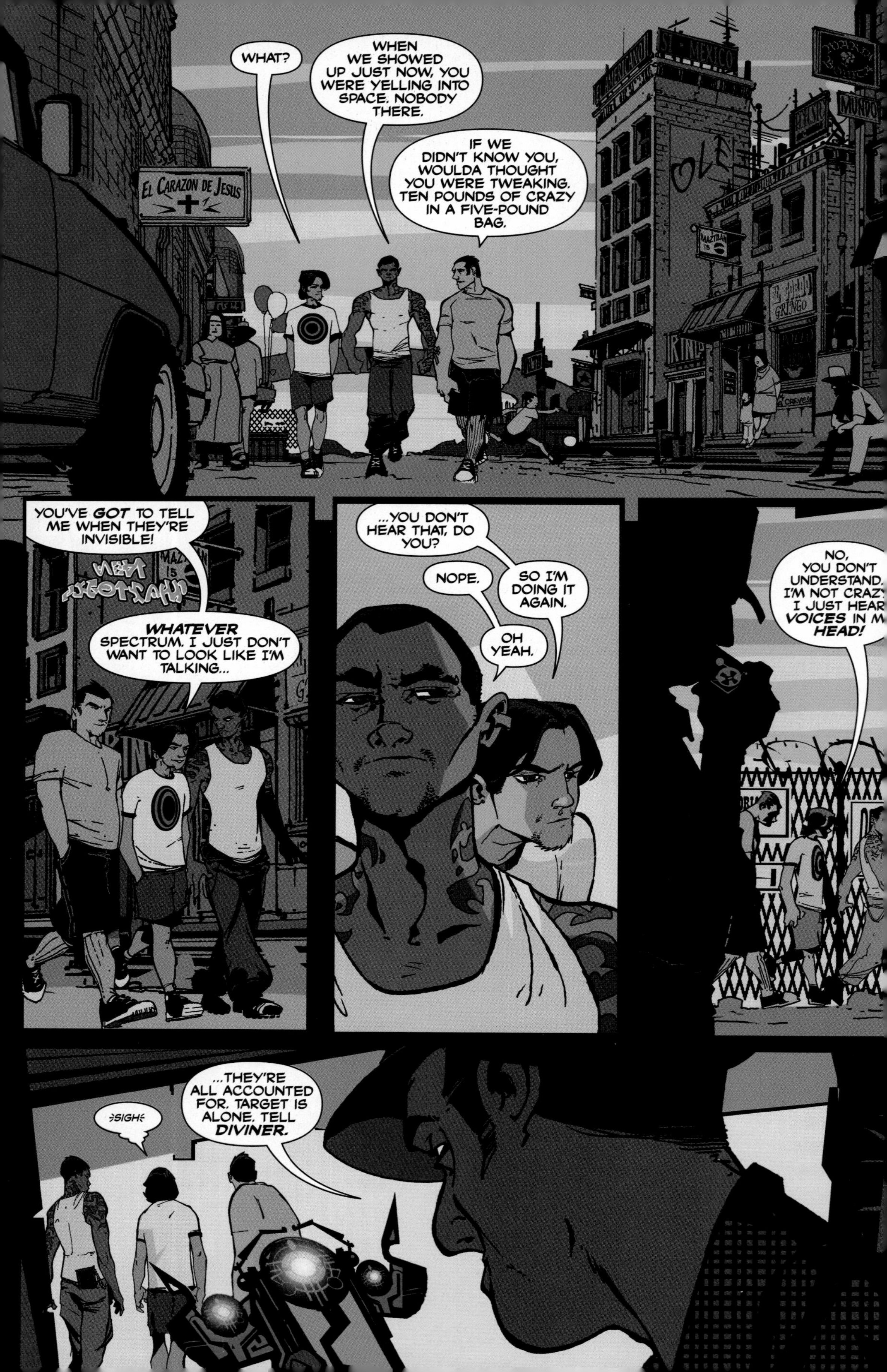
EL CARAZON DE JESUS
WHAT?
WHEN WE SHOWED UP JUST NOW, YOU WERE YELLING INTO SPACE. NOBODY THERE.
IF WE DIDN'T KNOW YOU, WOULDA THOUGHT YOU WERE TWEAKING. TEN POUNDS OF CRAZY IN A FIVE-POUND BAG.
YOU'VE *GOT* TO TELL ME WHEN THEY'RE INVISIBLE!
WHATEVER SPECTRUM. I JUST DON'T WANT TO LOOK LIKE I'M TALKING...
...YOU DON'T HEAR THAT, DO YOU?
NOPE.
SO I'M DOING IT AGAIN.
OH YEAH.
NO, YOU DON'T UNDERSTAND. I'M NOT CRAZ I JUST HEAR *VOICES* IN M *HEAD!*
›SIGH‹
...THEY'RE ALL ACCOUNTED FOR. TARGET IS ALONE. TELL *DINER.*

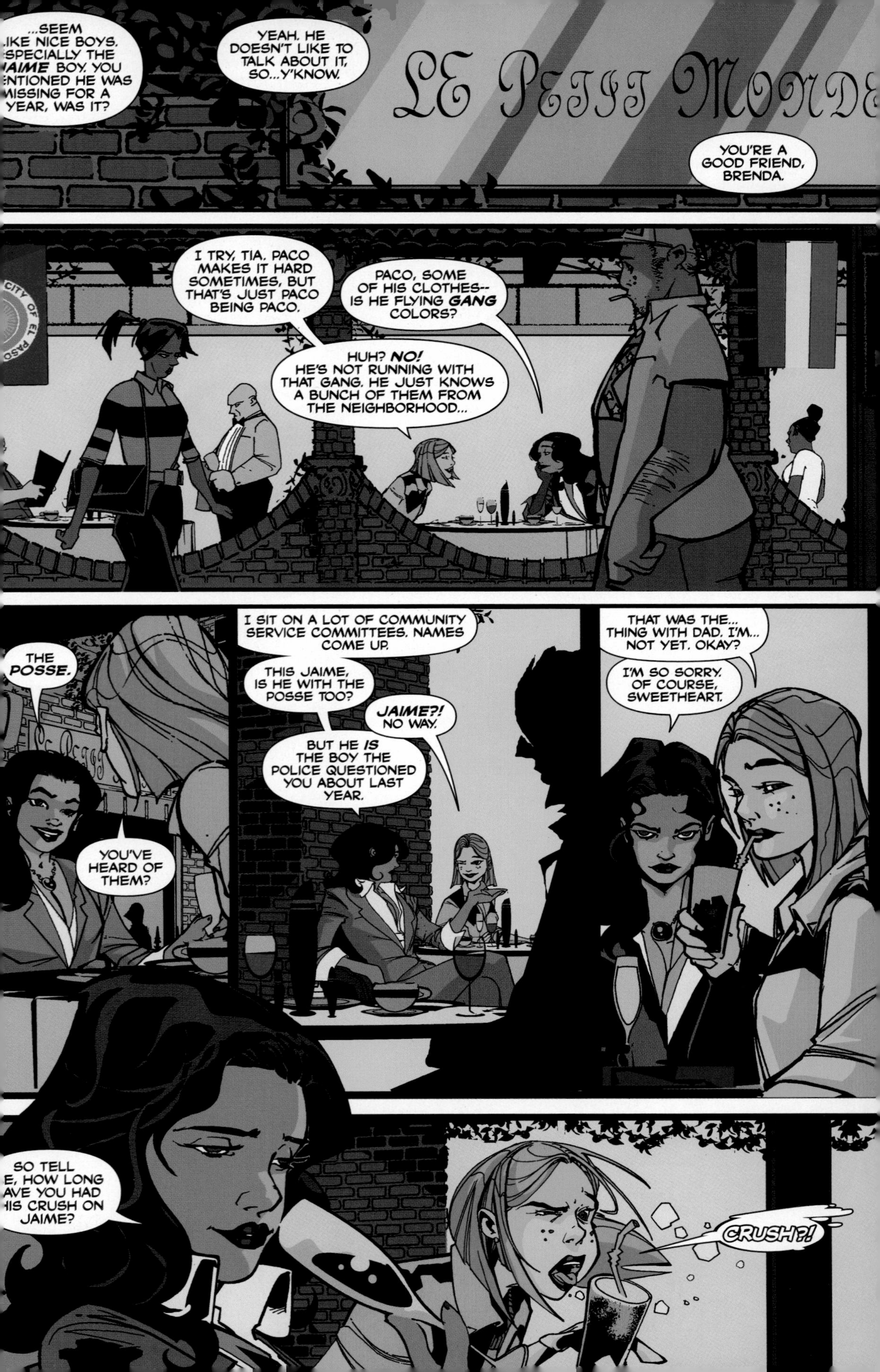

...SEEM
LIKE NICE BOYS.
ESPECIALLY THE
JAIME BOY. YOU
MENTIONED HE WAS
MISSING FOR A
YEAR, WAS IT?
YEAH. HE
DOESN'T LIKE TO
TALK ABOUT IT,
SO...Y'KNOW.
LE PETIT MONDE
YOU'RE A
GOOD FRIEND,
BRENDA.
I TRY, TIA. PACO
MAKES IT HARD
SOMETIMES, BUT
THAT'S JUST PACO
BEING PACO.
PACO, SOME
OF HIS CLOTHES--
IS HE FLYING GANG
COLORS?
HUH? NO!
HE'S NOT RUNNING WITH
THAT GANG. HE JUST KNOWS
A BUNCH OF THEM FROM
THE NEIGHBORHOOD...
THE
POSSE.
YOU'VE
HEARD OF
THEM?
I SIT ON A LOT OF COMMUNITY
SERVICE COMMITTEES. NAMES
COME UP.
THIS JAIME,
IS HE WITH THE
POSSE TOO?
JAIME?!
NO WAY.
BUT HE IS
THE BOY THE
POLICE QUESTIONED
YOU ABOUT LAST
YEAR.
THAT WAS THE...
THING WITH DAD. I'M...
NOT YET. OKAY?
I'M SO SORRY.
OF COURSE,
SWEETHEART.
SO TELL
ME, HOW LONG
HAVE YOU HAD
THIS CRUSH ON
JAIME?
CRUSH?!

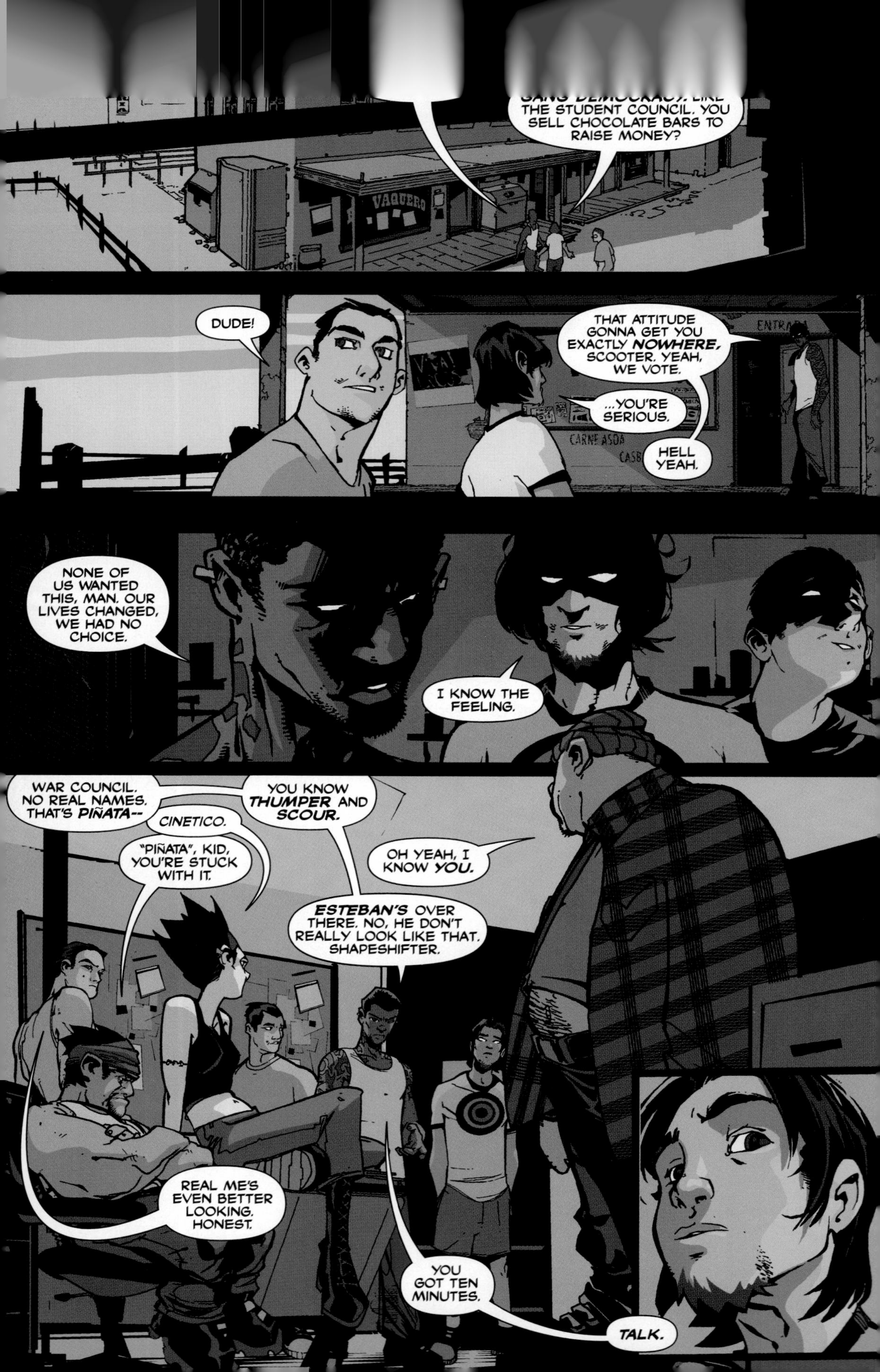
THE STUDENT COUNCIL. YOU SELL CHOCOLATE BARS TO RAISE MONEY?
VAQUERO
DUDE!
THAT ATTITUDE GONNA GET YOU EXACTLY NOWHERE, SCOOTER. YEAH, WE VOTE.
...YOU'RE SERIOUS.
HELL YEAH.
NONE OF US WANTED THIS, MAN. OUR LIVES CHANGED, WE HAD NO CHOICE.
I KNOW THE FEELING.
WAR COUNCIL. NO REAL NAMES. THAT'S PIÑATA--
CINETICO.
"PIÑATA", KID, YOU'RE STUCK WITH IT.
YOU KNOW THUMPER AND SCOUR.
OH YEAH, I KNOW YOU.
ESTEBAN'S OVER THERE. NO, HE DON'T REALLY LOOK LIKE THAT. SHAPESHIFTER.
REAL ME'S EVEN BETTER LOOKING, HONEST.
YOU GOT TEN MINUTES.
TALK.

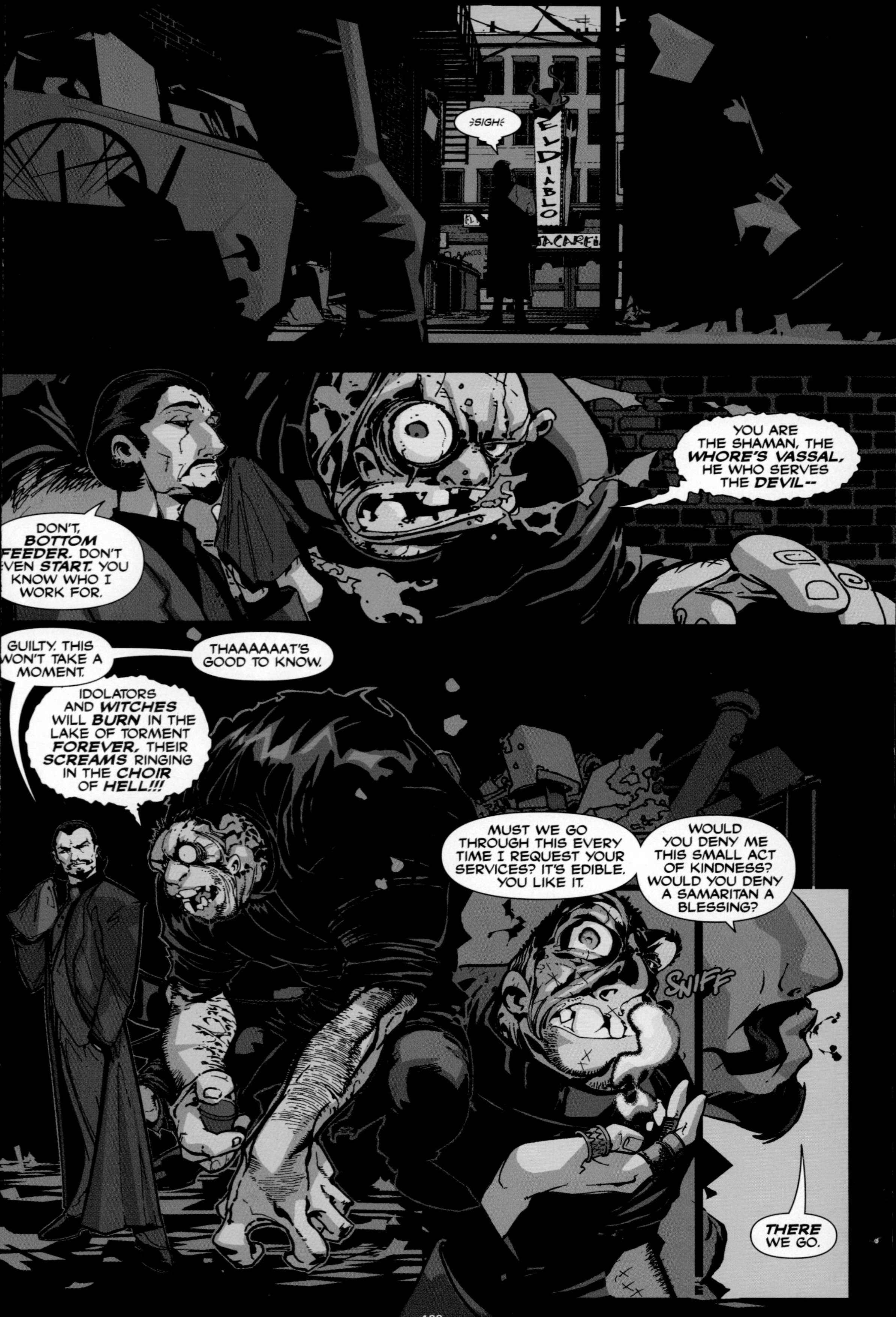

≥SIGH≤
EL DIABLO
TACARE
YOU ARE THE SHAMAN, THE WHORE'S VASSAL, HE WHO SERVES THE DEVIL--
DON'T, BOTTOM FEEDER. DON'T EVEN START. YOU KNOW WHO I WORK FOR.
GUILTY. THIS WON'T TAKE A MOMENT.
THAAAAAAT'S GOOD TO KNOW.
IDOLATORS AND WITCHES WILL BURN IN THE LAKE OF TORMENT FOREVER, THEIR SCREAMS RINGING IN THE CHOIR OF HELL!!!
MUST WE GO THROUGH THIS EVERY TIME I REQUEST YOUR SERVICES? IT'S EDIBLE. YOU LIKE IT.
WOULD YOU DENY ME THIS SMALL ACT OF KINDNESS? WOULD YOU DENY A SAMARITAN A BLESSING?
SNIFF
THERE WE GO.

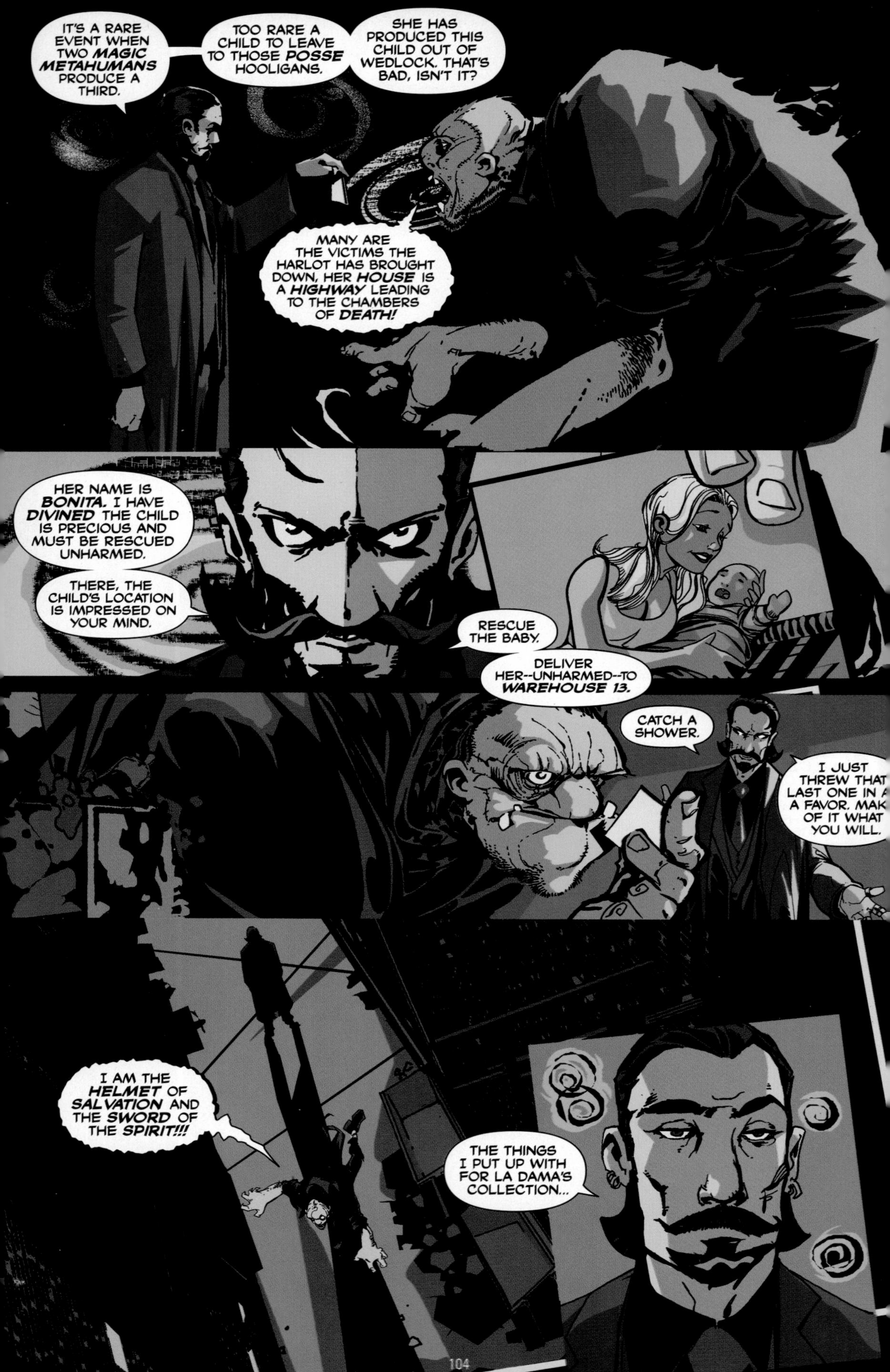
IT'S A RARE EVENT WHEN TWO MAGIC METAHUMANS PRODUCE A THIRD.
TOO RARE A CHILD TO LEAVE TO THOSE POSSE HOOLIGANS.
SHE HAS PRODUCED THIS CHILD OUT OF WEDLOCK. THAT'S BAD, ISN'T IT?
MANY ARE THE VICTIMS THE HARLOT HAS BROUGHT DOWN, HER HOUSE IS A HIGHWAY LEADING TO THE CHAMBERS OF DEATH!
HER NAME IS BONITA. I HAVE DIVINED THE CHILD IS PRECIOUS AND MUST BE RESCUED UNHARMED.
THERE, THE CHILD'S LOCATION IS IMPRESSED ON YOUR MIND.
RESCUE THE BABY.
DELIVER HER--UNHARMED--TO WAREHOUSE 13.
CATCH A SHOWER.
I JUST THREW THAT LAST ONE IN A A FAVOR. MAK OF IT WHAT YOU WILL.
I AM THE HELMET OF SALVATION AND THE SWORD OF THE SPIRIT!!!
THE THINGS I PUT UP WITH FOR LA DAMA'S COLLECTION...

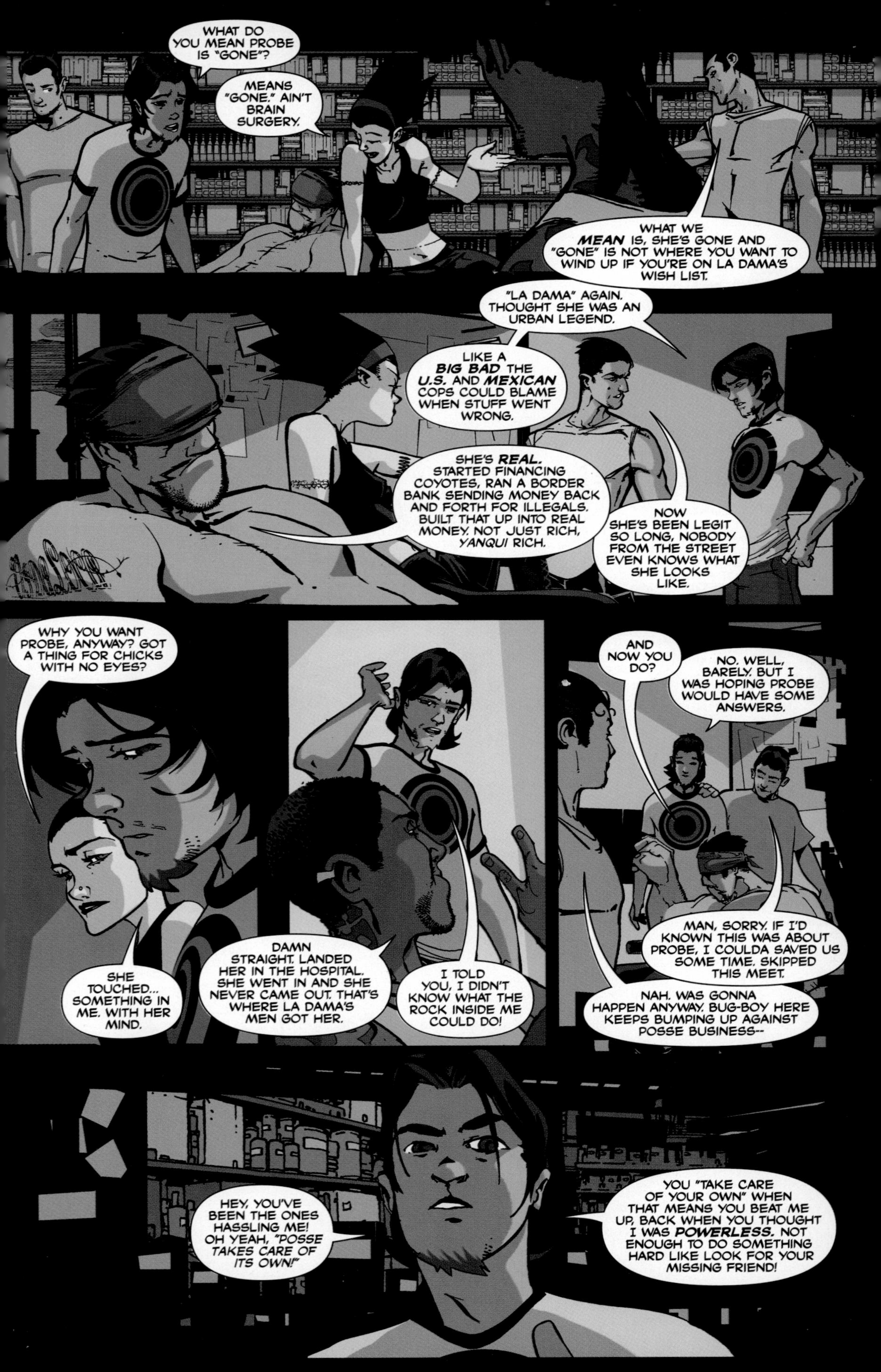
WHAT DO YOU MEAN PROBE IS "GONE"?
MEANS "GONE." AIN'T BRAIN SURGERY.
WHAT WE **MEAN** IS, SHE'S GONE AND "GONE" IS NOT WHERE YOU WANT TO WIND UP IF YOU'RE ON LA DAMA'S WISH LIST.
"LA DAMA" AGAIN. THOUGHT SHE WAS AN URBAN LEGEND.
LIKE A **BIG BAD** THE **U.S.** AND **MEXICAN** COPS COULD BLAME WHEN STUFF WENT WRONG.
SHE'S **REAL.** STARTED FINANCING COYOTES, RAN A BORDER BANK SENDING MONEY BACK AND FORTH FOR ILLEGALS. BUILT THAT UP INTO REAL MONEY. NOT JUST RICH, *YANQUI* RICH.
NOW SHE'S BEEN LEGIT SO LONG, NOBODY FROM THE STREET EVEN KNOWS WHAT SHE LOOKS LIKE.
WHY YOU WANT PROBE, ANYWAY? GOT A THING FOR CHICKS WITH NO EYES?
SHE TOUCHED... SOMETHING IN ME. WITH HER MIND.
DAMN STRAIGHT. LANDED HER IN THE HOSPITAL. SHE WENT IN AND SHE NEVER CAME OUT. THAT'S WHERE LA DAMA'S MEN GOT HER.
I TOLD YOU, I DIDN'T KNOW WHAT THE ROCK INSIDE ME COULD DO!
AND NOW YOU DO?
NO. WELL, BARELY. BUT I WAS HOPING PROBE WOULD HAVE SOME ANSWERS.
MAN, SORRY. IF I'D KNOWN THIS WAS ABOUT PROBE, I COULDA SAVED US SOME TIME. SKIPPED THIS MEET.
NAH. WAS GONNA HAPPEN ANYWAY. BUG-BOY HERE KEEPS BUMPING UP AGAINST POSSE BUSINESS--
HEY, YOU'VE BEEN THE ONES HASSLING ME! OH YEAH, *"POSSE TAKES CARE OF ITS OWN!"*
YOU "TAKE CARE OF YOUR OWN" WHEN THAT MEANS YOU BEAT ME UP, BACK WHEN YOU THOUGHT I WAS **POWERLESS.** NOT ENOUGH TO DO SOMETHING HARD LIKE LOOK FOR YOUR MISSING FRIEND!

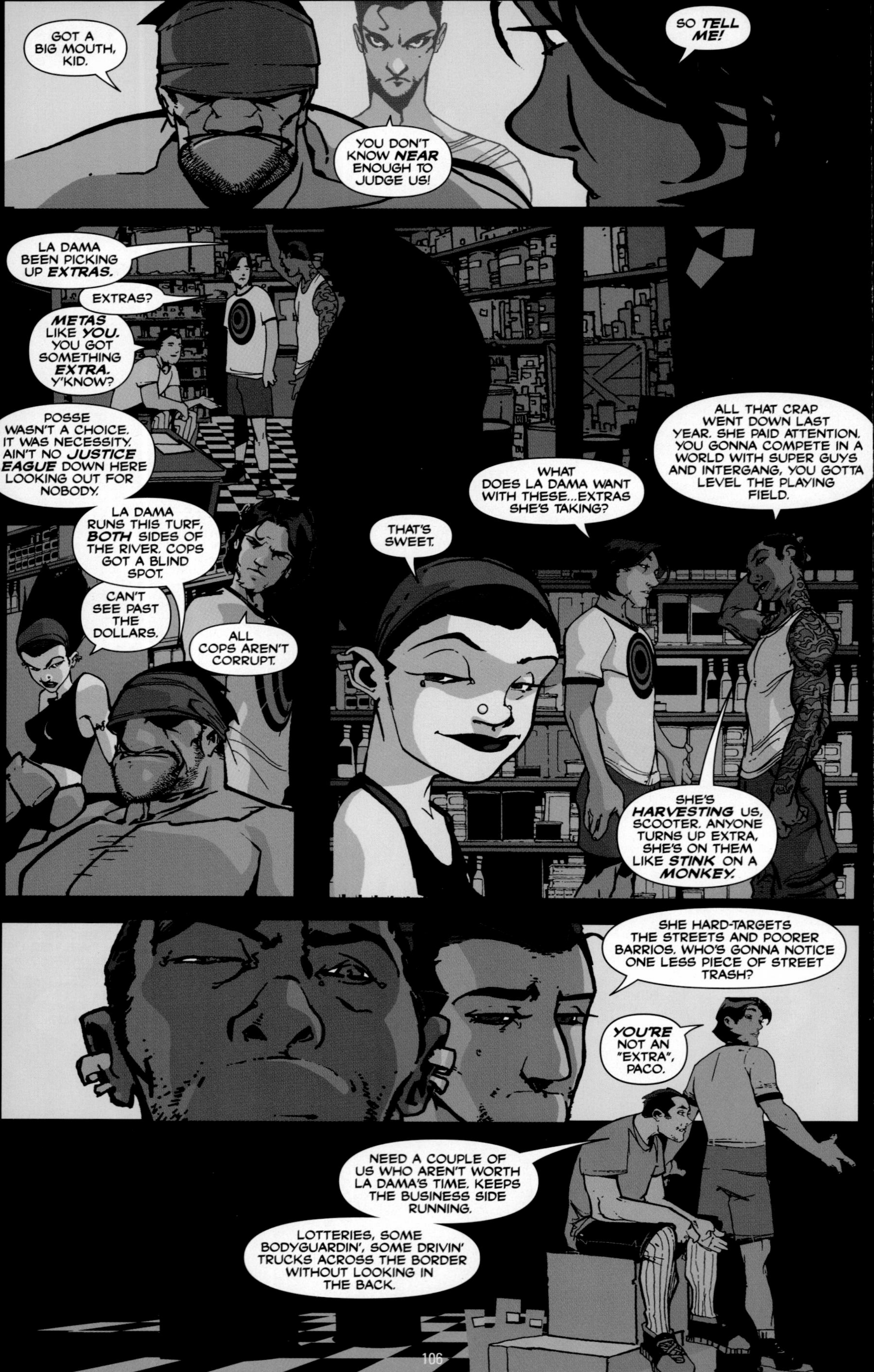
GOT A BIG MOUTH, KID.
YOU DON'T KNOW NEAR ENOUGH TO JUDGE US!
SO TELL ME!
LA DAMA BEEN PICKING UP EXTRAS.
EXTRAS?
METAS LIKE YOU. YOU GOT SOMETHING EXTRA. Y'KNOW?
POSSE WASN'T A CHOICE. IT WAS NECESSITY. AIN'T NO JUSTICE LEAGUE DOWN HERE LOOKING OUT FOR NOBODY.
LA DAMA RUNS THIS TURF, BOTH SIDES OF THE RIVER. COPS GOT A BLIND SPOT.
CAN'T SEE PAST THE DOLLARS.
ALL COPS AREN'T CORRUPT.
THAT'S SWEET.
WHAT DOES LA DAMA WANT WITH THESE...EXTRAS SHE'S TAKING?
ALL THAT CRAP WENT DOWN LAST YEAR. SHE PAID ATTENTION. YOU GONNA COMPETE IN A WORLD WITH SUPER GUYS AND INTERGANG, YOU GOTTA LEVEL THE PLAYING FIELD.
SHE'S HARVESTING US, SCOOTER. ANYONE TURNS UP EXTRA, SHE'S ON THEM LIKE STINK ON A MONKEY.
SHE HARD-TARGETS THE STREETS AND POORER BARRIOS. WHO'S GONNA NOTICE ONE LESS PIECE OF STREET TRASH?
YOU'RE NOT AN "EXTRA", PACO.
NEED A COUPLE OF US WHO AREN'T WORTH LA DAMA'S TIME. KEEPS THE BUSINESS SIDE RUNNING.
LOTTERIES, SOME BODYGUARDIN', SOME DRIVIN' TRUCKS ACROSS THE BORDER WITHOUT LOOKING IN THE BACK.

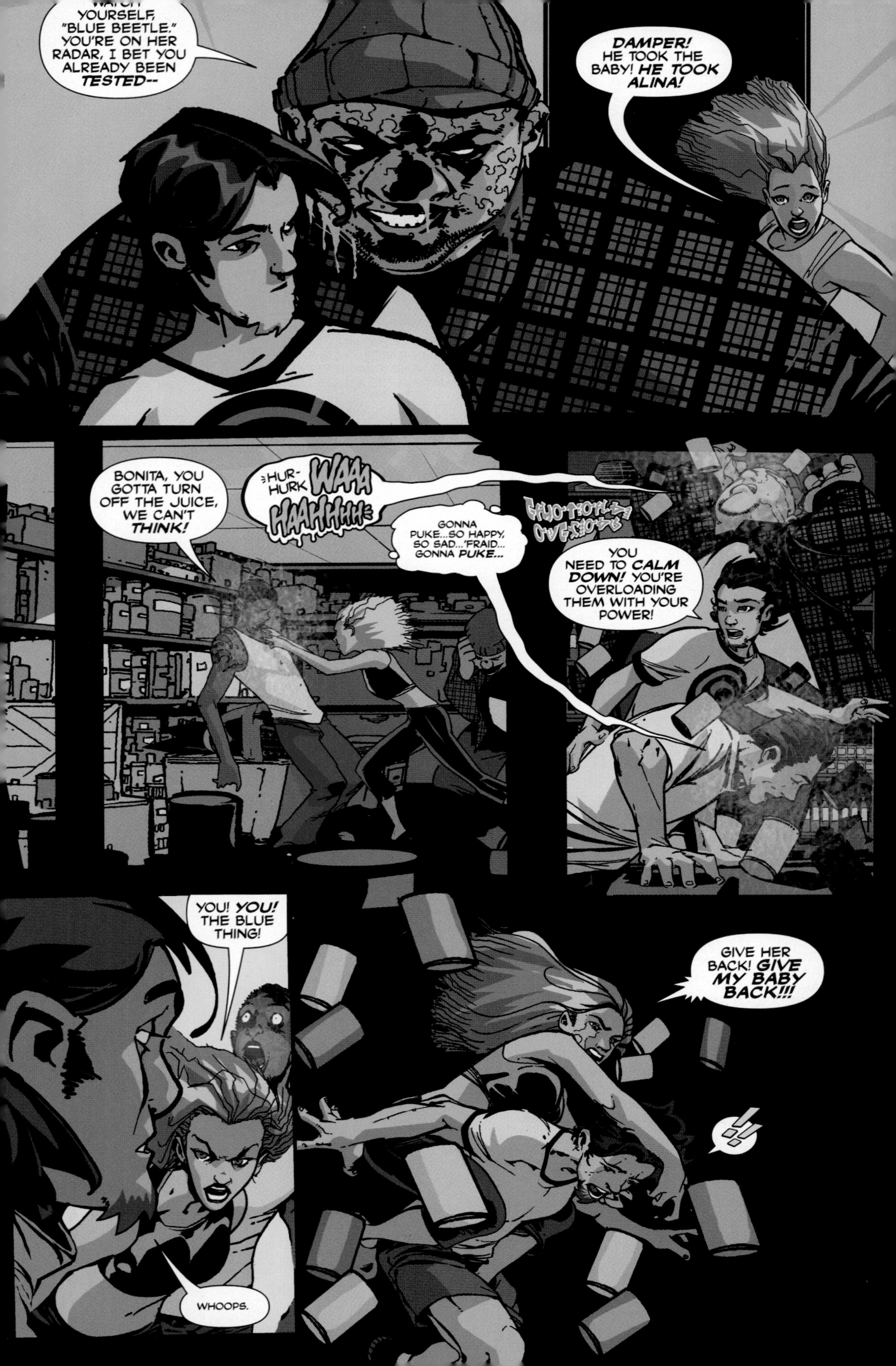
YOURSELF, "BLUE BEETLE." YOU'RE ON HER RADAR, I BET YOU ALREADY BEEN TESTED--
DAMPER! HE TOOK THE BABY! HE TOOK ALINA!
BONITA, YOU GOTTA TURN OFF THE JUICE, WE CAN'T THINK!
HUR-HURK WAAA HAAHHHH
GONNA PUKE...SO HAPPY, SO SAD...'FRAID... GONNA PUKE...
YOU NEED TO CALM DOWN! YOU'RE OVERLOADING THEM WITH YOUR POWER!
YOU! YOU! THE BLUE THING!
GIVE HER BACK! GIVE MY BABY BACK!!!
WHOOPS.

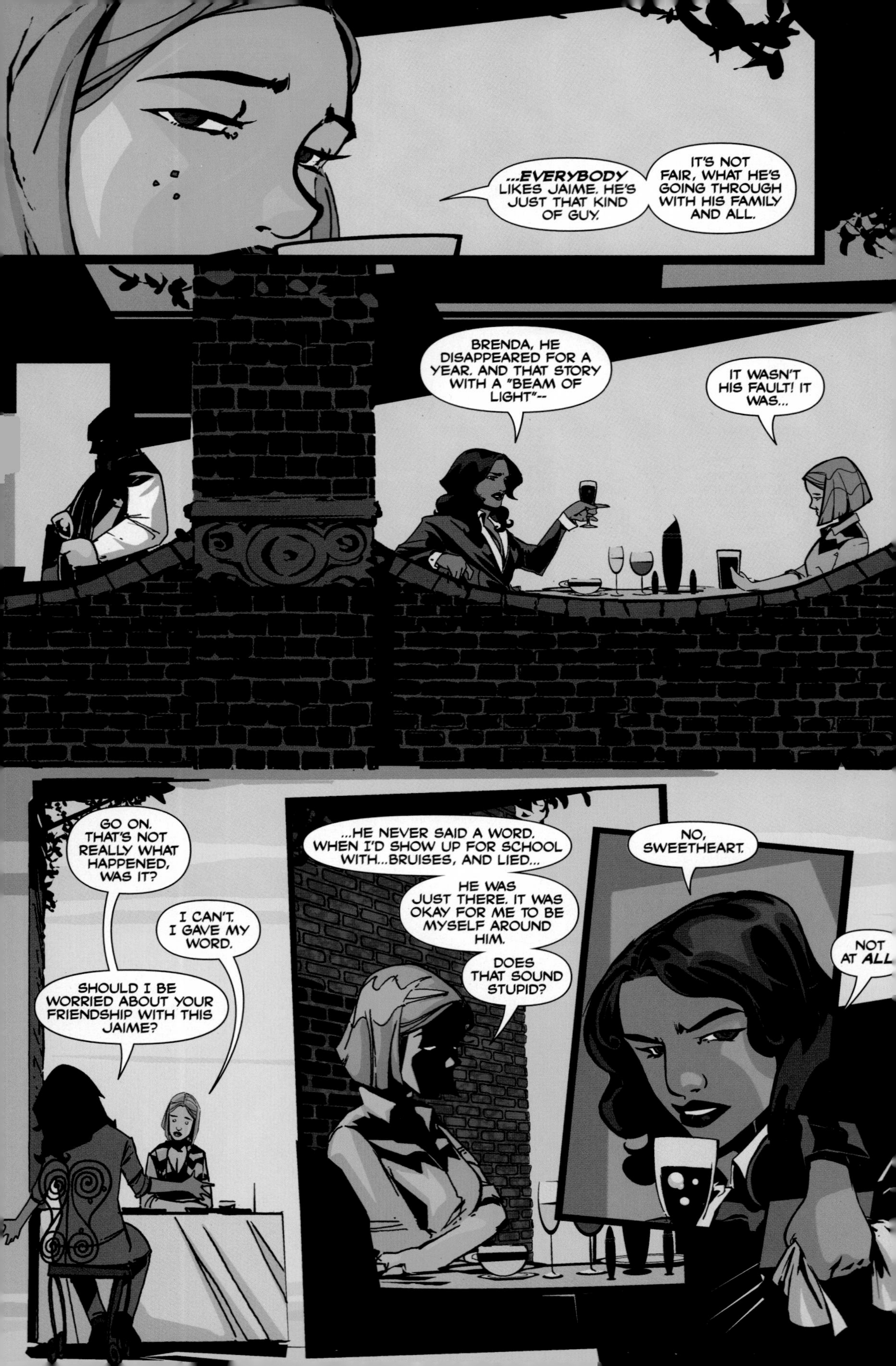

...*EVERYBODY* LIKES JAIME. HE'S JUST THAT KIND OF GUY.
IT'S NOT FAIR, WHAT HE'S GOING THROUGH WITH HIS FAMILY AND ALL.
BRENDA, HE DISAPPEARED FOR A YEAR. AND THAT STORY WITH A "BEAM OF LIGHT"--
IT WASN'T HIS FAULT! IT WAS...
GO ON. THAT'S NOT REALLY WHAT HAPPENED, WAS IT?
I CAN'T. I GAVE MY WORD.
SHOULD I BE WORRIED ABOUT YOUR FRIENDSHIP WITH THIS JAIME?
...HE NEVER SAID A WORD. WHEN I'D SHOW UP FOR SCHOOL WITH...BRUISES, AND LIED...
HE WAS JUST THERE. IT WAS OKAY FOR ME TO BE MYSELF AROUND HIM.
DOES THAT SOUND STUPID?
NO, SWEETHEART.
NOT AT *ALL*

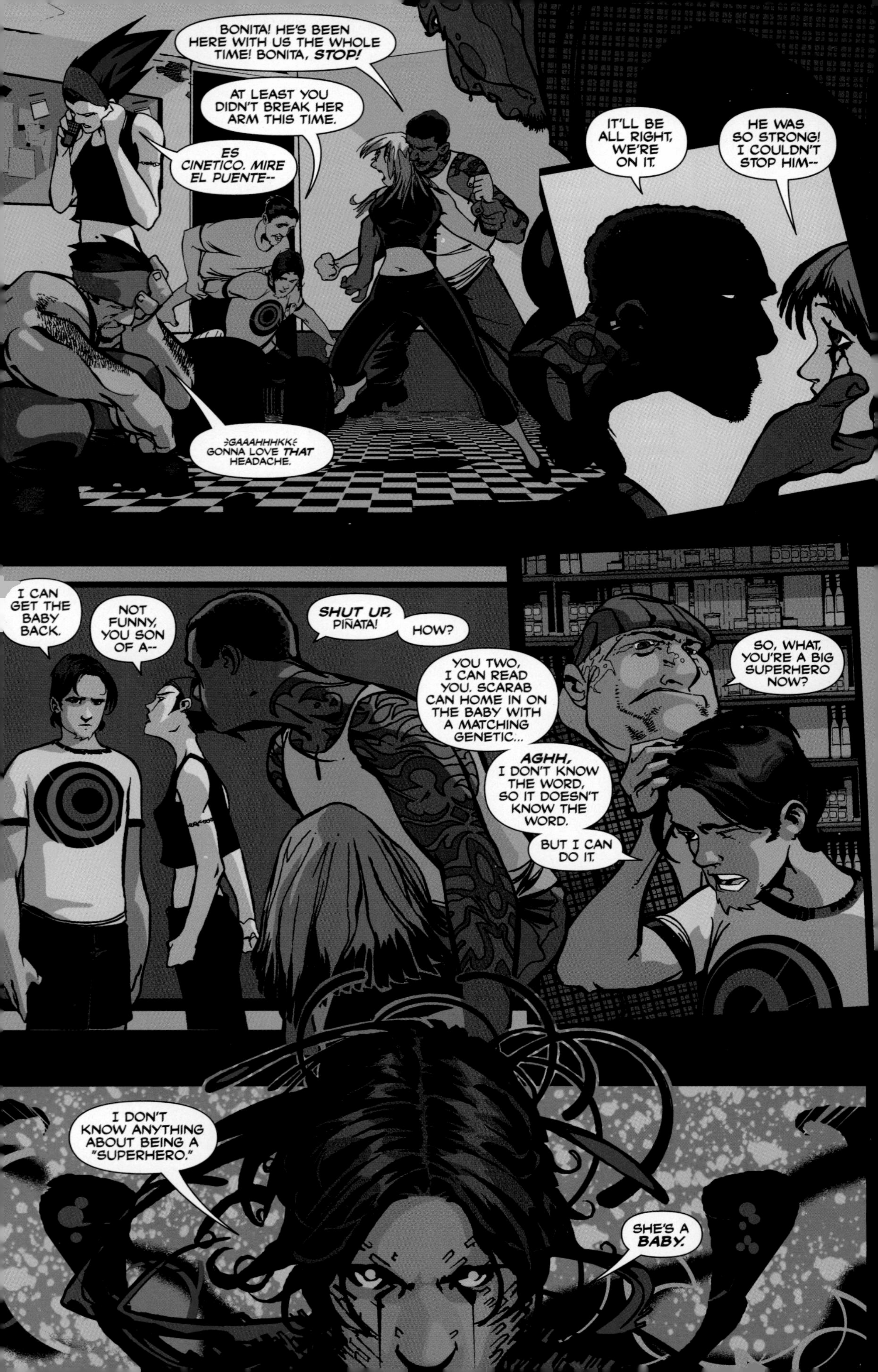
BONITA! HE'S BEEN HERE WITH US THE WHOLE TIME! BONITA, STOP!
AT LEAST YOU DIDN'T BREAK HER ARM THIS TIME.
ES CINETICO. MIRE EL PUENTE--
GAAAHHHKK GONNA LOVE THAT HEADACHE.
IT'LL BE ALL RIGHT, WE'RE ON IT.
HE WAS SO STRONG! I COULDN'T STOP HIM--
I CAN GET THE BABY BACK.
NOT FUNNY, YOU SON OF A--
SHUT UP, PIÑATA!
HOW?
YOU TWO, I CAN READ YOU. SCARAB CAN HOME IN ON THE BABY WITH A MATCHING GENETIC...
AGHH, I DON'T KNOW THE WORD, SO IT DOESN'T KNOW THE WORD.
BUT I CAN DO IT.
SO, WHAT, YOU'RE A BIG SUPERHERO NOW?
I DON'T KNOW ANYTHING ABOUT BEING A "SUPERHERO."
SHE'S A BABY.

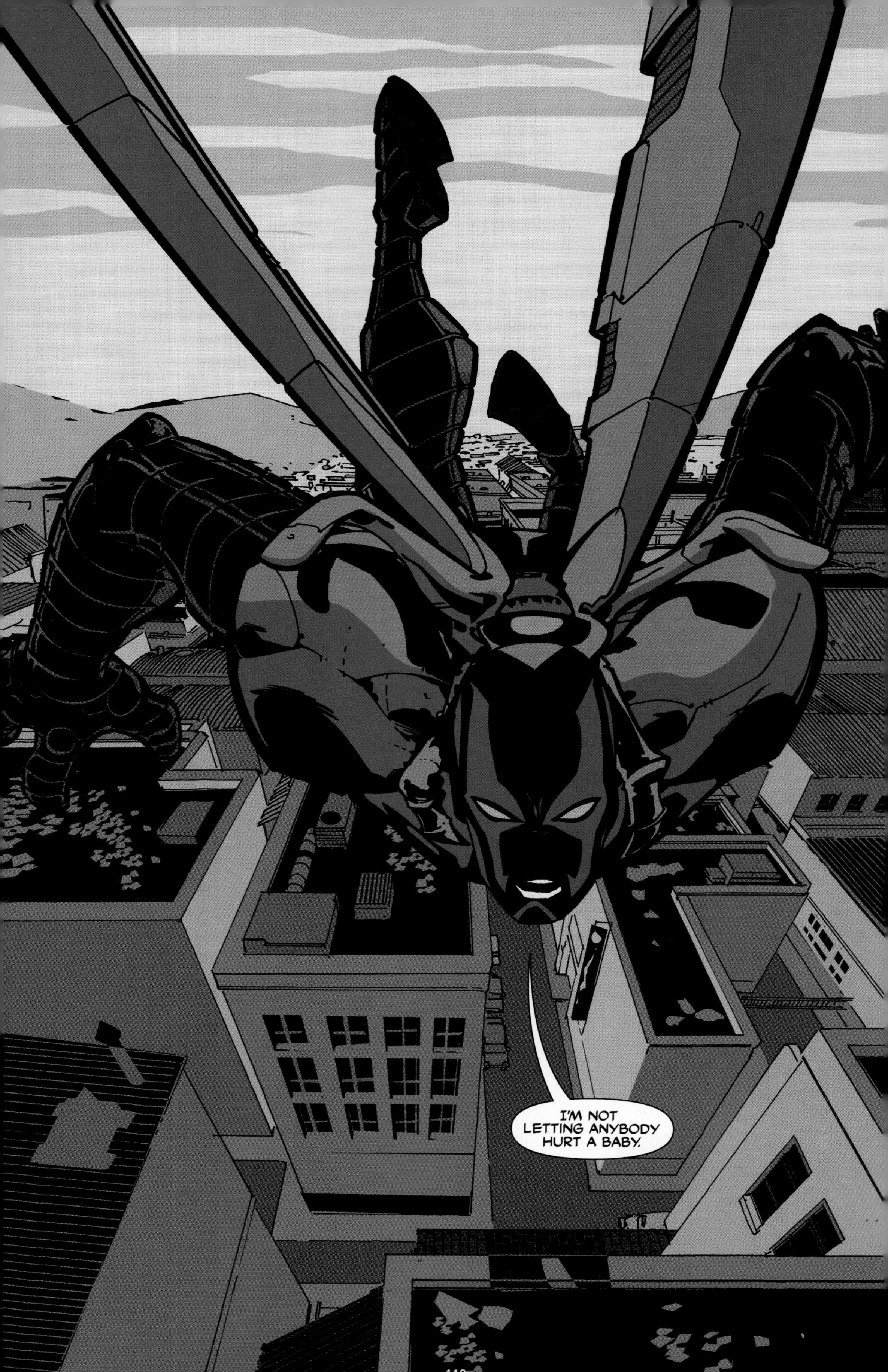
I'M NOT LETTING ANYBODY HURT A BABY.

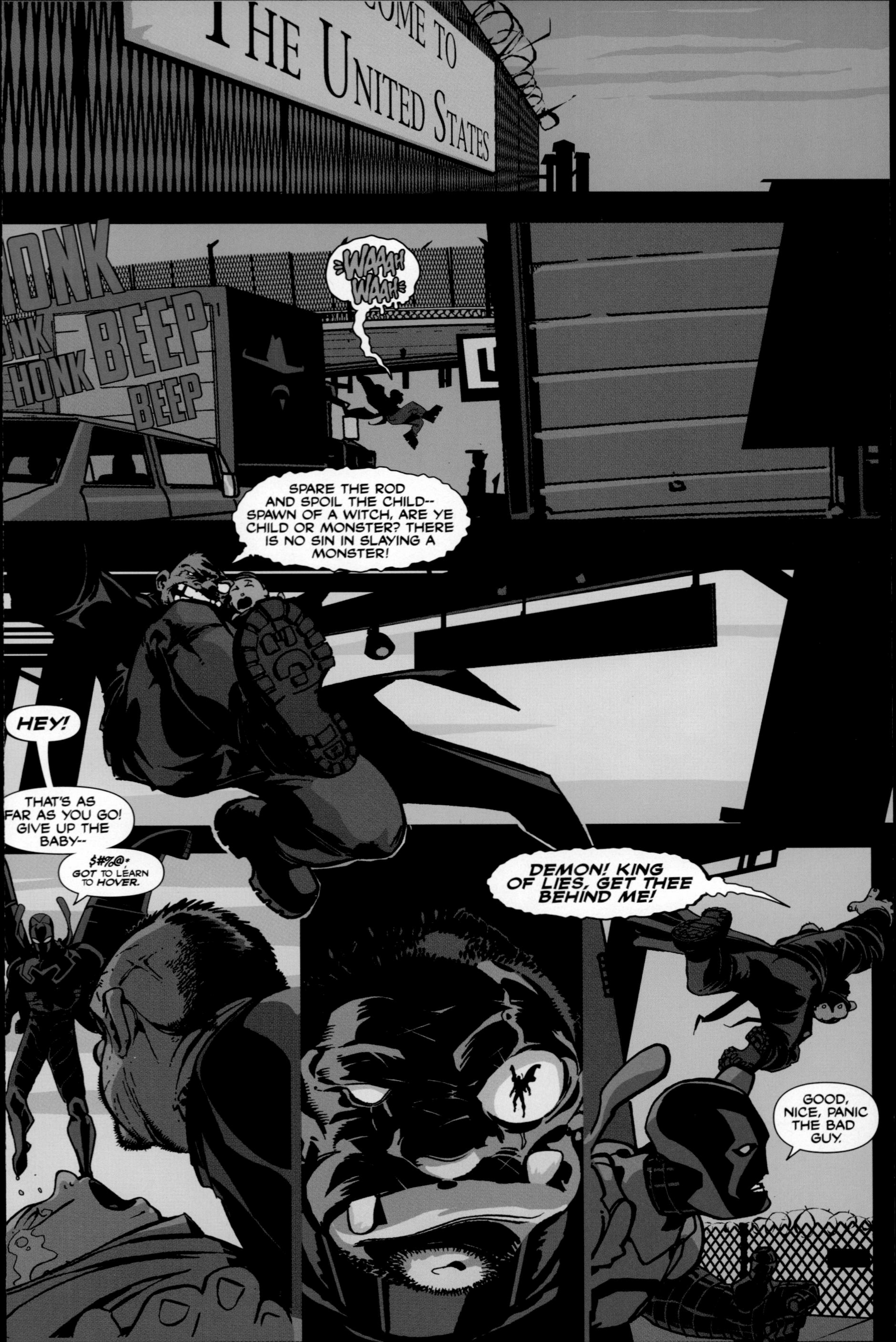

...COME TO
THE UNITED STATES
HONK
HONK
HONK
BEEP
BEEP
WAAAH! WAAH!
SPARE THE ROD AND SPOIL THE CHILD-- SPAWN OF A WITCH, ARE YE CHILD OR MONSTER? THERE IS NO SIN IN SLAYING A MONSTER!
HEY!
THAT'S AS FAR AS YOU GO! GIVE UP THE BABY--
$#%@* GOT TO LEARN TO HOVER.
DEMON! KING OF LIES, GET THEE BEHIND ME!
GOOD, NICE, PANIC THE BAD GUY.

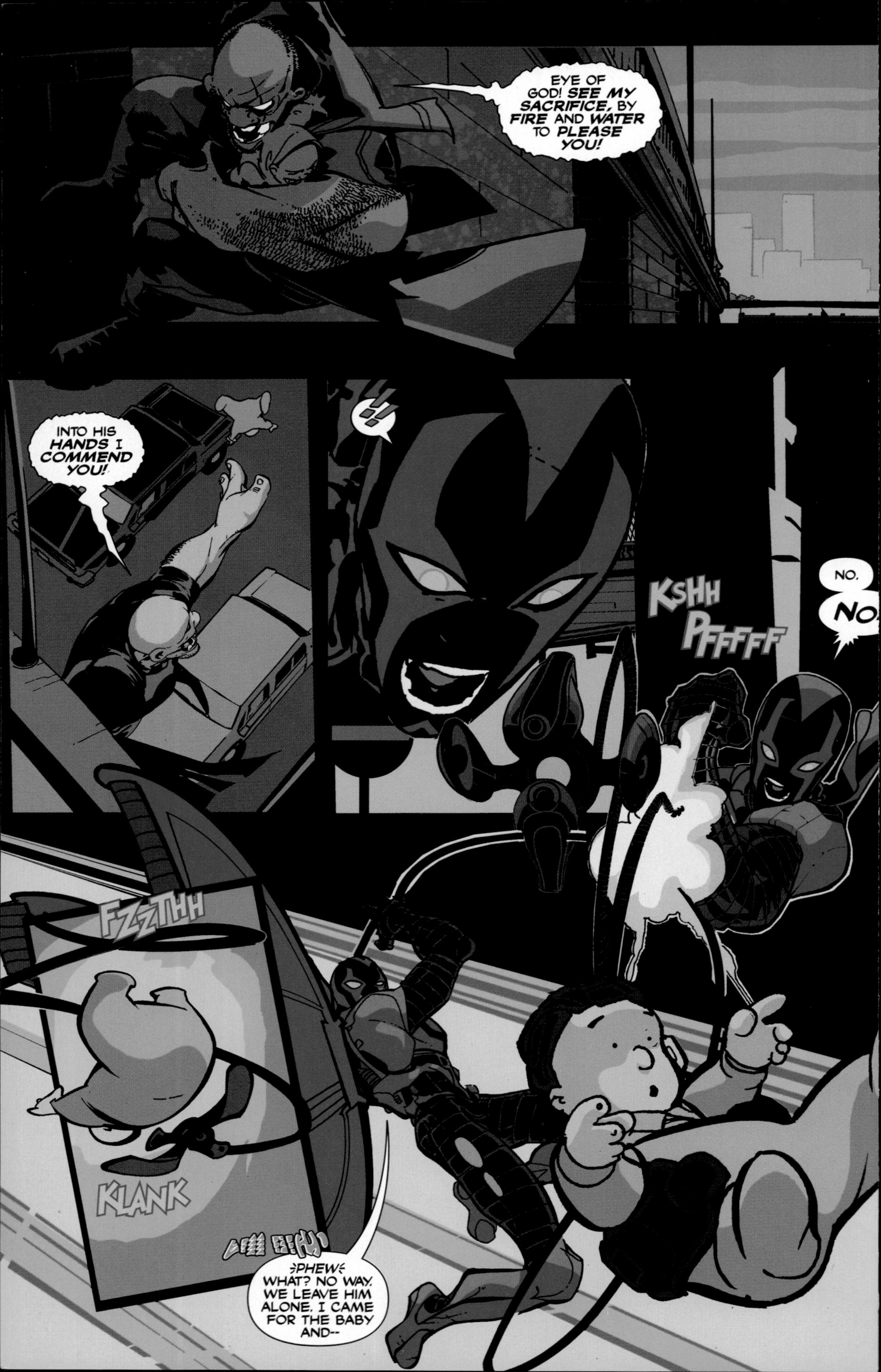
EYE OF GOD! SEE MY SACRIFICE, BY FIRE AND WATER TO PLEASE YOU!
INTO HIS HANDS I COMMEND YOU!
!!
KSHH
PFFFFF
NO.
NO.
FZZTHH
KLANK
PHEW
WHAT? NO WAY. WE LEAVE HIM ALONE. I CAME FOR THE BABY AND--

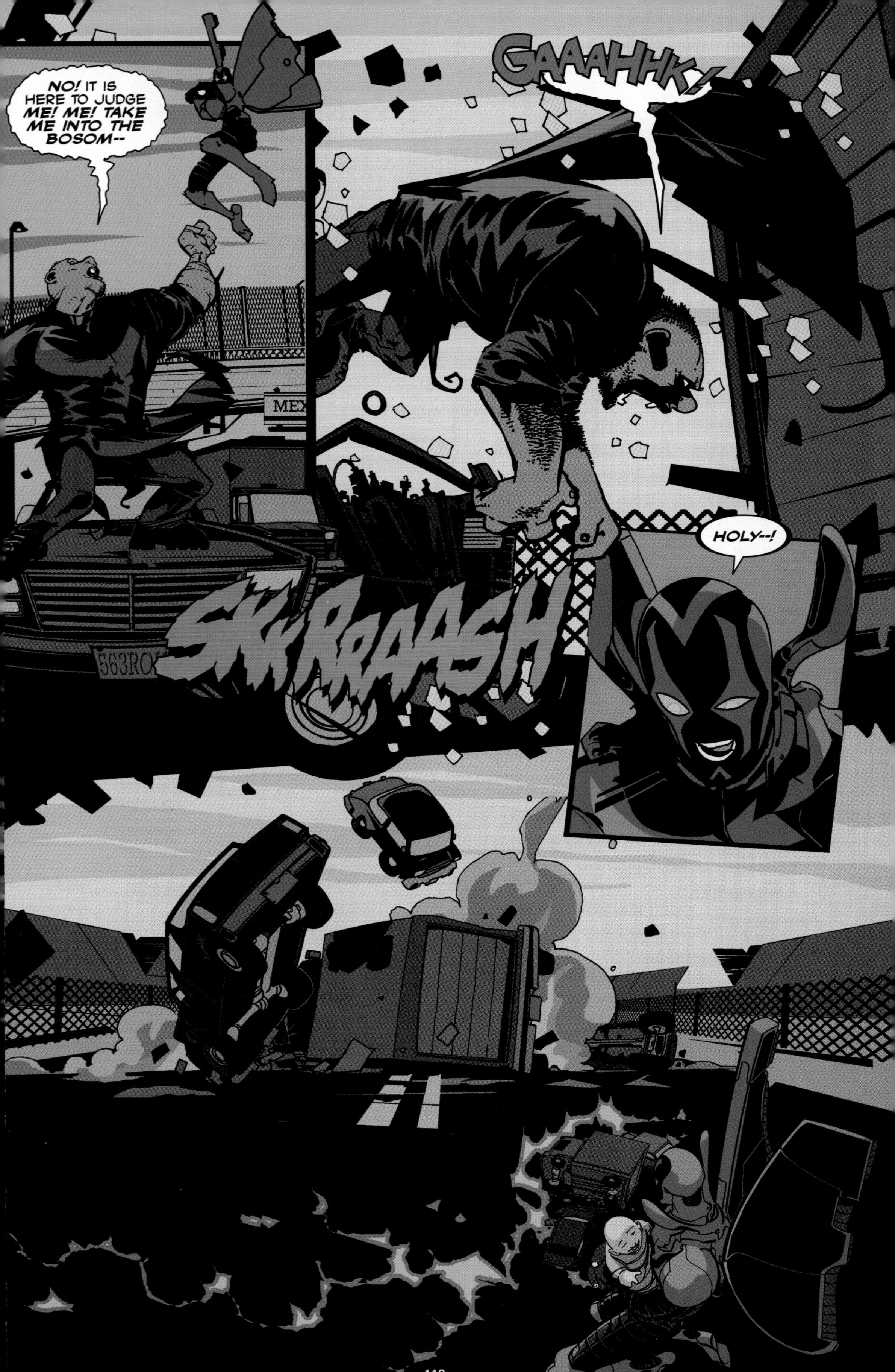
NO! IT IS HERE TO JUDGE ME! ME! TAKE ME INTO THE BOSOM--
GAAAHHK!
MEX
563RO
SKRRAASH
HOLY--!

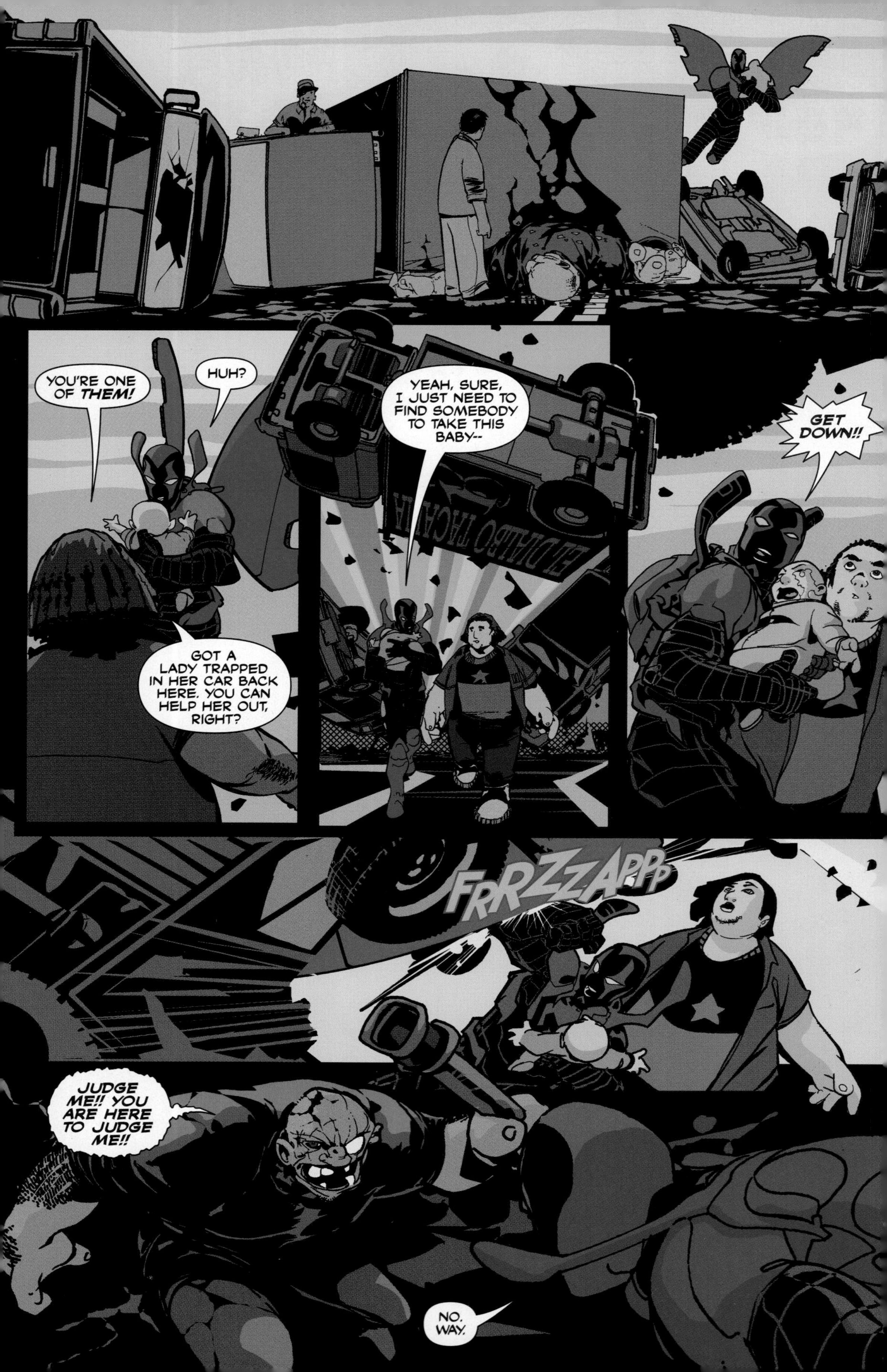
YOU'RE ONE OF THEM!
HUH?
GOT A LADY TRAPPED IN HER CAR BACK HERE. YOU CAN HELP HER OUT, RIGHT?
YEAH, SURE, I JUST NEED TO FIND SOMEBODY TO TAKE THIS BABY--
GET DOWN!!
FRRZZAPPP
JUDGE ME!! YOU ARE HERE TO JUDGE ME!!
NO. WAY.

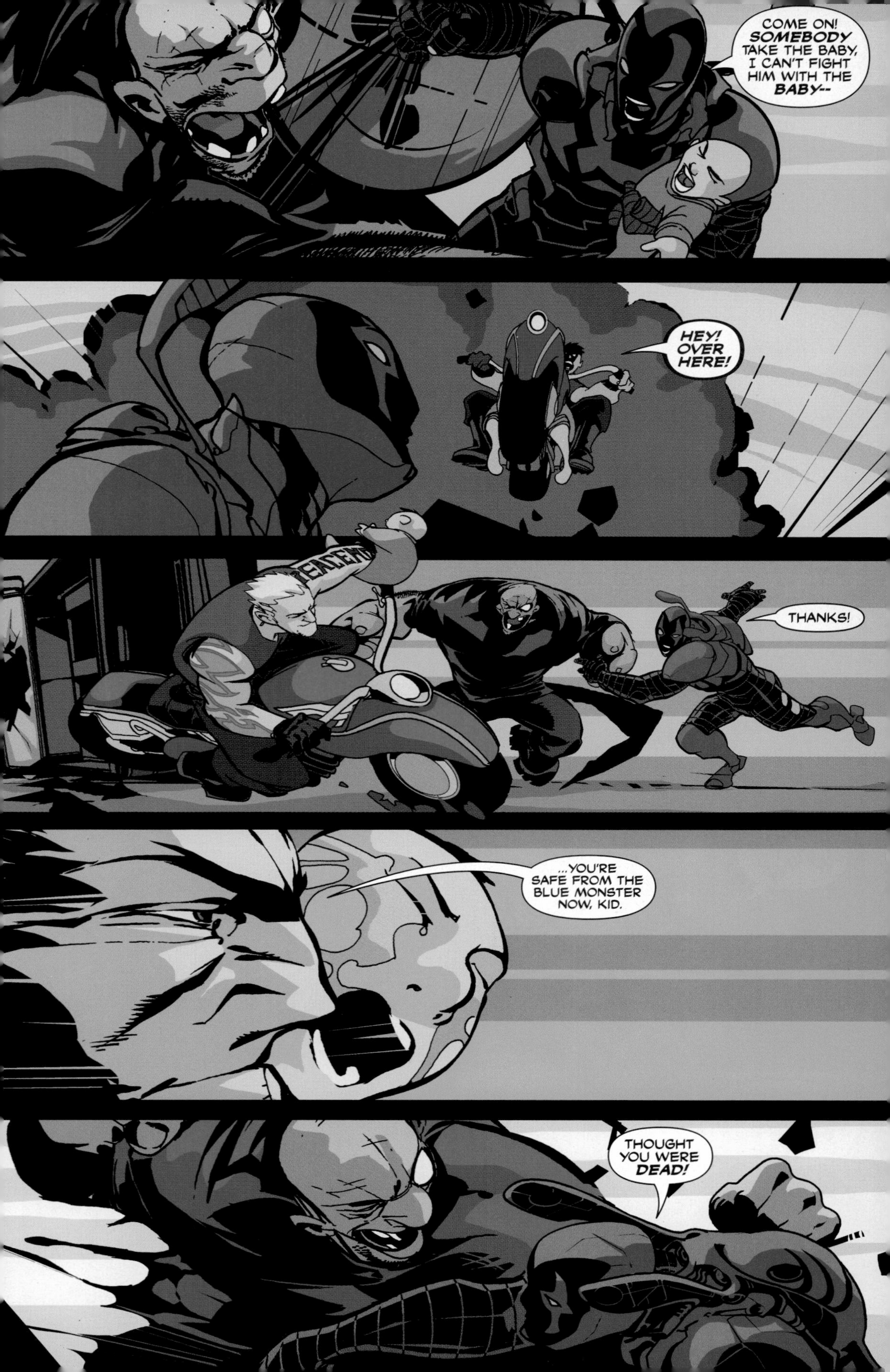
COME ON! SOMEBODY TAKE THE BABY, I CAN'T FIGHT HIM WITH THE BABY--
HEY! OVER HERE!
THANKS!
...YOU'RE SAFE FROM THE BLUE MONSTER NOW, KID.
THOUGHT YOU WERE DEAD!

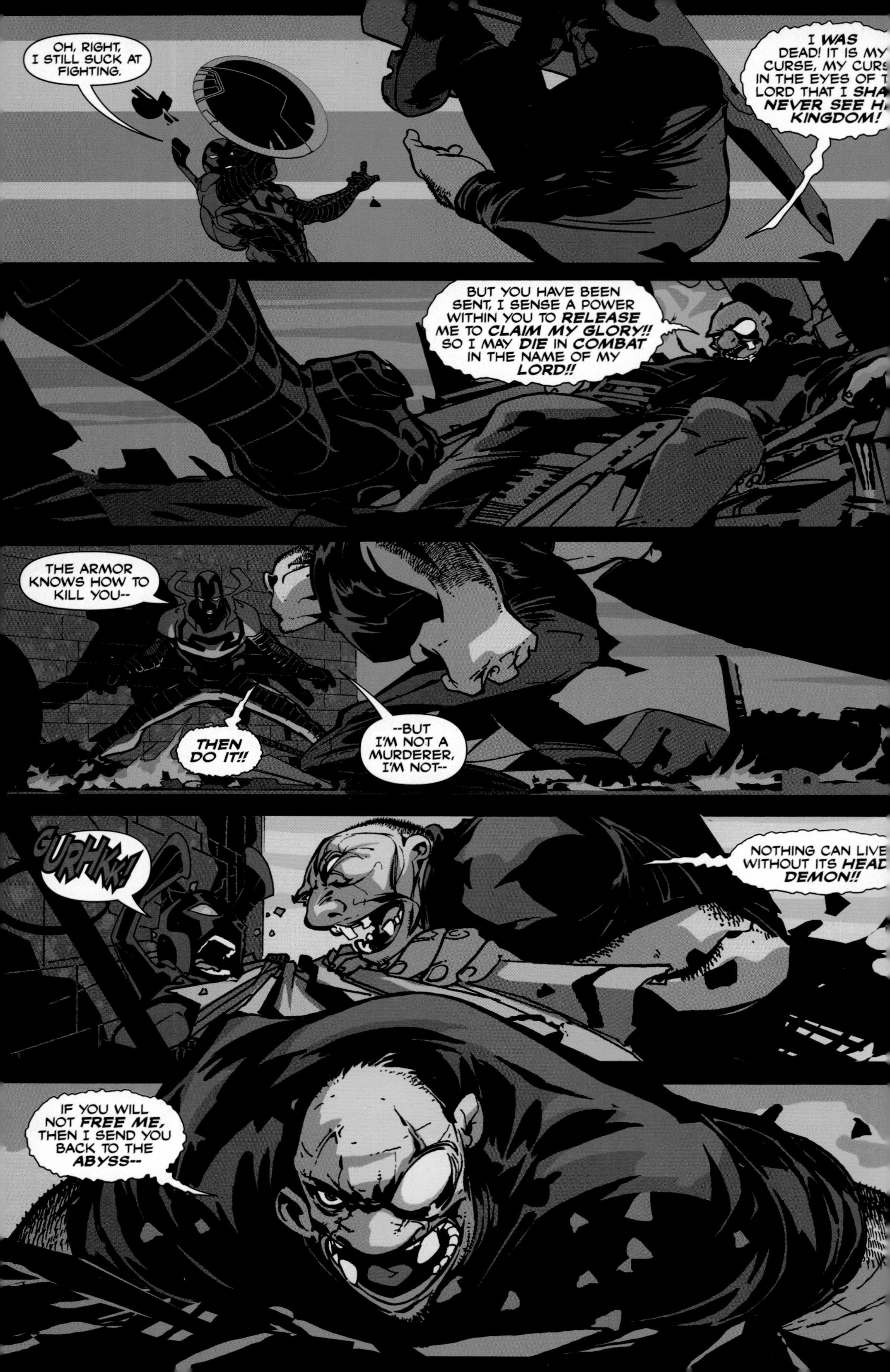
OH, RIGHT, I STILL SUCK AT FIGHTING.
I WAS DEAD! IT IS MY CURSE, MY CURS IN THE EYES OF T LORD THAT I SHA NEVER SEE HI KINGDOM!
BUT YOU HAVE BEEN SENT, I SENSE A POWER WITHIN YOU TO RELEASE ME TO CLAIM MY GLORY!! SO I MAY DIE IN COMBAT IN THE NAME OF MY LORD!!
THE ARMOR KNOWS HOW TO KILL YOU--
THEN DO IT!!
--BUT I'M NOT A MURDERER, I'M NOT--
GURHKK!
NOTHING CAN LIVE WITHOUT ITS HEAD DEMON!!
IF YOU WILL NOT FREE ME, THEN I SEND YOU BACK TO THE ABYSS--

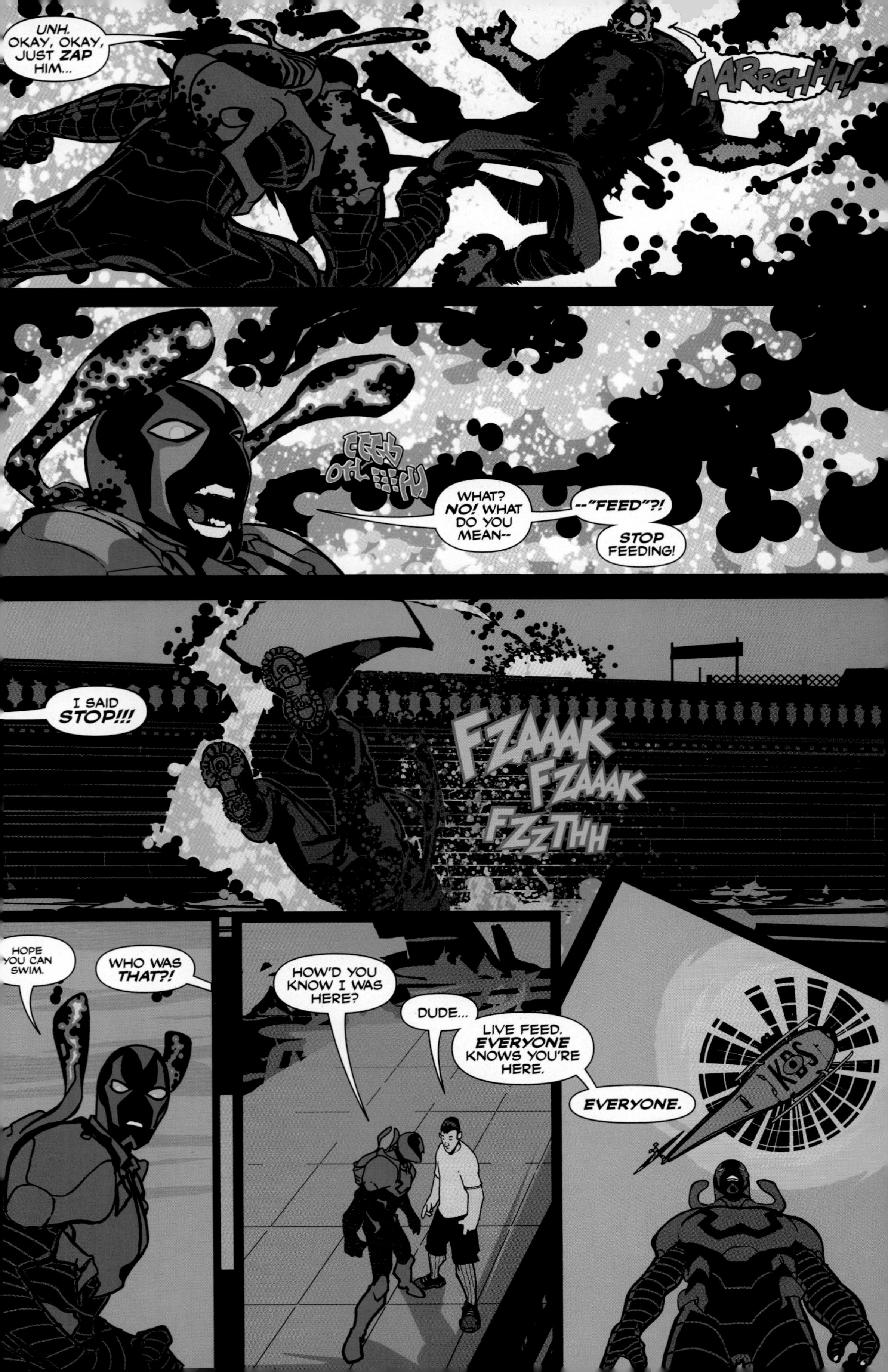
UNH. OKAY, OKAY, JUST ZAP HIM...
AARRGHHH!
WHAT? NO! WHAT DO YOU MEAN--
--"FEED"?!
STOP FEEDING!
I SAID STOP!!!
FZAAAK
FZAAAK
FZZTHH
HOPE YOU CAN SWIM.
WHO WAS THAT?!
HOW'D YOU KNOW I WAS HERE?
DUDE...
LIVE FEED. EVERYONE KNOWS YOU'RE HERE.
EVERYONE.
KBS

BLUE BEETLE #6
Cover by Duncan Rouleau
Interior art by Cynthia Martin & Phil Moy,
Kevin West & Jack Purcell

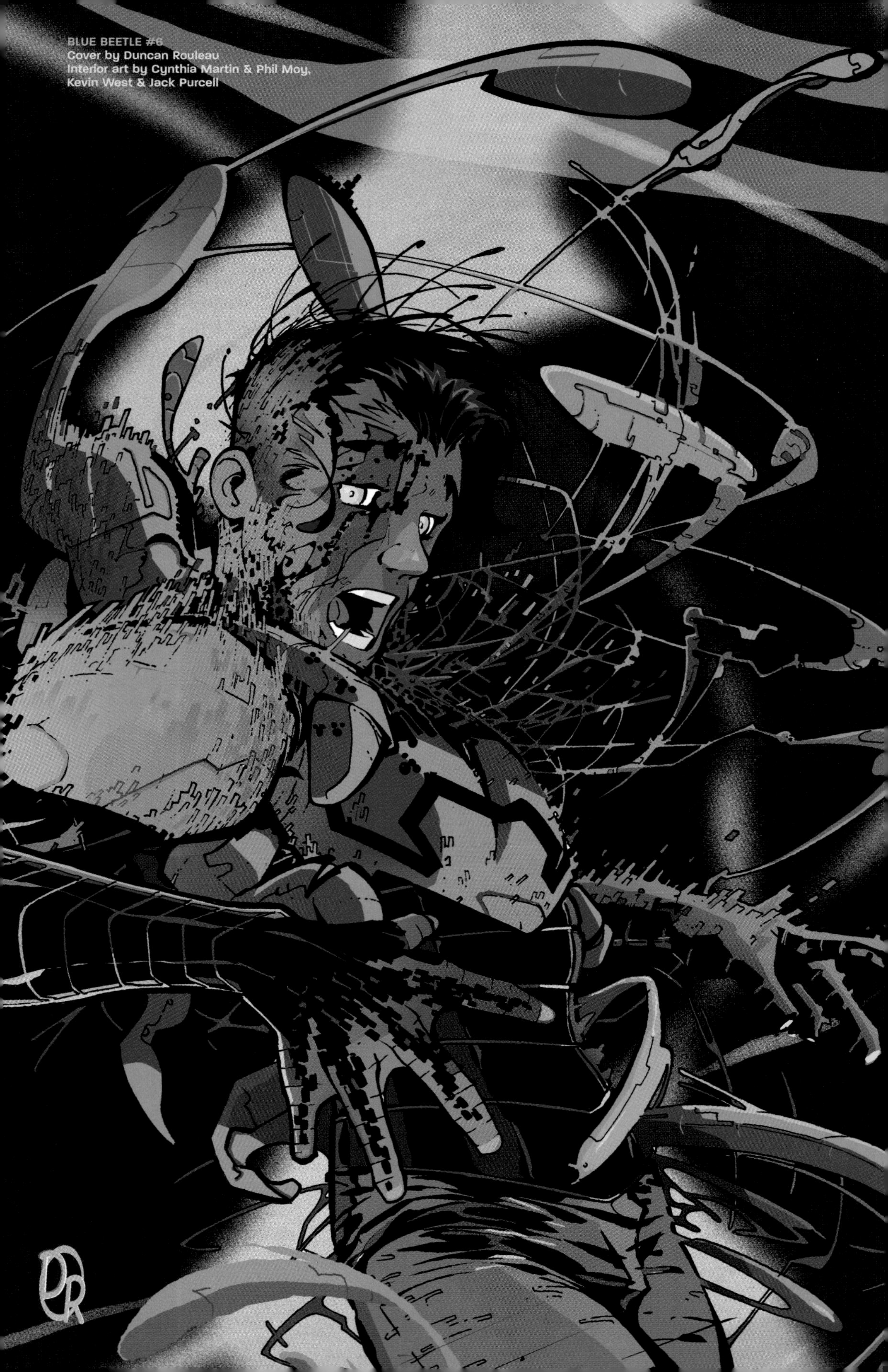

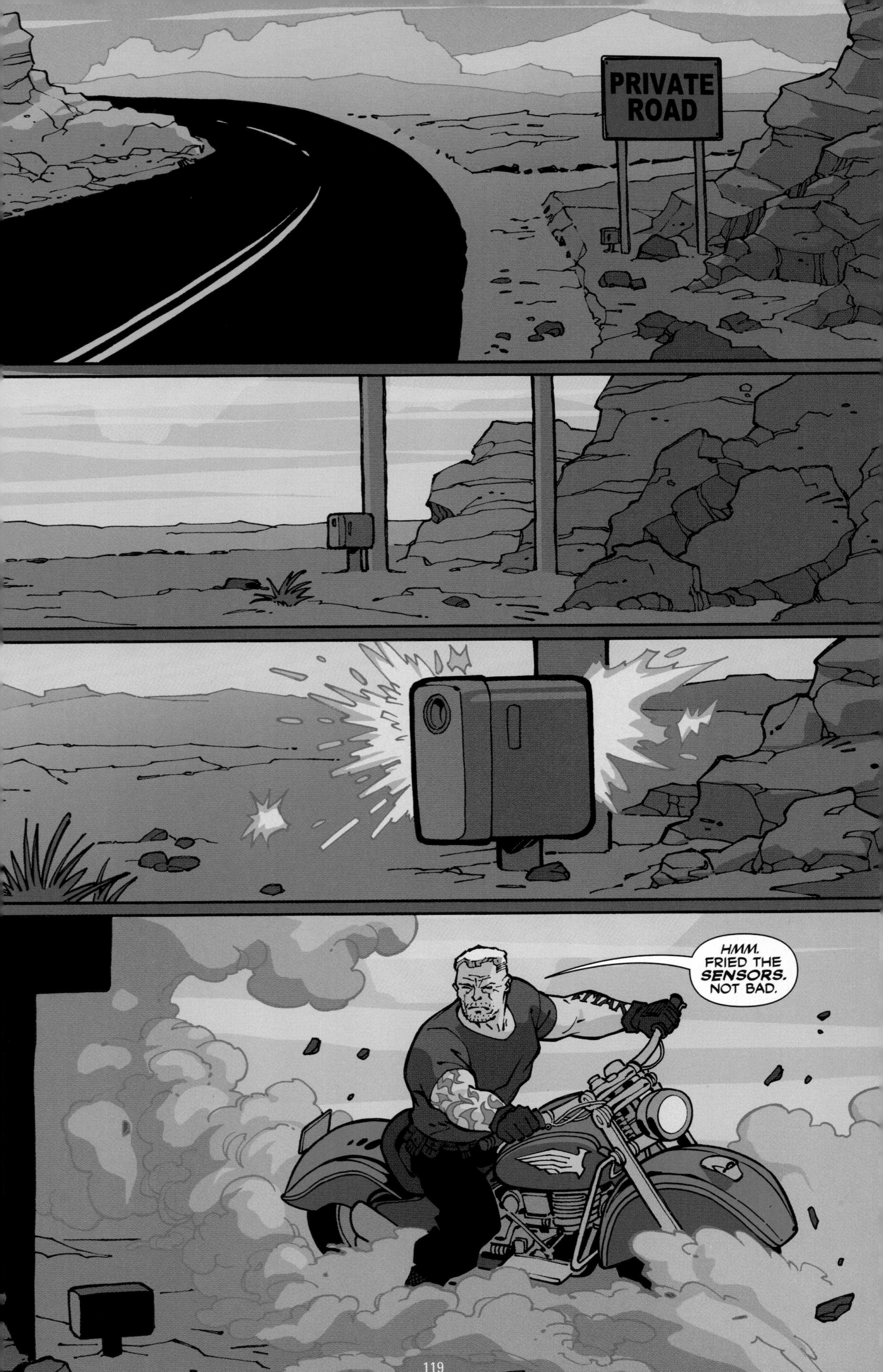
PRIVATE ROAD
HMM. FRIED THE SENSORS. NOT BAD.

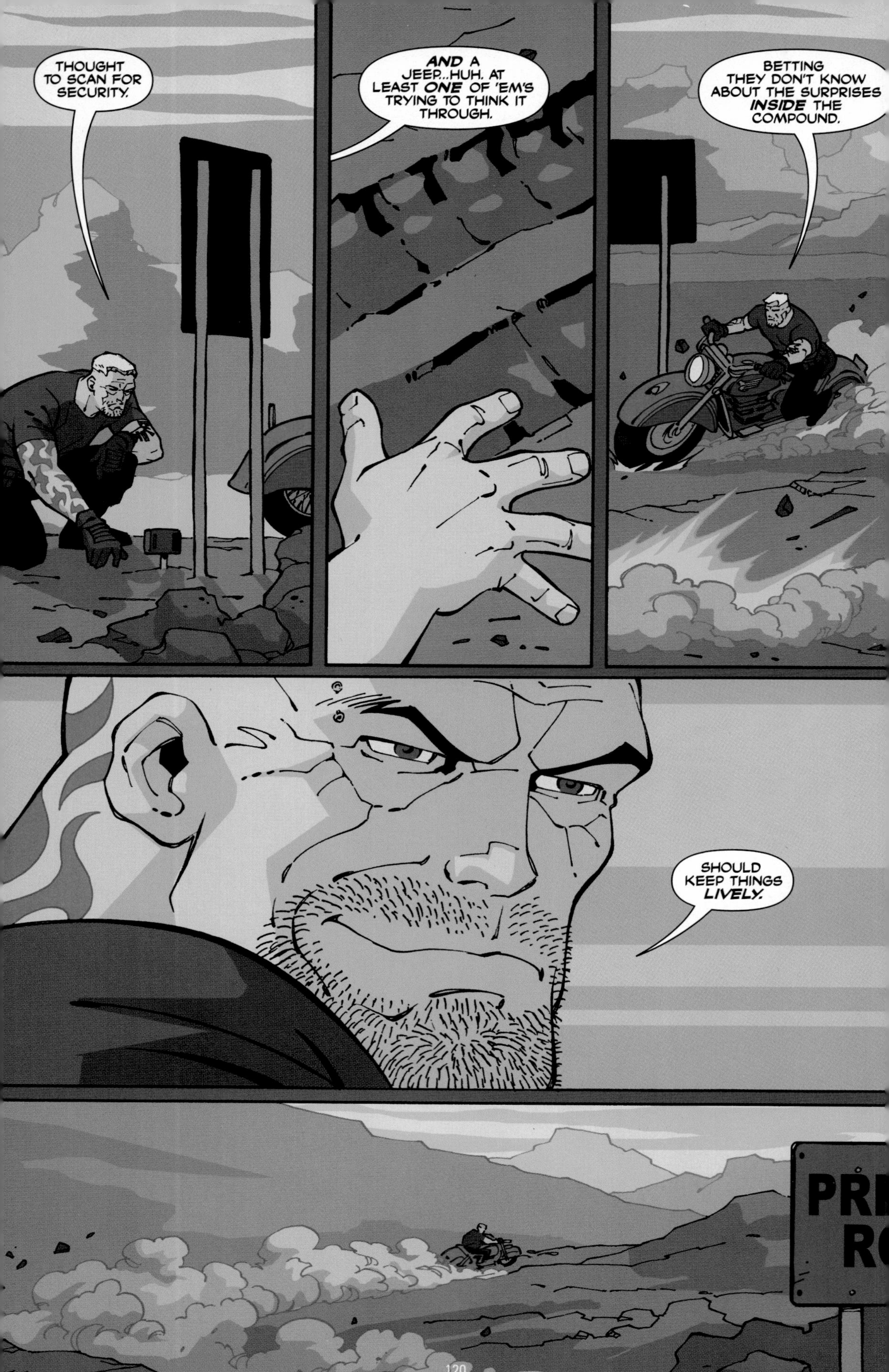
THOUGHT TO SCAN FOR SECURITY.
AND A JEEP...HUH. AT LEAST ONE OF 'EM'S TRYING TO THINK IT THROUGH.
BETTING THEY DON'T KNOW ABOUT THE SURPRISES INSIDE THE COMPOUND.
SHOULD KEEP THINGS LIVELY.

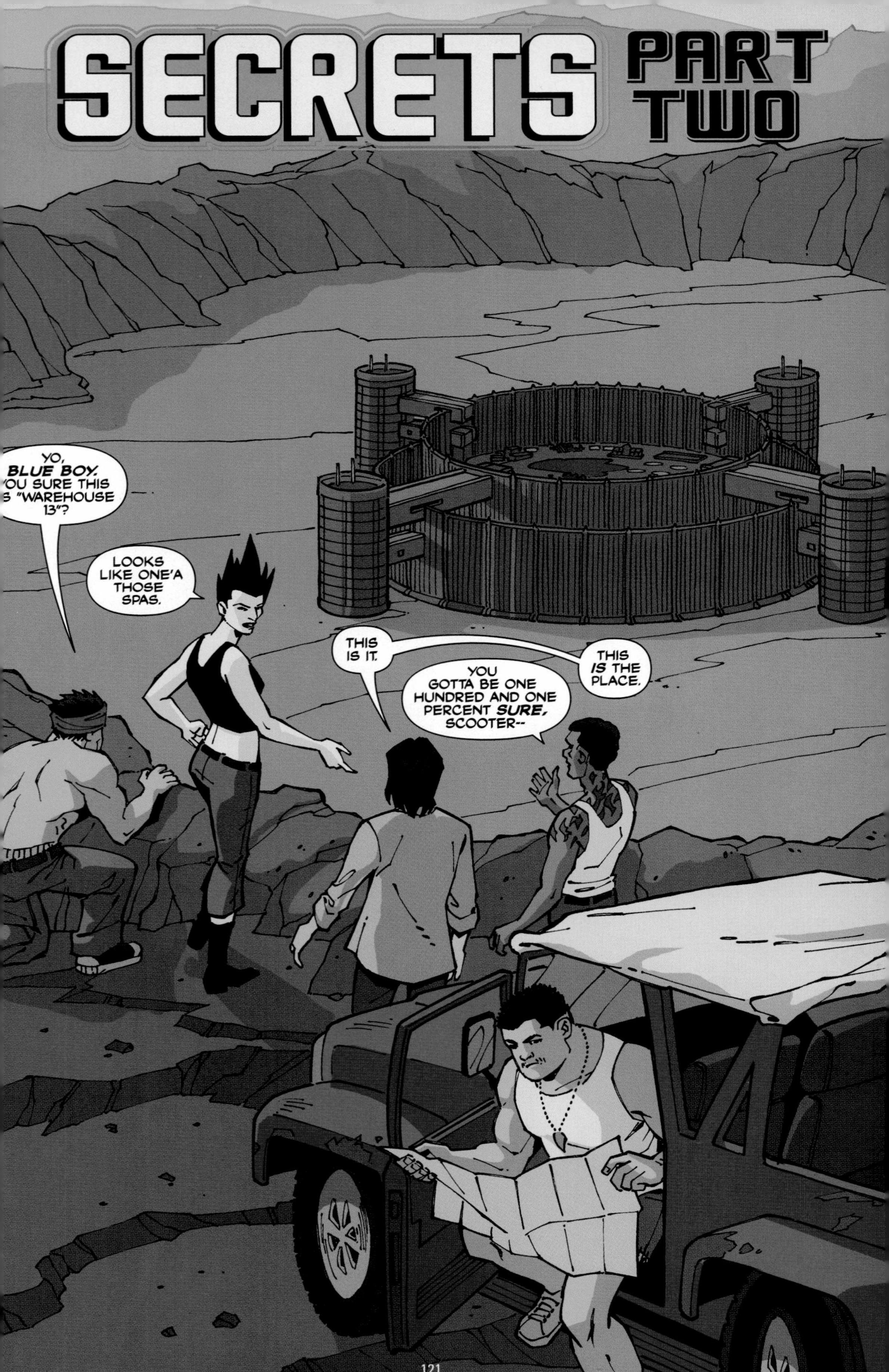
SECRETS PART TWO
YO, BLUE BOY. YOU SURE THIS IS "WAREHOUSE 13"?
LOOKS LIKE ONE'A THOSE SPAS.
THIS IS IT.
THIS IS THE PLACE.
YOU GOTTA BE ONE HUNDRED AND ONE PERCENT SURE, SCOOTER--

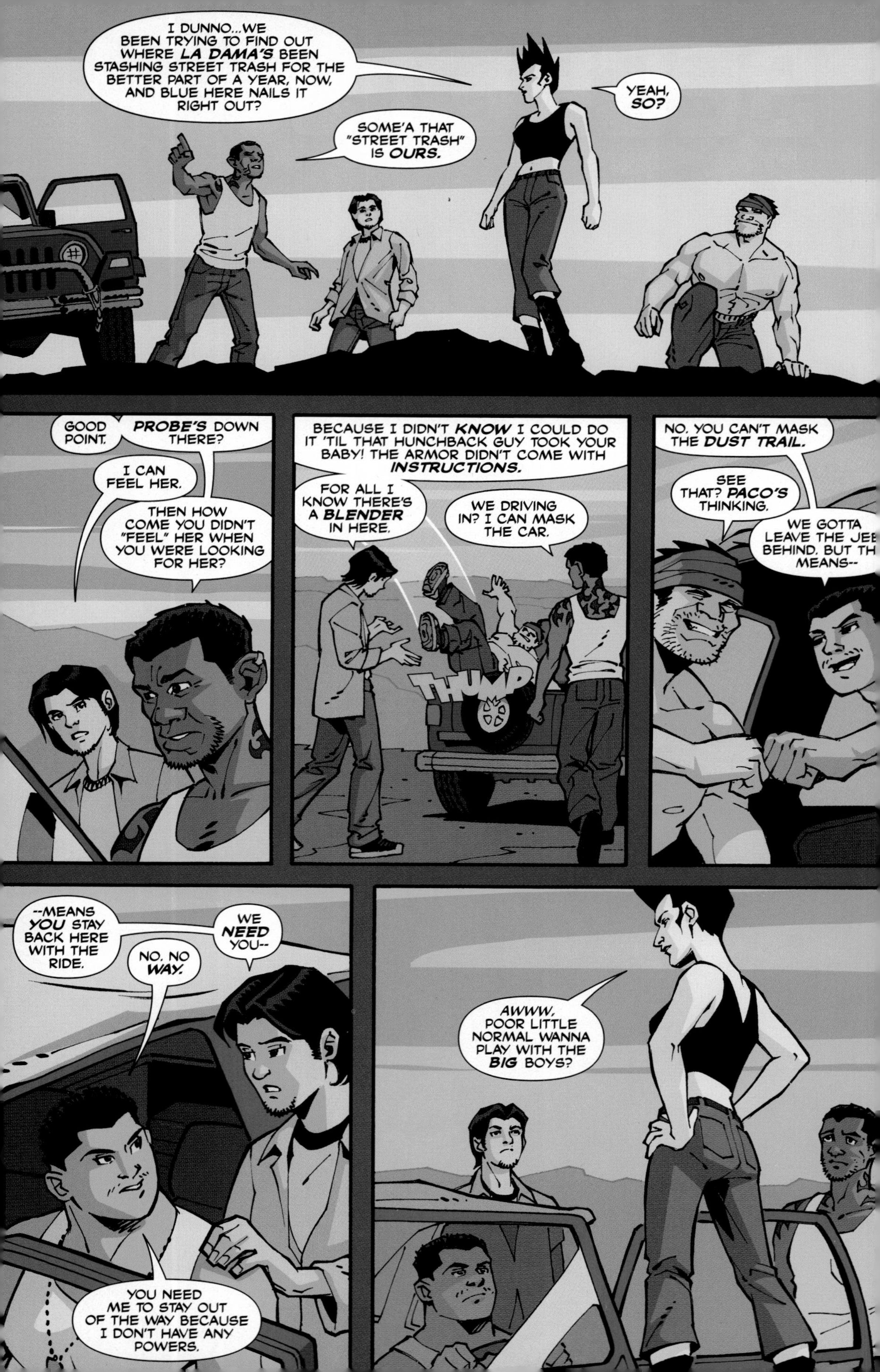

I DUNNO...WE BEEN TRYING TO FIND OUT WHERE LA DAMA'S BEEN STASHING STREET TRASH FOR THE BETTER PART OF A YEAR, NOW, AND BLUE HERE NAILS IT RIGHT OUT?
YEAH, SO?
SOME'A THAT "STREET TRASH" IS OURS.
GOOD POINT.
PROBE'S DOWN THERE?
I CAN FEEL HER.
THEN HOW COME YOU DIDN'T "FEEL" HER WHEN YOU WERE LOOKING FOR HER?
BECAUSE I DIDN'T KNOW I COULD DO IT 'TIL THAT HUNCHBACK GUY TOOK YOUR BABY! THE ARMOR DIDN'T COME WITH INSTRUCTIONS.
FOR ALL I KNOW THERE'S A BLENDER IN HERE.
WE DRIVING IN? I CAN MASK THE CAR.
THUMP
NO. YOU CAN'T MASK THE DUST TRAIL.
SEE THAT? PACO'S THINKING.
WE GOTTA LEAVE THE JEE BEHIND. BUT TH MEANS--
--MEANS YOU STAY BACK HERE WITH THE RIDE.
WE NEED YOU--
NO. NO WAY.
YOU NEED ME TO STAY OUT OF THE WAY BECAUSE I DON'T HAVE ANY POWERS.
AWWW, POOR LITTLE NORMAL WANNA PLAY WITH THE BIG BOYS?

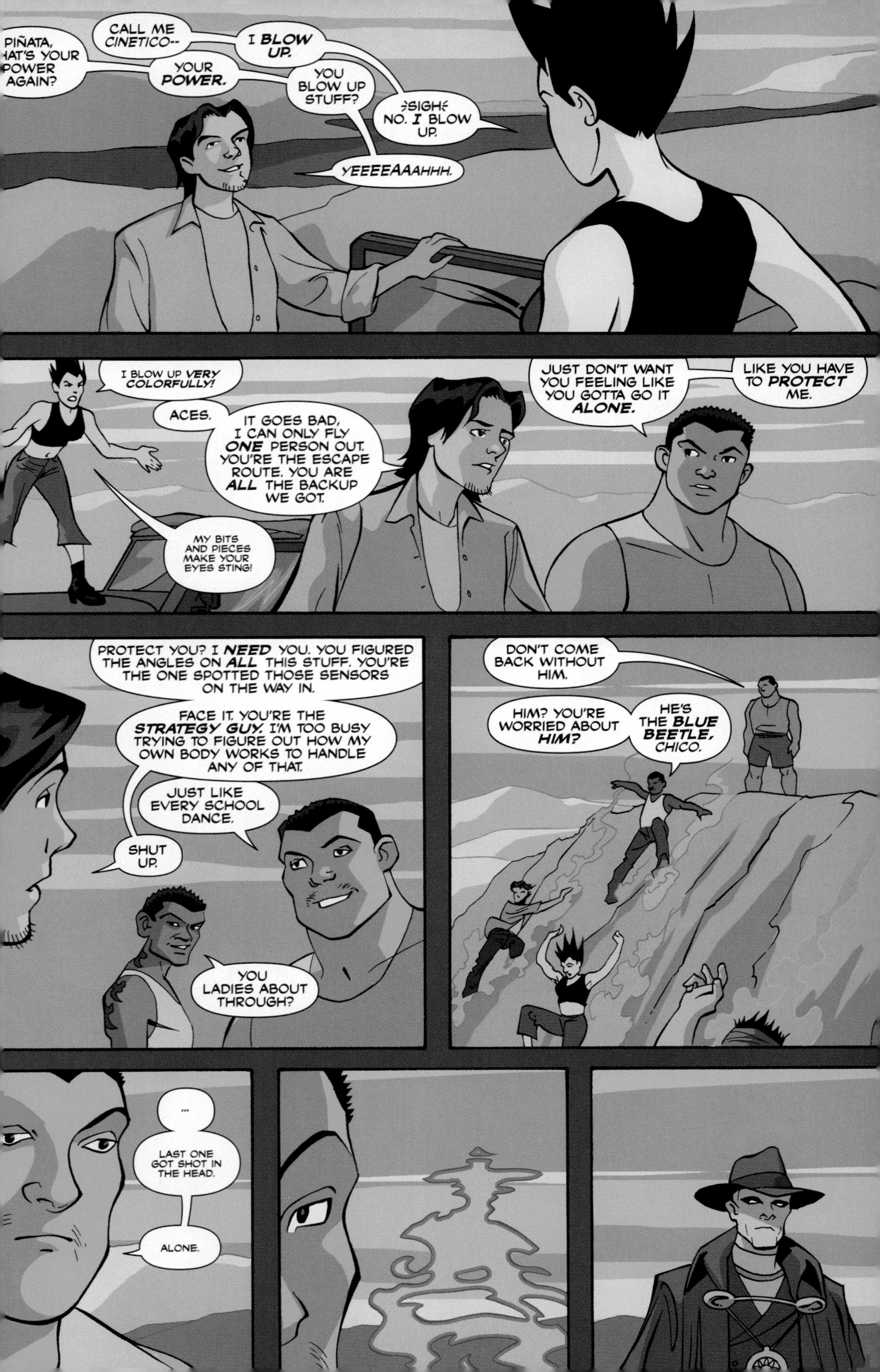
PIÑATA, THAT'S YOUR POWER AGAIN?
CALL ME CINETICO--
YOUR POWER.
I BLOW UP.
YOU BLOW UP STUFF?
≯SIGH≮ NO. I BLOW UP.
YEEEEAAAHHH.
I BLOW UP VERY COLORFULLY!
ACES.
IT GOES BAD, I CAN ONLY FLY ONE PERSON OUT. YOU'RE THE ESCAPE ROUTE. YOU ARE ALL THE BACKUP WE GOT.
MY BITS AND PIECES MAKE YOUR EYES STING!
JUST DON'T WANT YOU FEELING LIKE YOU GOTTA GO IT ALONE.
LIKE YOU HAVE TO PROTECT ME.
PROTECT YOU? I NEED YOU. YOU FIGURED THE ANGLES ON ALL THIS STUFF. YOU'RE THE ONE SPOTTED THOSE SENSORS ON THE WAY IN.
FACE IT. YOU'RE THE STRATEGY GUY. I'M TOO BUSY TRYING TO FIGURE OUT HOW MY OWN BODY WORKS TO HANDLE ANY OF THAT.
JUST LIKE EVERY SCHOOL DANCE.
SHUT UP.
YOU LADIES ABOUT THROUGH?
DON'T COME BACK WITHOUT HIM.
HIM? YOU'RE WORRIED ABOUT HIM?
HE'S THE BLUE BEETLE, CHICO.
...
LAST ONE GOT SHOT IN THE HEAD.
ALONE.

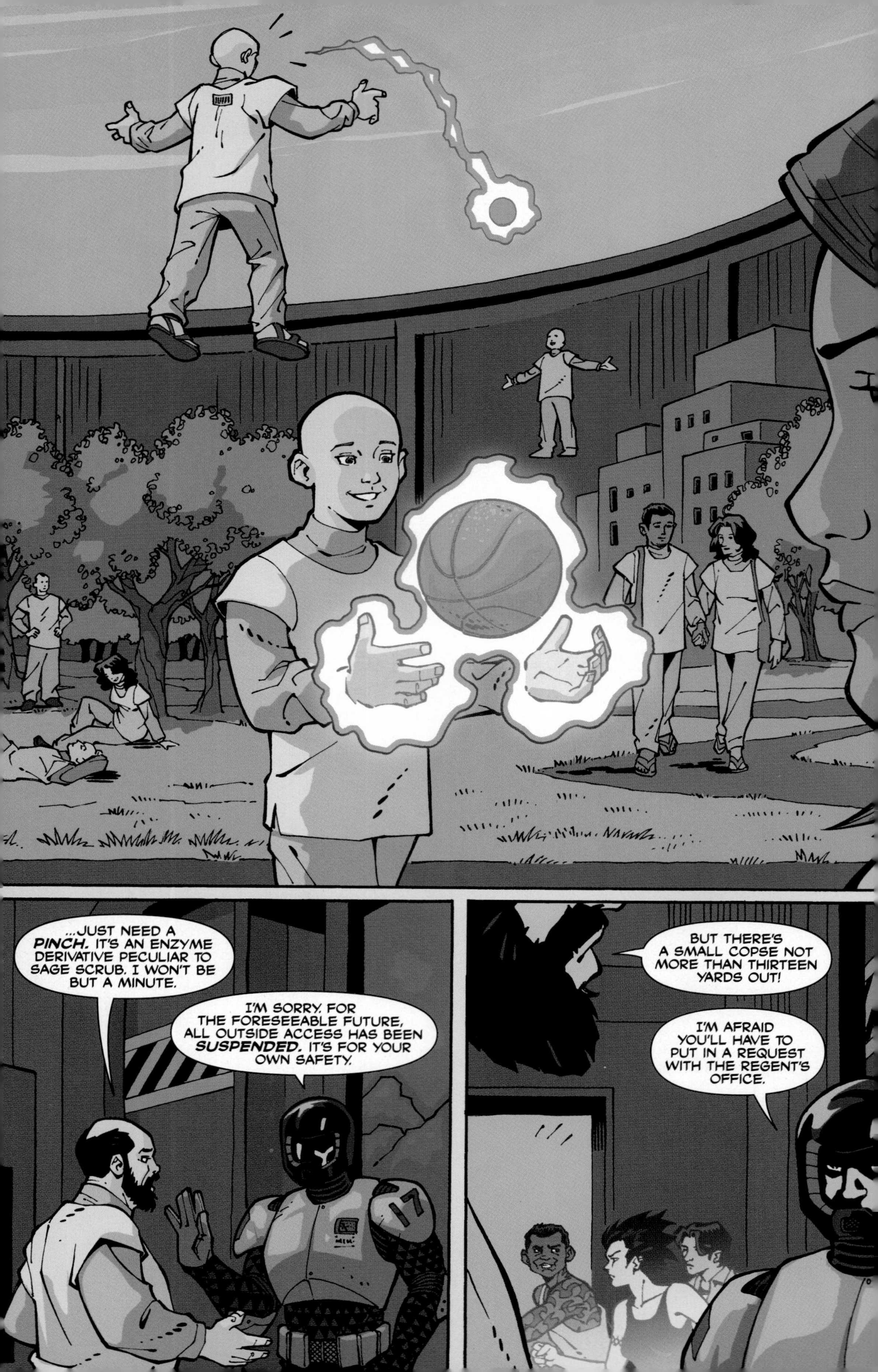
...JUST NEED A PINCH. IT'S AN ENZYME DERIVATIVE PECULIAR TO SAGE SCRUB. I WON'T BE BUT A MINUTE.
I'M SORRY. FOR THE FORESEEABLE FUTURE, ALL OUTSIDE ACCESS HAS BEEN SUSPENDED. IT'S FOR YOUR OWN SAFETY.
BUT THERE'S A SMALL COPSE NOT MORE THAN THIRTEEN YARDS OUT!
I'M AFRAID YOU'LL HAVE TO PUT IN A REQUEST WITH THE REGENT'S OFFICE.

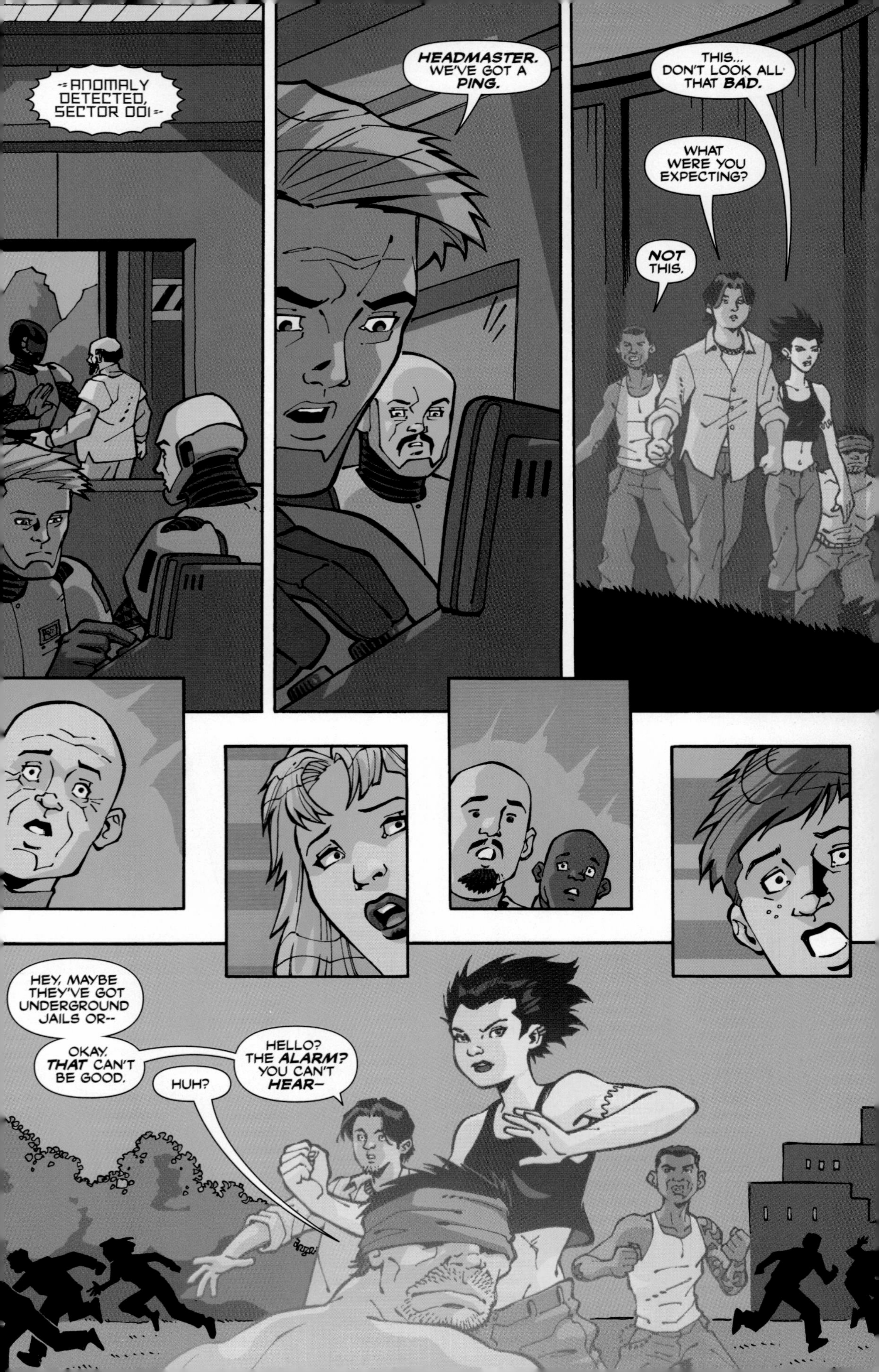
-= ANOMALY DETECTED, SECTOR 001 =-
HEADMASTER. WE'VE GOT A PING.
THIS... DON'T LOOK ALL THAT BAD.
WHAT WERE YOU EXPECTING?
NOT THIS.
HEY, MAYBE THEY'VE GOT UNDERGROUND JAILS OR--
OKAY. THAT CAN'T BE GOOD.
HELLO? THE ALARM? YOU CAN'T HEAR--
HUH?

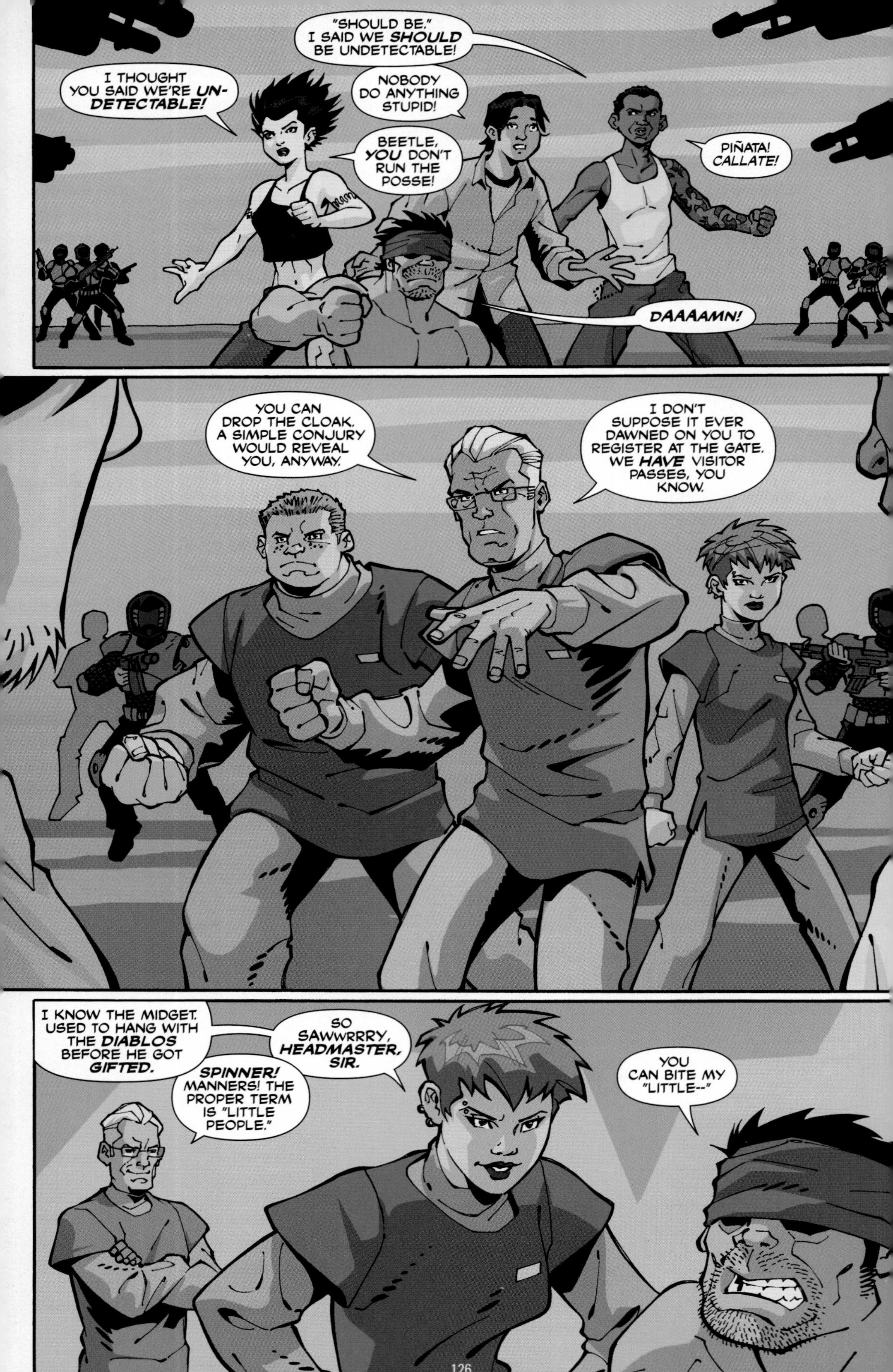
I THOUGHT YOU SAID WE'RE UN-DETECTABLE!
"SHOULD BE." I SAID WE SHOULD BE UNDETECTABLE!
NOBODY DO ANYTHING STUPID!
BEETLE, YOU DON'T RUN THE POSSE!
PIÑATA! CALLATE!
DAAAAMN!
YOU CAN DROP THE CLOAK. A SIMPLE CONJURY WOULD REVEAL YOU, ANYWAY.
I DON'T SUPPOSE IT EVER DAWNED ON YOU TO REGISTER AT THE GATE. WE HAVE VISITOR PASSES, YOU KNOW.
I KNOW THE MIDGET. USED TO HANG WITH THE DIABLOS BEFORE HE GOT GIFTED.
SPINNER! MANNERS! THE PROPER TERM IS "LITTLE PEOPLE."
SO SAWWRRRY, HEADMASTER, SIR.
YOU CAN BITE MY "LITTLE--"

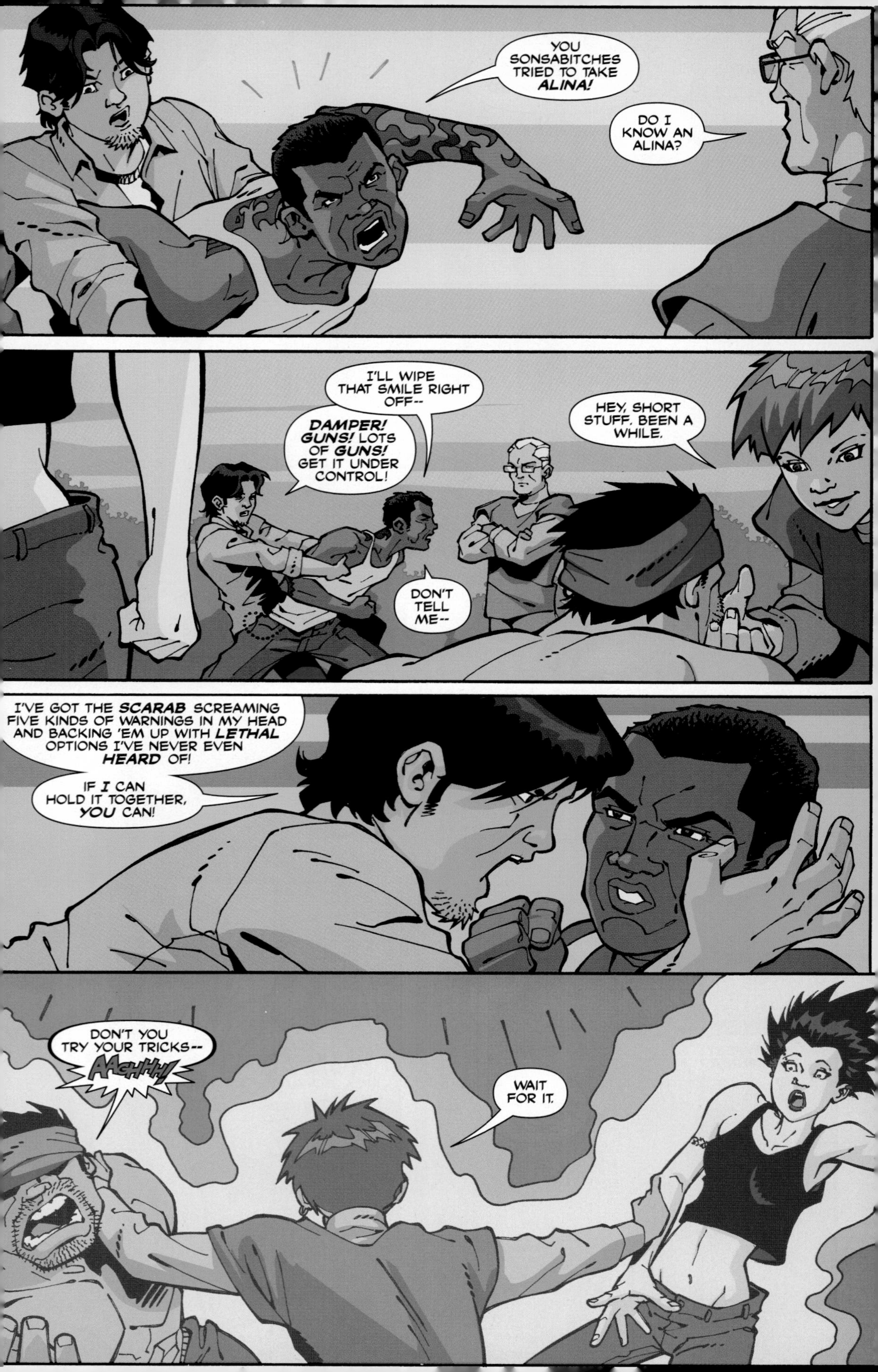
YOU SONSABITCHES TRIED TO TAKE ALINA!
DO I KNOW AN ALINA?
I'LL WIPE THAT SMILE RIGHT OFF--
DAMPER! GUNS! LOTS OF GUNS! GET IT UNDER CONTROL!
HEY, SHORT STUFF, BEEN A WHILE.
DON'T TELL ME--
I'VE GOT THE SCARAB SCREAMING FIVE KINDS OF WARNINGS IN MY HEAD AND BACKING 'EM UP WITH LETHAL OPTIONS I'VE NEVER EVEN HEARD OF!
IF I CAN HOLD IT TOGETHER, YOU CAN!
DON'T YOU TRY YOUR TRICKS--
AAGHHH!
WAIT FOR IT.

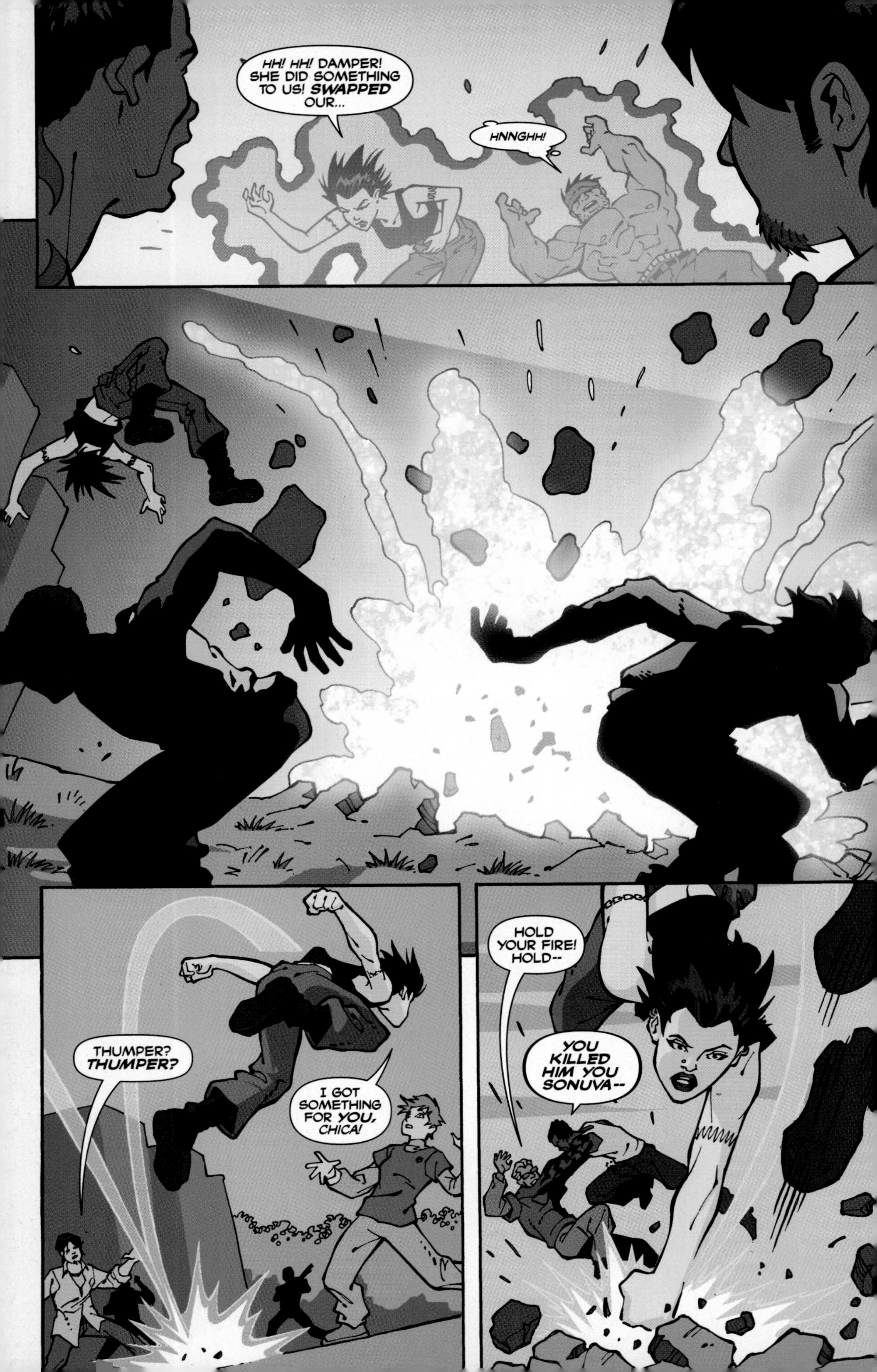
HH! HH! DAMPER! SHE DID SOMETHING TO US! SWAPPED OUR...
HNNGHH!
THUMPER? THUMPER?
I GOT SOMETHING FOR YOU, CHICA!
HOLD YOUR FIRE! HOLD--
YOU KILLED HIM YOU SONUVA--

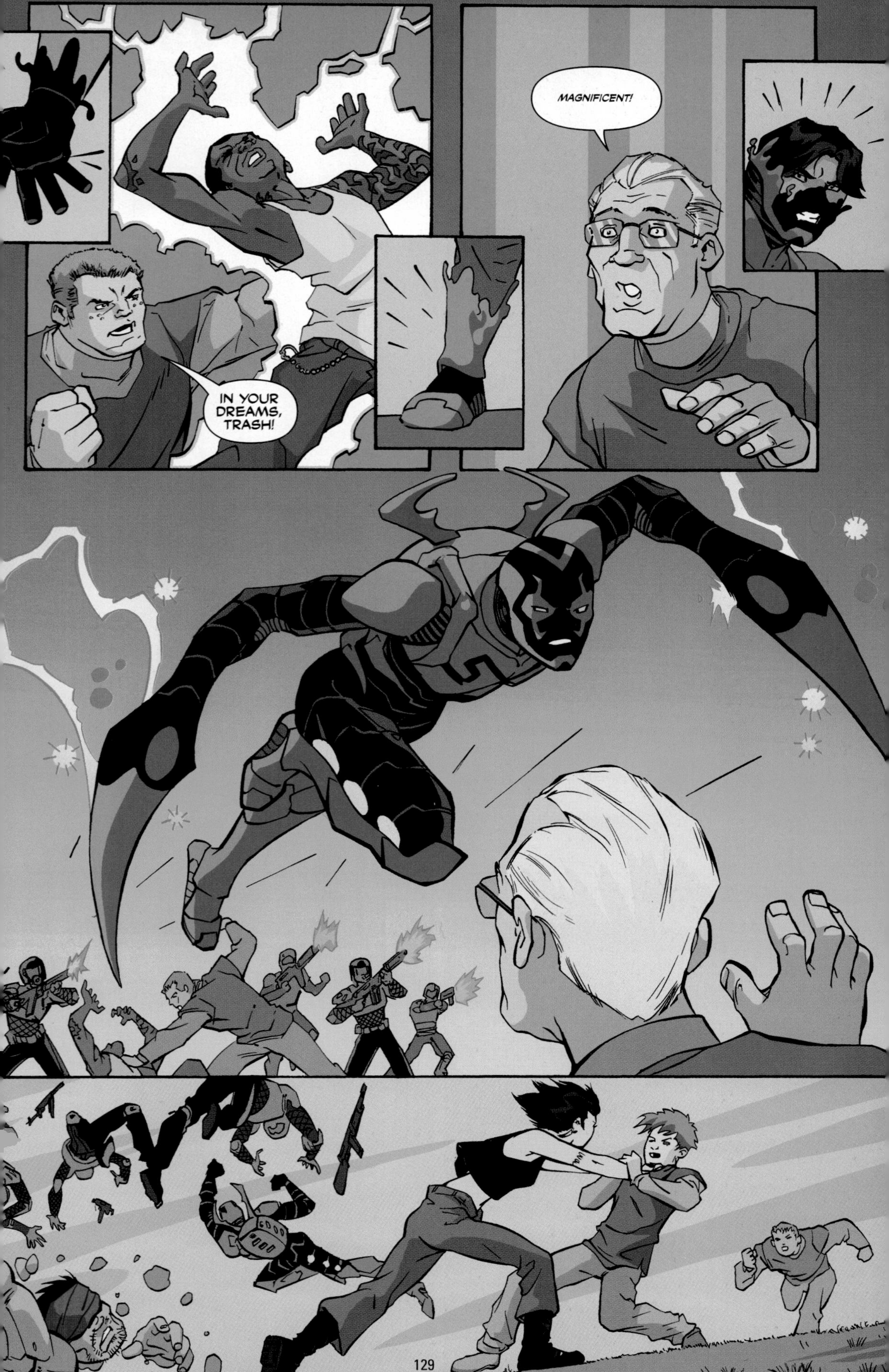
IN YOUR DREAMS, TRASH!
MAGNIFICENT!

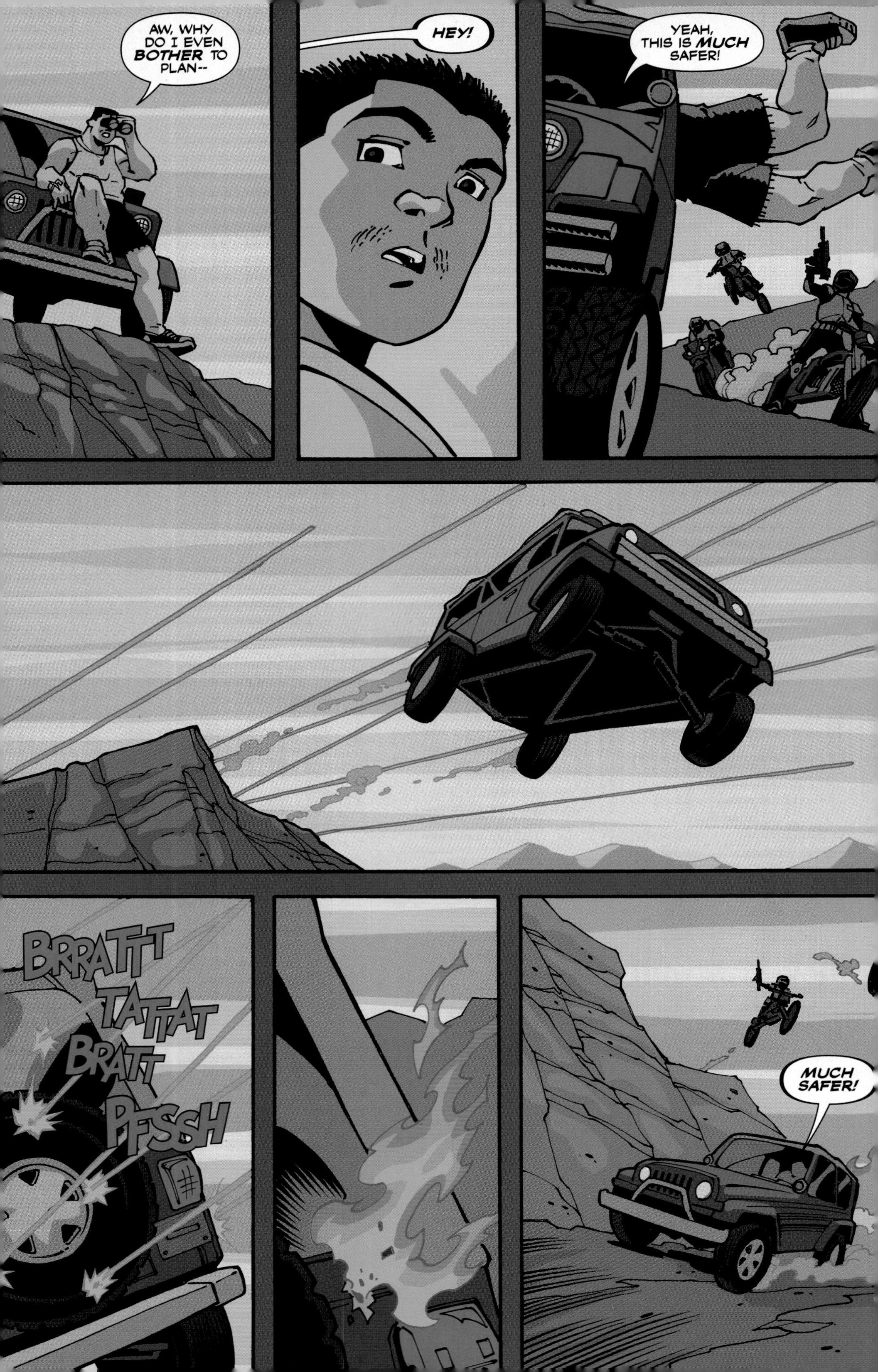
AW, WHY DO I EVEN BOTHER TO PLAN--
HEY!
YEAH, THIS IS MUCH SAFER!
BRRATTT
TATTAT
BRATT
PFSSH
MUCH SAFER!

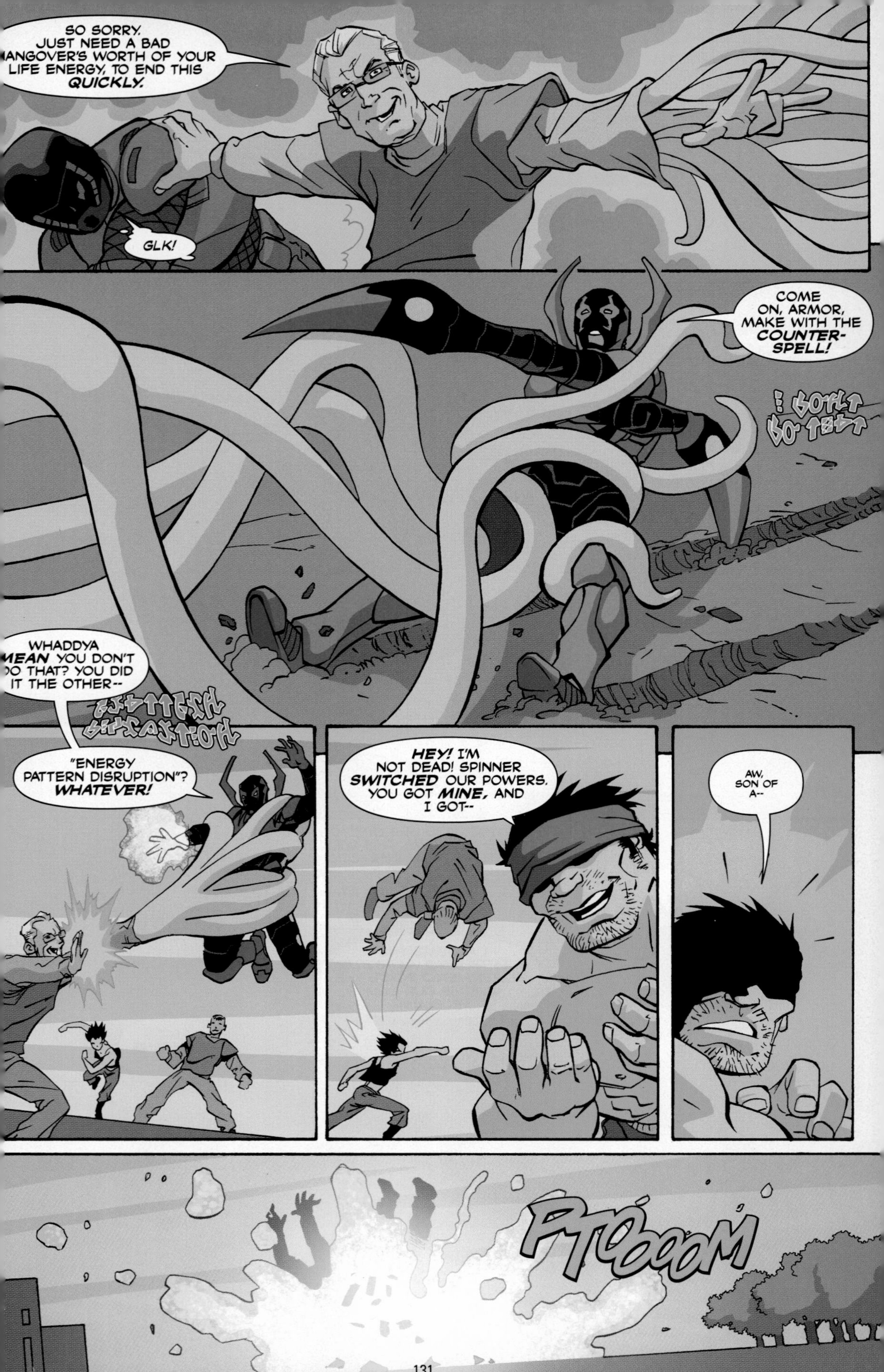

SO SORRY. JUST NEED A BAD HANGOVER'S WORTH OF YOUR LIFE ENERGY, TO END THIS QUICKLY.
GLK!
COME ON, ARMOR, MAKE WITH THE COUNTER-SPELL!
WHADDYA MEAN YOU DON'T DO THAT? YOU DID IT THE OTHER--
"ENERGY PATTERN DISRUPTION"? WHATEVER!
HEY! I'M NOT DEAD! SPINNER SWITCHED OUR POWERS. YOU GOT MINE, AND I GOT--
AW, SON OF A--
PTOOOOM

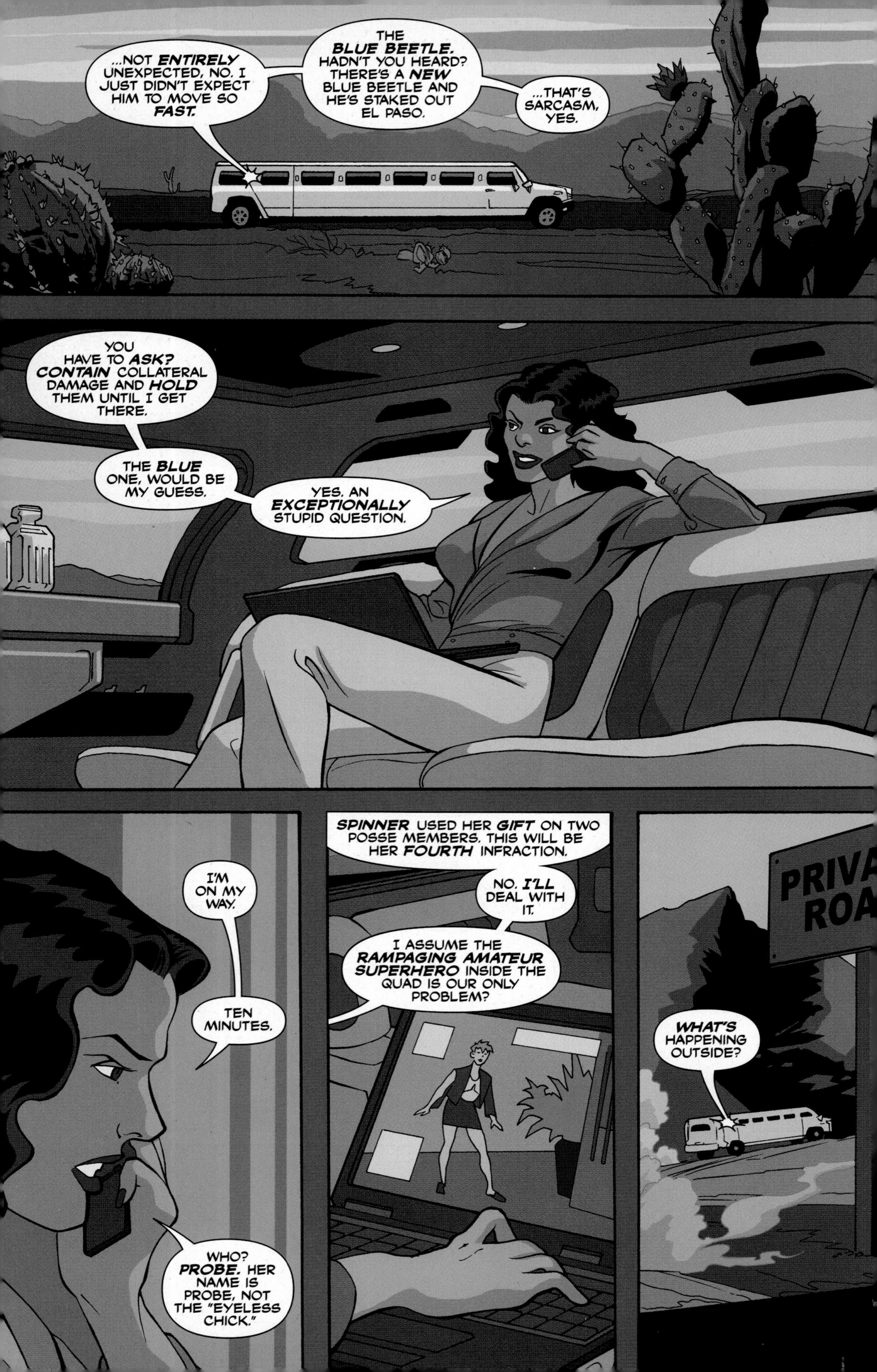
...NOT ENTIRELY UNEXPECTED, NO. I JUST DIDN'T EXPECT HIM TO MOVE SO FAST.
THE BLUE BEETLE. HADN'T YOU HEARD? THERE'S A NEW BLUE BEETLE AND HE'S STAKED OUT EL PASO.
...THAT'S SARCASM, YES.
YOU HAVE TO ASK? CONTAIN COLLATERAL DAMAGE AND HOLD THEM UNTIL I GET THERE.
THE BLUE ONE, WOULD BE MY GUESS.
YES, AN EXCEPTIONALLY STUPID QUESTION.
I'M ON MY WAY.
TEN MINUTES.
WHO? PROBE. HER NAME IS PROBE, NOT THE "EYELESS CHICK."
SPINNER USED HER GIFT ON TWO POSSE MEMBERS. THIS WILL BE HER FOURTH INFRACTION.
NO. I'LL DEAL WITH IT.
I ASSUME THE RAMPAGING AMATEUR SUPERHERO INSIDE THE QUAD IS OUR ONLY PROBLEM?
PRIVA
ROA
WHAT'S HAPPENING OUTSIDE?

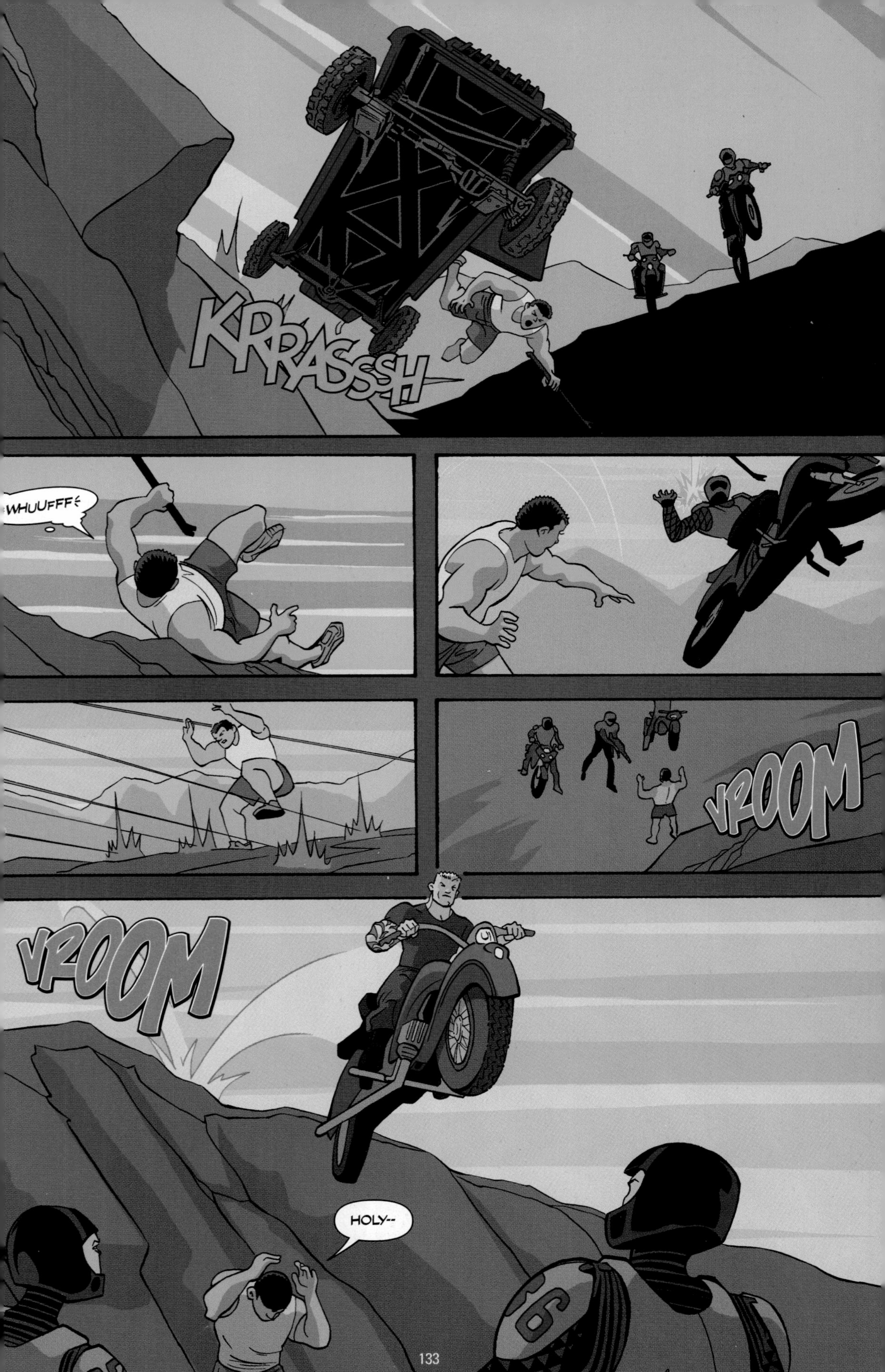
KRRASSH
WHUUFFF
VROOM
VROOM
HOLY--

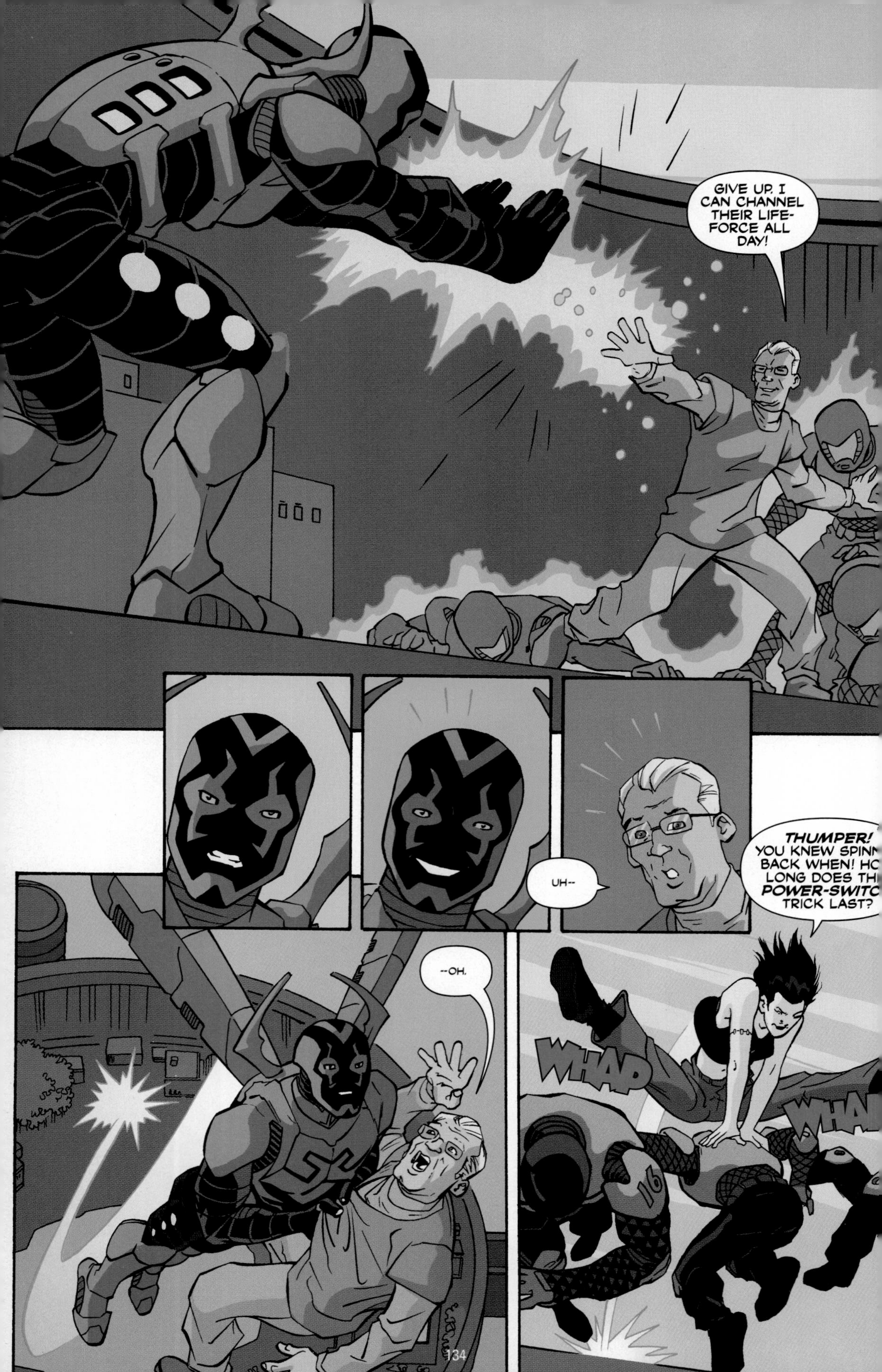
GIVE UP. I CAN CHANNEL THEIR LIFE-FORCE ALL DAY!
UH--
THUMPER! YOU KNEW SPINN BACK WHEN! HO LONG DOES TH POWER-SWITC TRICK LAST?
--OH.
WHAP
WHA

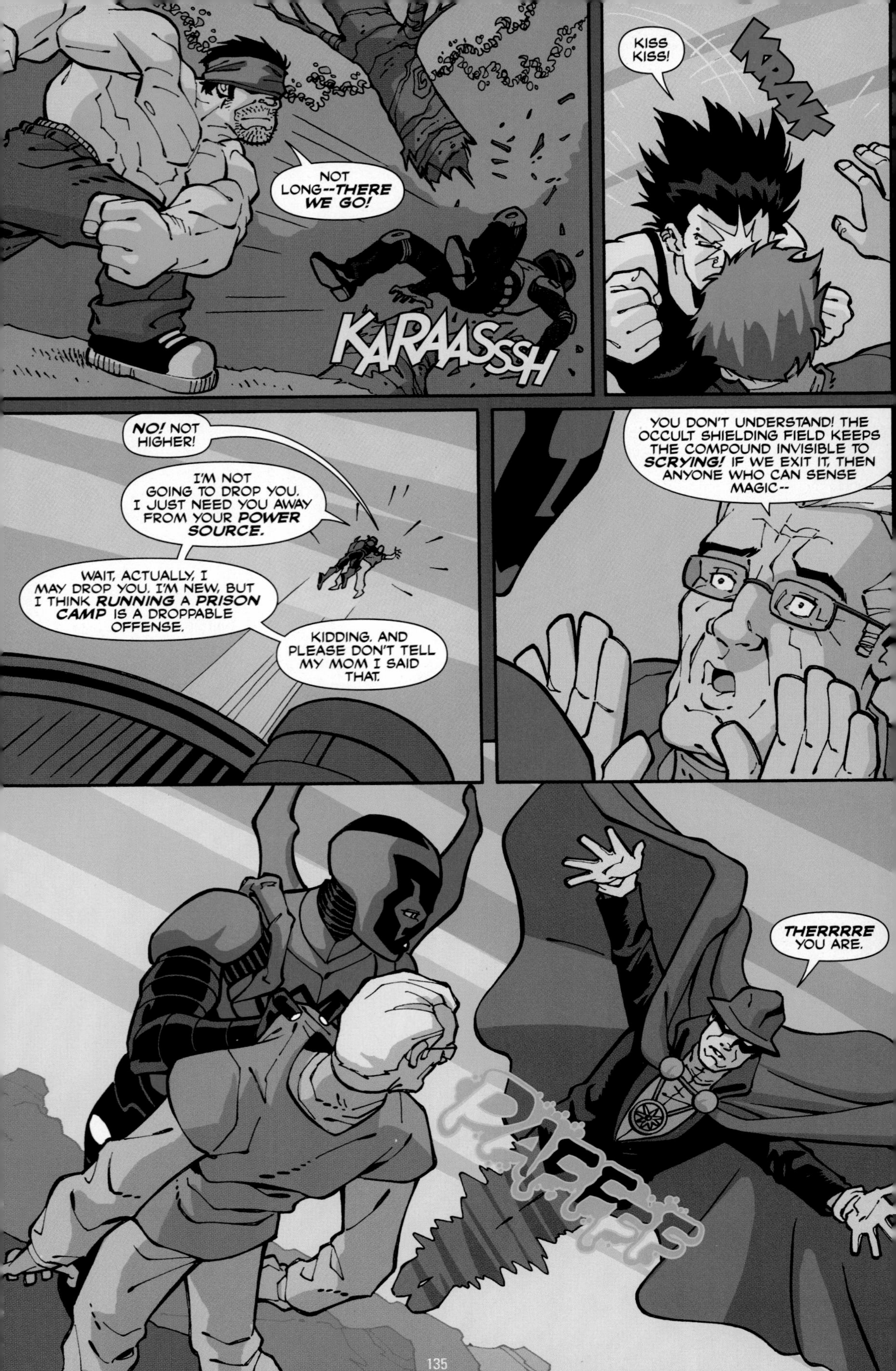
NOT LONG--THERE WE GO!
KARAASSSH
KISS KISS!
KRAK
NO! NOT HIGHER!
I'M NOT GOING TO DROP YOU. I JUST NEED YOU AWAY FROM YOUR POWER SOURCE.
WAIT, ACTUALLY, I MAY DROP YOU. I'M NEW, BUT I THINK RUNNING A PRISON CAMP IS A DROPPABLE OFFENSE.
KIDDING. AND PLEASE DON'T TELL MY MOM I SAID THAT.
YOU DON'T UNDERSTAND! THE OCCULT SHIELDING FIELD KEEPS THE COMPOUND INVISIBLE TO SCRYING! IF WE EXIT IT, THEN ANYONE WHO CAN SENSE MAGIC--
THERRRRE YOU ARE.

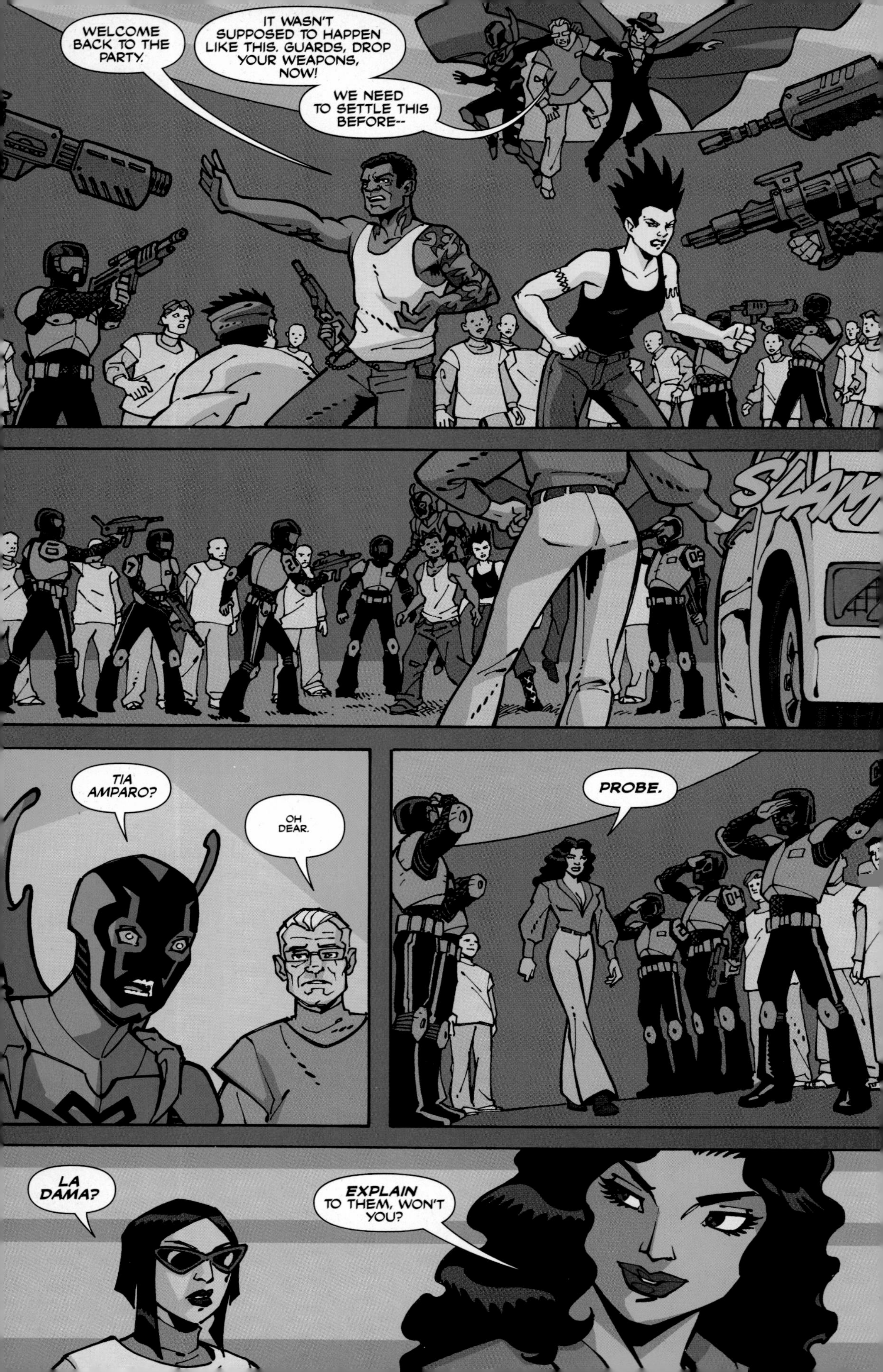
WELCOME BACK TO THE PARTY.
IT WASN'T SUPPOSED TO HAPPEN LIKE THIS. GUARDS, DROP YOUR WEAPONS, NOW!
WE NEED TO SETTLE THIS BEFORE--
SLAM
TIA AMPARO?
OH DEAR.
PROBE.
LA DAMA?
EXPLAIN TO THEM, WON'T YOU?

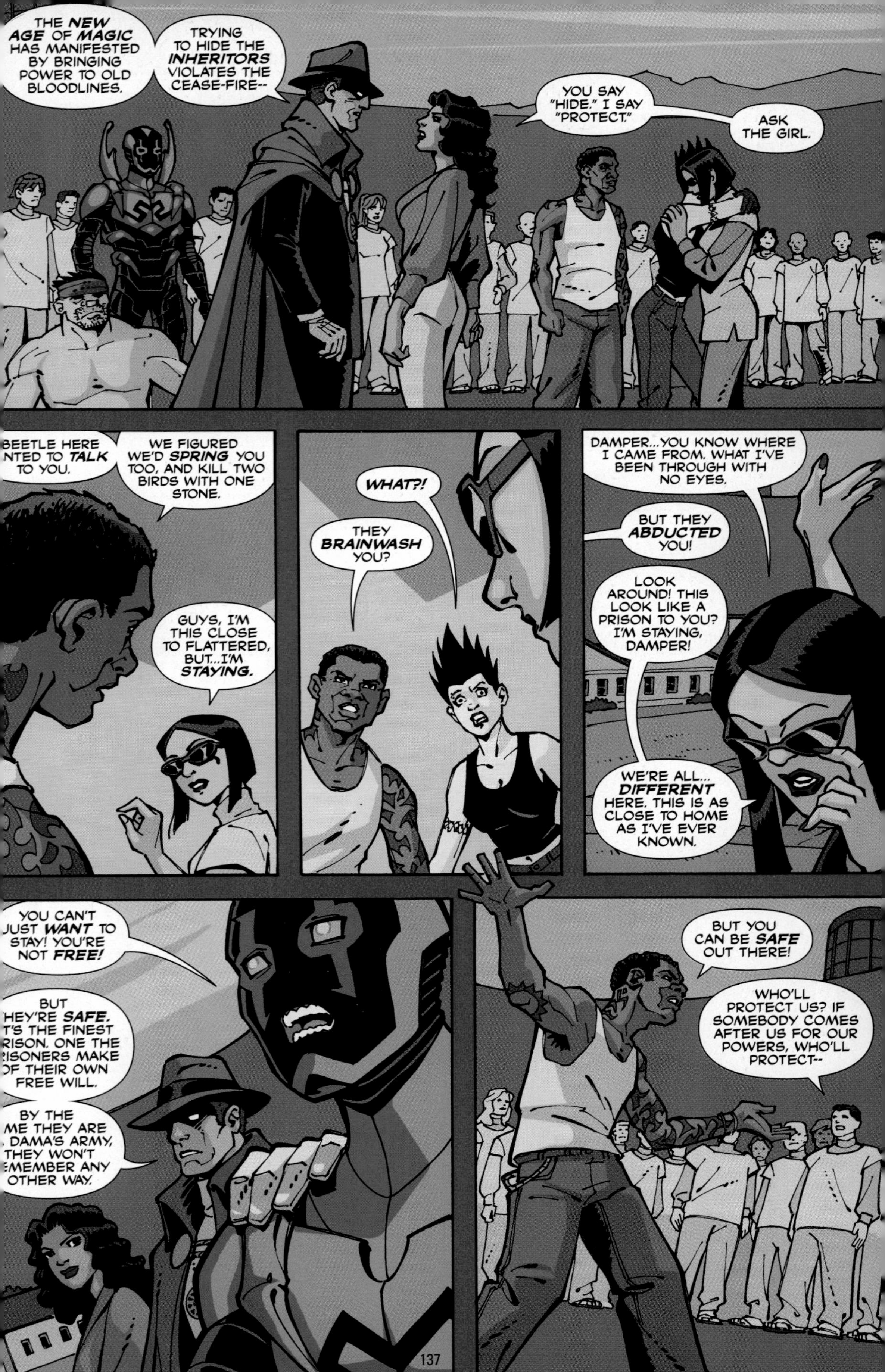
THE NEW AGE OF MAGIC HAS MANIFESTED BY BRINGING POWER TO OLD BLOODLINES.
TRYING TO HIDE THE INHERITORS VIOLATES THE CEASE-FIRE--
YOU SAY "HIDE." I SAY "PROTECT."
ASK THE GIRL.
BEETLE HERE NTED TO TALK TO YOU.
WE FIGURED WE'D SPRING YOU TOO, AND KILL TWO BIRDS WITH ONE STONE.
GUYS, I'M THIS CLOSE TO FLATTERED, BUT...I'M STAYING.
WHAT?!
THEY BRAINWASH YOU?
DAMPER...YOU KNOW WHERE I CAME FROM. WHAT I'VE BEEN THROUGH WITH NO EYES.
BUT THEY ABDUCTED YOU!
LOOK AROUND! THIS LOOK LIKE A PRISON TO YOU? I'M STAYING, DAMPER!
WE'RE ALL... DIFFERENT HERE. THIS IS AS CLOSE TO HOME AS I'VE EVER KNOWN.
YOU CAN'T JUST WANT TO STAY! YOU'RE NOT FREE!
BUT HEY'RE SAFE. T'S THE FINEST RISON. ONE THE RISONERS MAKE OF THEIR OWN FREE WILL.
BY THE ME THEY ARE DAMA'S ARMY, THEY WON'T EMEMBER ANY OTHER WAY.
BUT YOU CAN BE SAFE OUT THERE!
WHO'LL PROTECT US? IF SOMEBODY COMES AFTER US FOR OUR POWERS, WHO'LL PROTECT--

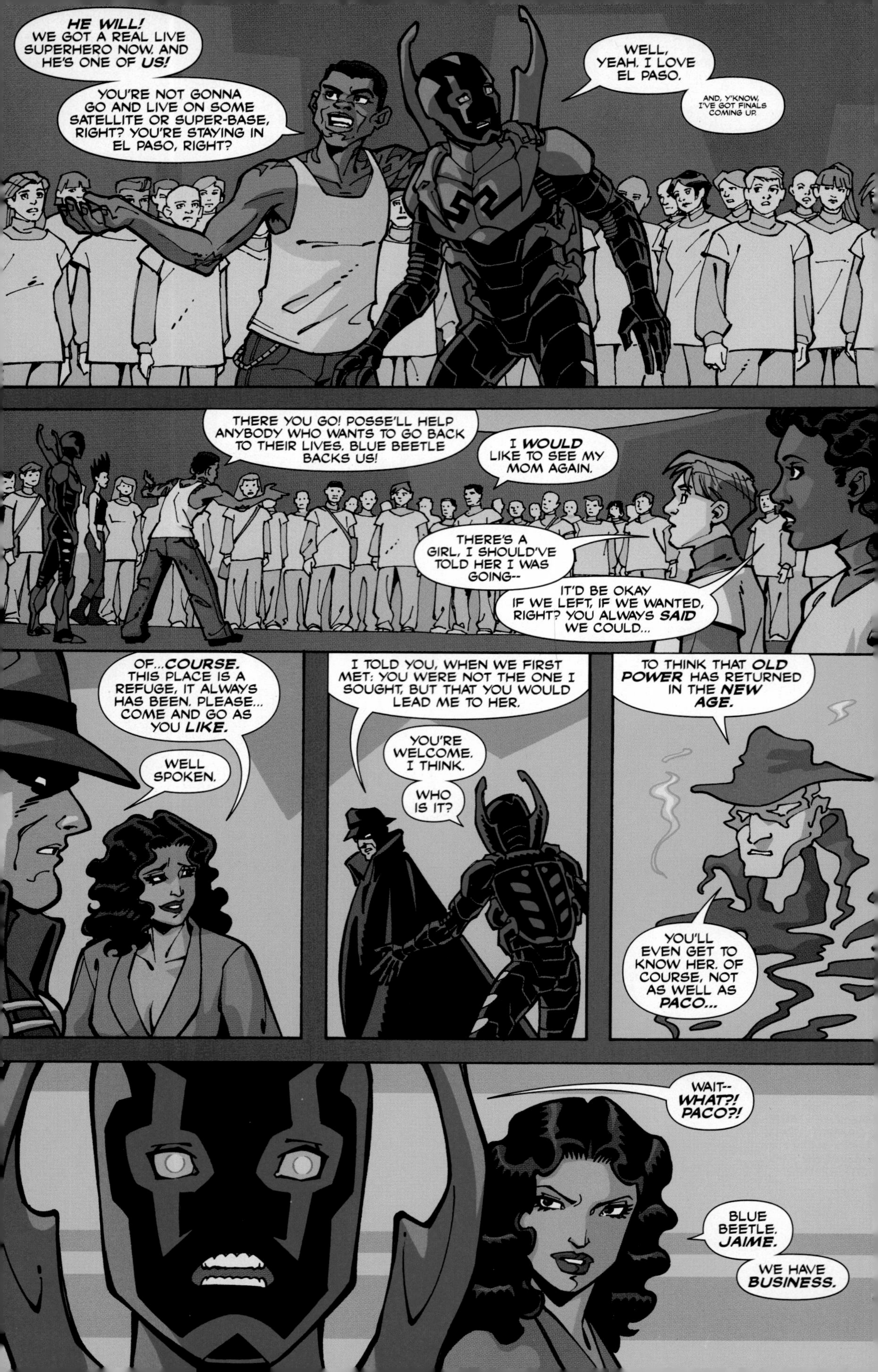

HE WILL! WE GOT A REAL LIVE SUPERHERO NOW. AND HE'S ONE OF US!
YOU'RE NOT GONNA GO AND LIVE ON SOME SATELLITE OR SUPER-BASE, RIGHT? YOU'RE STAYING IN EL PASO, RIGHT?
WELL, YEAH. I LOVE EL PASO.
AND, Y'KNOW, I'VE GOT FINALS COMING UP.
THERE YOU GO! POSSE'LL HELP ANYBODY WHO WANTS TO GO BACK TO THEIR LIVES. BLUE BEETLE BACKS US!
I WOULD LIKE TO SEE MY MOM AGAIN.
THERE'S A GIRL, I SHOULD'VE TOLD HER I WAS GOING--
IT'D BE OKAY IF WE LEFT, IF WE WANTED, RIGHT? YOU ALWAYS SAID WE COULD...
OF...COURSE. THIS PLACE IS A REFUGE, IT ALWAYS HAS BEEN. PLEASE... COME AND GO AS YOU LIKE.
WELL SPOKEN.
I TOLD YOU, WHEN WE FIRST MET: YOU WERE NOT THE ONE I SOUGHT, BUT THAT YOU WOULD LEAD ME TO HER.
YOU'RE WELCOME. I THINK.
WHO IS IT?
TO THINK THAT OLD POWER HAS RETURNED IN THE NEW AGE.
YOU'LL EVEN GET TO KNOW HER. OF COURSE, NOT AS WELL AS PACO...
WAIT-- WHAT?! PACO?!
BLUE BEETLE. JAIME.
WE HAVE BUSINESS.

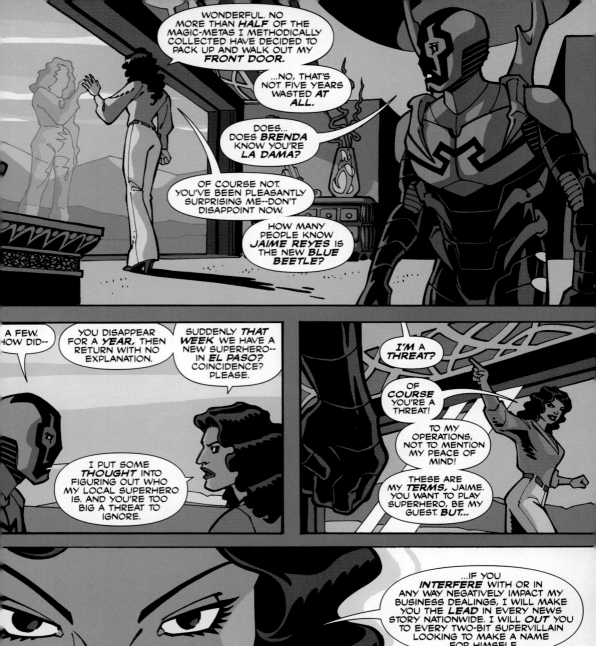

WONDERFUL. NO MORE THAN *HALF* OF THE MAGIC-METAS I METHODICALLY COLLECTED HAVE DECIDED TO PACK UP AND WALK OUT MY *FRONT DOOR.*

...NO, THAT'S NOT FIVE YEARS WASTED *AT ALL.*

DOES... DOES *BRENDA* KNOW YOU'RE *LA DAMA?*

OF COURSE NOT. YOU'VE BEEN PLEASANTLY SURPRISING ME--DON'T DISAPPOINT NOW.

HOW MANY PEOPLE KNOW *JAIME REYES* IS THE NEW *BLUE BEETLE?*

A FEW. HOW DID--

YOU DISAPPEAR FOR A *YEAR,* THEN RETURN WITH NO EXPLANATION.

SUDDENLY *THAT WEEK* WE HAVE A NEW SUPERHERO-- IN *EL PASO?* COINCIDENCE? PLEASE.

I PUT SOME *THOUGHT* INTO FIGURING OUT WHO MY LOCAL SUPERHERO IS, AND YOU'RE TOO BIG A THREAT TO IGNORE.

I'M A *THREAT?*

OF *COURSE* YOU'RE A THREAT!

TO MY OPERATIONS, NOT TO MENTION MY PEACE OF MIND!

THESE ARE MY *TERMS,* JAIME. YOU WANT TO PLAY SUPERHERO, BE MY GUEST. *BUT...*

...IF YOU *INTERFERE* WITH OR IN ANY WAY NEGATIVELY IMPACT MY BUSINESS DEALINGS, I WILL MAKE YOU THE *LEAD* IN EVERY NEWS STORY NATIONWIDE. I WILL *OUT* YOU TO EVERY TWO-BIT SUPERVILLAIN LOOKING TO MAKE A NAME FOR HIMSELF.

YOU DON'T KNOW WHAT I'VE DONE--WHAT I *HAD* TO DO, WHAT I WAS *RIGHT* TO DO-- FOR MY LIFE. FOR MY *FAMILY.*

YOU HURT ANYTHING OR ANYONE I CARE ABOUT--I WILL *END* YOU.

...

YOU... YOU DID IT, DIDN'T YOU?

YOU *KILLED* BRENDA'S FATHER.

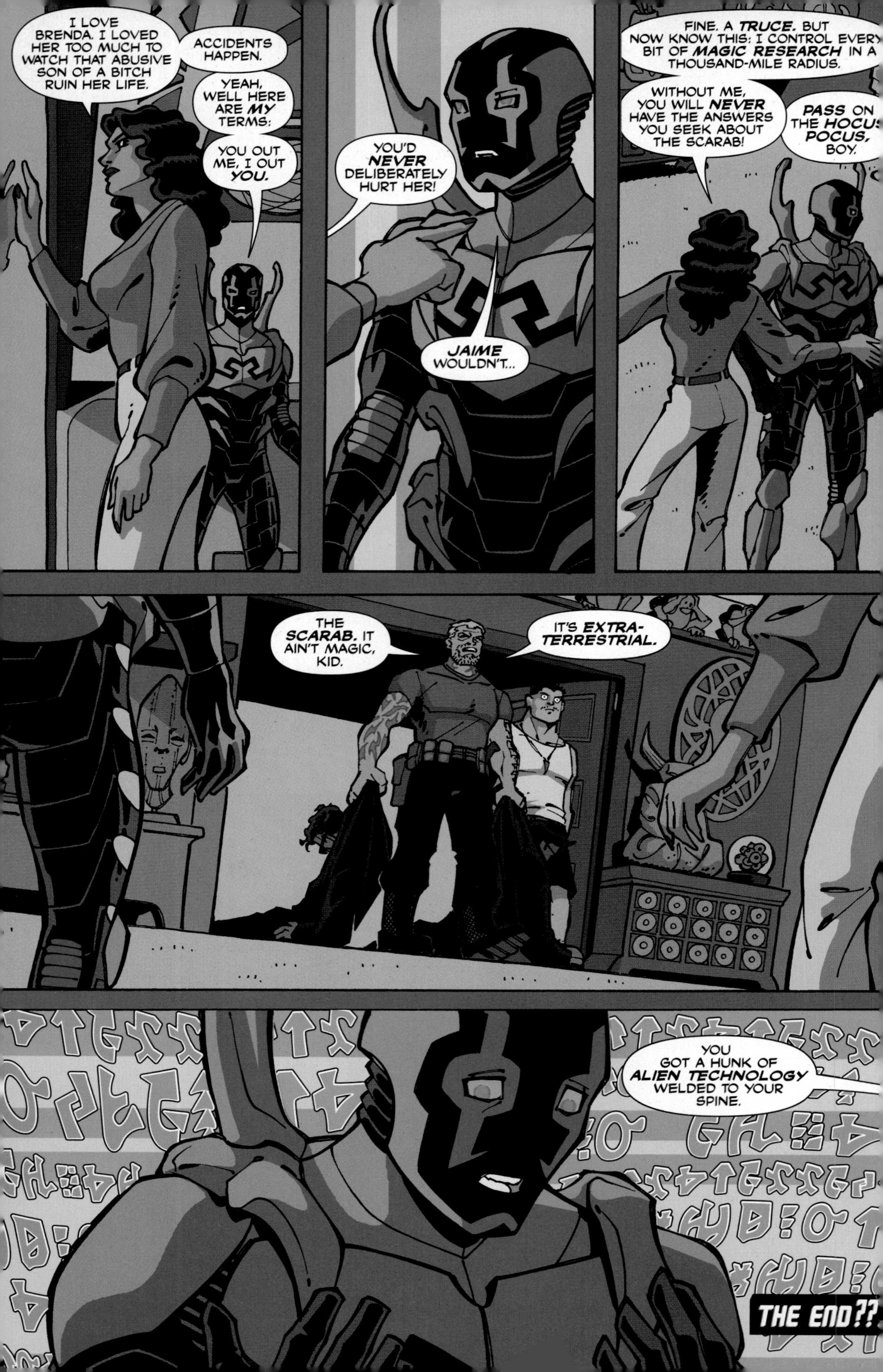
I LOVE BRENDA. I LOVED HER TOO MUCH TO WATCH THAT ABUSIVE SON OF A BITCH RUIN HER LIFE.
ACCIDENTS HAPPEN.
YEAH, WELL HERE ARE MY TERMS:
YOU OUT ME, I OUT YOU.
YOU'D NEVER DELIBERATELY HURT HER!
JAIME WOULDN'T...
FINE. A TRUCE. BUT NOW KNOW THIS: I CONTROL EVERY BIT OF MAGIC RESEARCH IN A THOUSAND-MILE RADIUS.
WITHOUT ME, YOU WILL NEVER HAVE THE ANSWERS YOU SEEK ABOUT THE SCARAB!
PASS ON THE HOCUS POCUS, BOY.
THE SCARAB. IT AIN'T MAGIC, KID.
IT'S EXTRA-TERRESTRIAL.
YOU GOT A HUNK OF ALIEN TECHNOLOGY WELDED TO YOUR SPINE.
THE END??

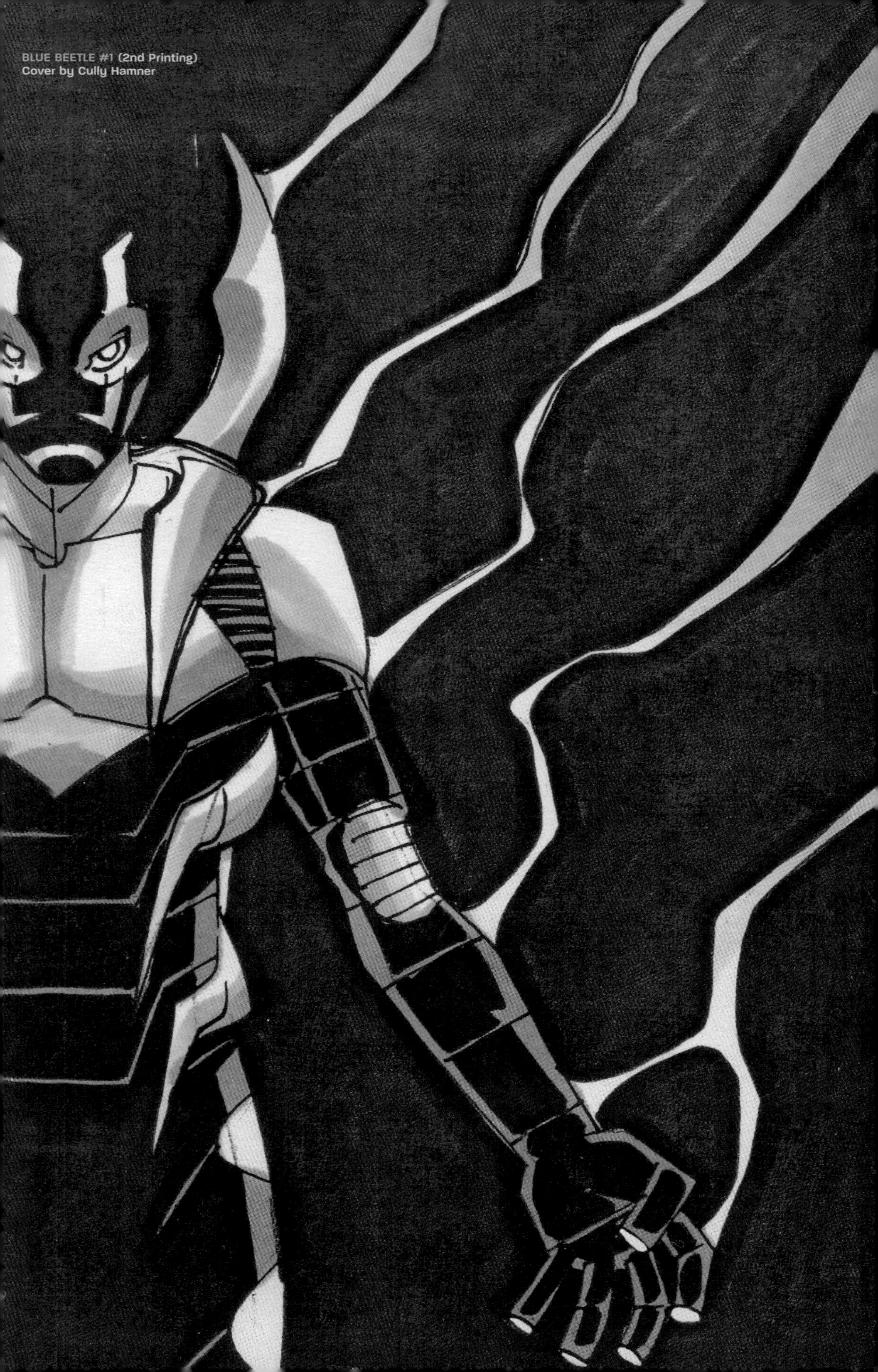

BLUE BEETLE #1 (2nd Printing)
Cover by Cully Hamner

BLUE BEETLE #1 (3rd Printing)
Cover by Cully Hamner

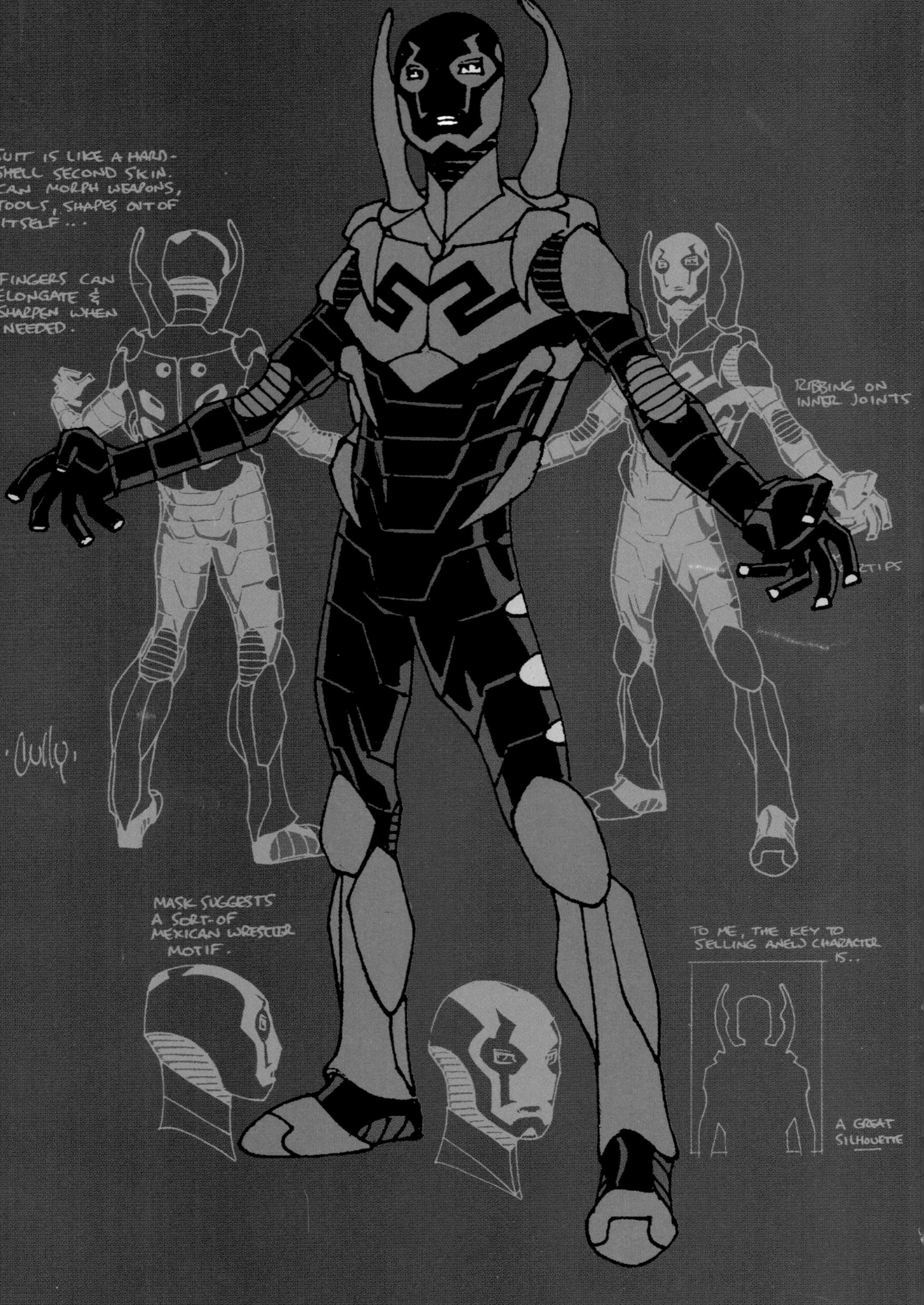

SUIT IS LIKE A HARD-SHELL SECOND SKIN. CAN MORPH WEAPONS, TOOLS, SHAPES OUT OF ITSELF...
FINGERS CAN ELONGATE & SHARPEN WHEN NEEDED.
RIBBING ON INNER JOINTS
CULLY
MASK SUGGESTS A SORT-OF MEXICAN WRESTLER MOTIF.
TO ME, THE KEY TO SELLING A NEW CHARACTER IS..
A GREAT SILHOUETTE

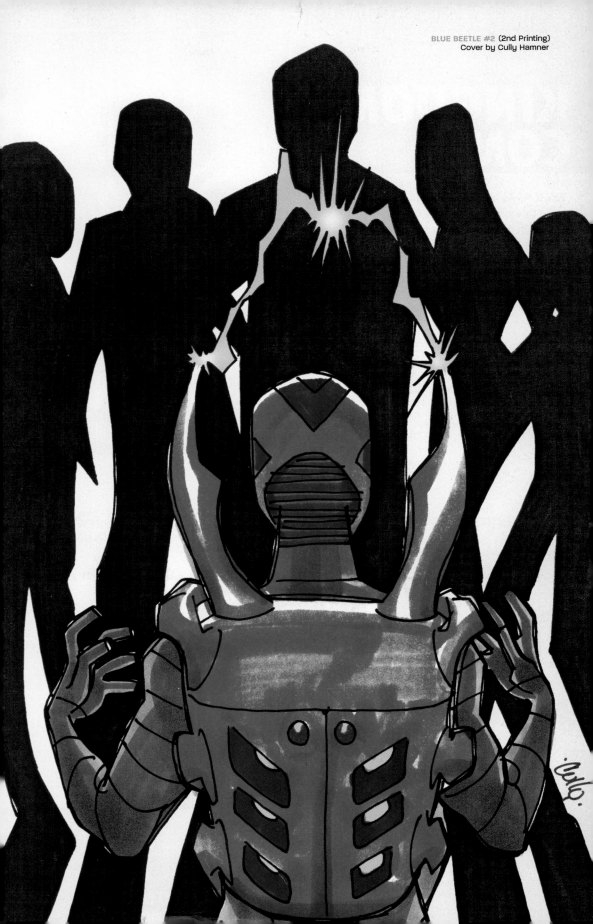

BLUE BEETLE #2 (2nd Printing)
Cover by Cully Hamner

READ MORE ADVENTURES OF YOUR FAVORITE HEROES IN THESE COLLECTIONS FROM DC COMICS:

KINGDOM COME

THE GREATEST SUPER HERO EPIC OF TOMORROW!
KINGDOM COME
Mark WAID
Alex ROSS

Mark Waid and **Alex Ross** deliver a grim tale of youth versus experience, tradition versus change and what defines a hero. KINGDOM COME is a riveting story pitting the old guard — Superman, Batman, Wonder Woman and their peers — against a new uncompromising generation.

WINNER OF FIVE EISNER AND HARVEY AWARDS, INCLUDING BEST LIMITED SERIES AND BEST ARTIST

IDENTITY CRISIS

RAGS MORALES

BRAD MELTZER
RAGS MORALES
MICHAEL BAIR

MARV WOLFMAN
GEORGE PÉREZ

E NEW FRONTIER VOLUME 1

VOLUME ONE
DAVE STEWART

DARWYN COOKE
DAVE STEWART

SEARCH THE GRAPHIC NOVELS SECTION OF

www.DCCOMICS.com

FOR ART AND INFORMATION ON ALL OF OUR BOOKS!

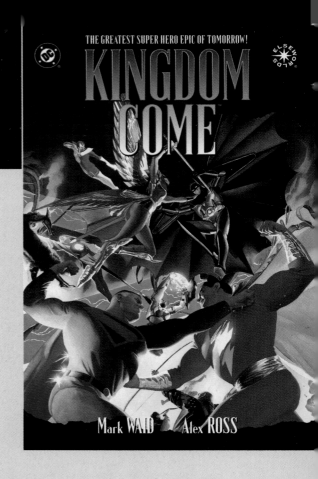

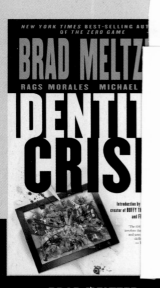